FUNNY ON PURPOSE

Funny On Purpose

THE DEFINITIVE GUIDE TO AN UNPREDICTABLE CAREER IN COMEDY

STANDUP + IMPROV +
SKETCH + TV + WRITING +
DIRECTING + YOUTUBE

By Joe Randazzo

Illustrations by R. Sikoryak
Foreword by John Hodgman

CHRONICLE BOOKS
SAN FRANCISCO

FOR KAT AND CORMAC AND AUGUST

Library of Congress Cataloging-in-Publication Data

Randazzo, Joe, 1978-
  Funny on purpose : the definitive guide to an unpredictable career in comedy : standup + improv + sketch + tv + writing + directing + youtube / Joe Randazzo ; foreword by John Hodgman.
      pages cm
  Includes index.
  ISBN 978-1-4521-2839-9 (alk. paper)
  1. Wit and humor—Authorship. 2. Comedy—Authorship. 3. Stand-up comedy. I. Title.

PN6149.A88R36 2014
808.7—dc23

2014031094

Manufactured in China

MIX
Paper from
responsible sources
FSC® C008047

Cover design by Neil Egan
Interior design by Alissa Faden and Neil Egan
Illustrations by R. Sikoryak
Illustrations on pages 142–143 by Amanda Sims

10 9 8 7 6 5 4 3 2 1

Chronicle Books LLC
680 Second Street
San Francisco, California 94107
www.chroniclebooks.com

CONTENTS

Foreword

BY
JOHN HODGMAN

Some years ago, I had stopped being a literary agent and was looking for a new job. I chose writing for magazines because those still existed then, and they still paid money, so now you know I am very old.

I was writing in my best magazine style: long, twisty sentences full of clever wordplay and profound thoughts and adverbs. I didn't want my prose to be merely luminous; I wanted it to be luminously. It was dumb. I was just writing about cheese and whiskey and junk. After a while my editor, Mark Adams, told me to calm down. He told me to be myself: "Go ahead and be funny," he said. I was offended—deeply, naturally, luminously—that he would boil me down to that one dumb word. Anyone could be funny. But Mark corrected me: funny is an asset. Not everyone can do it.

George Saunders has talked about how the day he realized it was okay to be funny was like the day he realized he had been fighting his whole life with one hand tied behind his back, and now he was able to use both fists. (If you don't know, George Saunders is a very famous mixed martial arts fighter. He is notorious for his ground game, which is extremely brutal, but also hilarious, with hints of the surreal.)

Now, I have never punched a human into a blood puddle like George Saunders has. But it is true: once I took Mark's advice, I knew what Saunders meant. I got more paid work with funny, yes. But more, being funny allowed me to get serious as a writer in a way I never had. Because I was being myself. And myself wanted to write seven hundred hobo nicknames in a book of hundreds of fake facts (we also had books then). And that is why you know me as the famous American fake-fact humorist JOHN HODGMAN and not as that guy who wrote about cheese for *Men's Journal* that time.

Also I went on *The Daily Show*. That helped, too.

So there you have the secret to having a career in comedy. Be funny. Be yourself. Go on television. Of the three, television is the easiest to accomplish, because there is so much of it now. Or so much television-equivalent mass media. Recall that when my story began, in the ancient past, the web was still largely the province of a small group of relatively affluent, tech-savvy Caucasian people, and getting your work in front of a wide audience still meant scraping before sundry media gatekeepers. Even RADIO, the most ridiculously old-timey and nonprofitable of mass media, was tightly controlled by a cabal of public-radio programmers who met once a year in a secret tomb beneath the Fitzgerald Theater in St. Paul.

But by the end of the last decade, phones had put both the Internet and pretty good A/V equipment in the hands of a much broader population, video and podcasting gave all those people instant access to a massive global audience, and Twitter proved that Mark Adams was actually wrong: pretty much everyone can be funny, at least a little bit, from time to time.

Because humans like comedy, and comedy tends to attract young people who have the Internet and live as much on attention as food, that means there is a lot more of it out there than there used to be. In fact, more careers in comedy have been launched in the past five years than in the previous five thousand (factoring in smaller populations and the Black Death, which was a bad time for standup).

I hope you are sobered by this statistical fact even though I made it up, because it is true, and also you drink too much. But I hope you will not give up. As in all of the arts, fortune favors the persistent much more than the merely talented. And with Randazzo's book in hand, you have a tool that has never existed before.

Like many crafts, comedy as both a practice and a business requires a set of skills that historically have been closely guarded by a guild of bitter weirdos. The etiquette of submitting packets to TV shows, how to ease yourself into a writers' room, how to handle failing onstage—this is the kind of nutty, bolty wisdom that is normally only passed down verbally, from elder to apprentice, in unguarded moments in some green room full of cast-off couches and a tub of moldering hummus.

The difference with Joe is that, unlike almost everyone else in comedy, he is not secretly a monster who wants you to fail so he can continue to scrape out a livelihood in a professional landscape he doesn't understand anymore. He has gathered this information and stripped it of all sabotage, plus he has written it down, so you can enjoy it with your own, fresh hummus.

But if getting on television or a television-equivalent isn't as difficult as it used to be, it means that the first two secrets—being funny and being yourself—are even harder. And this is the real value of this book. Read the interview with Paul F. Tompkins; read the interview with Pete Holmes; and read the ones with so many others contained herein who recount when they stopped imitating (which is where all art begins and bad standup stops) and how they began to understand their own taste, their own preoccupations, their own voices.

Every time you take to the stage or the page, you are presuming to waste the time of strangers, and it is best to appreciate early that, in reality, no one cares about your dumb musings. The imperative to speak comes from you, so you had better know why you are doing it. This sounds like a big question, but if I can offer only one thing to the wisdom Joe has expressed and collected here, it's this: it's a really small question.

When I was asked to talk comedy at the Radio and Television Correspondents' Dinner in Washington in front of the president of the United States, I said yes automatically because: free drinks, and I love to ride that Acela. I began to write some jokes, but they were all terrible. Because it turns out, most jokes are not funny. Is there anything more depressing and unfunny than a joke book?

I realized that this was a very specific and strange opportunity, and there was no point trying to be funny until I understood what I specifically wanted to say to the president of the United States. The true but unprofound answer was: I just wanted to know if the story I had heard was true. Did he actually give Leonard Nimoy the "Live Long and Prosper" salute when passing him on the streets of Chicago? Was the president a nerd?

Now you may have seen the president and I exchanging the split-fingered greeting that night on YouTube, and you may think my grilling of the president on his nerd credentials was not very funny. Luke Russert didn't like it either. Maybe you two should be pals.

But I have never been badly served by stopping before typing a word or taking a step on a stage and asking myself: Why am I doing this? What do I have to say—*need* to say—on this specific day, to this group of people? It takes rigor, and a certain brave honesty, because sometimes the answer is small and dumb. Even if the answer in that moment is, "I hate Mondays, but I love lasagna," if that's the truth, then you have made something that no one else in the world can (except for Jim Davis).

I know why I am writing this. First, because Joe told me to. And also because I feel compelled to say to you: In a comedy-saturation era, where every joke you can think of has already been made five times, twelve minutes ago, knowing yourself is not merely essential to being funny (and for that matter, being human), it is more important than being funny. Because truly not everyone can do it.

Introduction:

WHAT TO EXPECT FROM THIS BOOK IN TERMS OF INTRODUCTIONS

I woke up one recent morning, and rather than shake off the veil of sleepy confusion and push the dread of daily life deeper into the pit of my stomach like I normally do, I realized that I was content. Happy, even. I realized that I had managed to make something of my life. Moreover, I'd done so by doing what I am good at, while maintaining integrity and making about as much money as a poorly paid doctor. Perhaps one of those doctors who got their degree at a sketchy Caribbean medical school, struggled with alcoholism and a gambling addiction, and now makes ends meet by doing black-market veterinary work on fighting dogs.

Anyway, I was making about as much money as that disgraced doctor, and I had also worked for two of the most respected and independent-spirited comedy organizations in the country: *The Onion* and Adult Swim. It didn't seem real, lying there for those few minutes, thinking about it all. It seemed like a thin reflection of reality, a nice, fleeting fantasy that would soon come to an end. But it didn't. It was real life.

As I looked back, wondering how I got here, I noticed certain patterns emerge, benchmarks and qualities that other people I admired had also talked about as necessary in their own lives. I got to wondering: Was there a series of qualities shared by successful comedy people? I wanted to find out.

I explored this question deeply for over a year, interviewing people, reading books, consuming media, and generally experiencing and reflecting on the life of the comedy professional. After countless hours and conversations, I finally came up with this:

THE SEVEN TRAITS OF HIGHLY SUCCESSFUL COMEDY PEOPLE

1 Self-Doubt
2 Excellent Procrastination
  Skills
3 Fear of the Unknown
4 Laziness
5 Fear of Failure
6 Poor Planning
7 A Need to Express
  Something to the World

These are the only things you need to become a successful comedy person. (I almost listed eight, but I couldn't choose between Indecision and Impulsive Behavior, so I just said, "Fuck it!" and left them both off.) They seem so obvious, don't they? But for me and all the professionally funny people I know, these seven traits are absolutely vital, and without them, we'd probably have just wound up as lawyers or investment bankers or software engineers or entrepreneurs or something.

For someone considering a career in comedy, having all seven is obviously ideal, but you can get started even if you only possess a few. For instance, Self-Doubt and Fear of the Unknown can set you on the path to being a great standup comedian, while Laziness and Excellent Procrastination Skills are common among some of the best TV writers in the world. It's all about finding the ones that best apply to you and learning how you can use them to fulfill No. 7, your Need to Express Something to the World.

However, if you read this list and feel that you don't possess any of these qualities, then you should seriously consider pursuing another career. You're confident and content, and I'm afraid you just don't have what it takes to work in comedy.

Otherwise, this book is for you!

Comedy is a hard life. It's full of disappointment and frustration. There's a lot of competition out there, and the public's idea of What Is Funny changes from year to year and week to week. But it's a very rewarding life: you get to create, and you get to make people laugh. If you're really good, you get to make money, too.

It's difficult to know where to start—not just in practical terms, like *where can I start telling jokes in public*, but when to decide that, from this moment on, *I am going to make a career out of comedy. I am going to do this for my life.*

My hope is that this book can help you with both.

First, let me tell you very quickly how I got here: I always liked comedy, and I was always funny. In high school, as I was preparing to enter the real world, I seriously considered becoming an orthodontist or going into cryogenics. They both seemed like growth industries. The thing is, I am terrible at math and science. Soon thereafter I discovered Ira Glass and *This American Life*, so I went to college for broadcast journalism, thinking, since it's impossible to make a career in comedy, maybe I can make a career at NPR, and maybe do kind of what Ira Glass does. My senior year of college, I finally got the nerve to start doing comedy: I did standup and wrote a show and wound up winning a comedy scholarship. With that money, I moved to New York and tried, and failed, to get a job at NPR. So I started working in reality TV: *The Apprentice, Survivor,* and the short-lived *Ultimate Hustler* with Damon Dash. These jobs made me want to kill myself. So I went to work at a fruit basket company (Manhattan Fruitier, great fruit baskets), and eventually, this job made me want to kill myself. So I started doing improv at the Magnet Theater. There I met people who worked at *The Onion*, one thing led to another, and I tested for a job there and got it. Yay! I rose through the ranks to become an editor. When *The Onion* moved to Chicago, I stayed in

New York and started a website called Thing X, which was later folded into AdultSwim.com. Now I am writing this book. In between, I did a lot of every other kind of comedy and made friends with some of the best people working in the industry. There. So that's me.

As in my story above, there are two things that almost everyone I talked to said about their comedy careers: (1) they didn't even realize it was something you could make a career out of, and (2) the worst advice they ever got was to have a backup plan.

I will address these two main themes to show that (1) comedy *is* something you can make a career out of, and (2) you will not *need* a backup plan if you really want it. This book is written primarily from my own experience and perspective, but it is made whole with information gleaned through research and conversations. I also interviewed some of my favorite Comedy People to provide commentary, wisdom, perspective, and expertise.

In hindsight, I realize that I did not include everything I might have or talked to everyone I know. There are also people I talked to whose interviews didn't make it into the book, and I feel bad about that. I wasn't able to cover every single aspect of comedy, nor include the perspective of every type of person or professional comedian, mainly because of space considerations, but also because I'm not sure that is possible. In the end, this book was written by me, and flavored by my experiences and biases, and while I tried to be fair and thorough, I think there's value in informed subjectivity. But I'm biased.

Everyone's path is different. You could try to follow in my footsteps, or in Jack Handey's or Kelly Oxford's, but you would look like an insane person. No one gets there in the same way, and where "there" is depends entirely on the person. This book, along with the Seven Traits of Highly Successful Comedy People, will give you some of the information and inspiration that you need to start forging your life in comedy. Or so I hope. Besides, if you're anything like me or the people in this book:

You can't do anything else.

Part 1

WRITING COMEDY

the foundation for the basis of the structure in the center of the comedy

At the heart of all great comedy, no matter the language or style, is one core element: a big tubby fatso falling out of his teeny chair face-first into a steaming plate of spaghetti and meatballs.

But there is often a second thing, and that thing, which is also important, is writing. Almost all comedy starts with writing, and scripts provide the blueprint for everything from a one-minute sketch to a feature-length film. The best sitcoms are built in the writers' room, where ideas are hatched and honed and turned into twenty-three minutes of comedy. The monologues delivered by our late-night talk show hosts are weaned from dozens or hundreds of one-liners churned out by a team of joke writers and contributors. Awards shows, speeches, cartoons, even Geico commercials: All require writers. Writing is where so many Comedy People start out—and where many happily stay—partly because there are more jobs in writing than in being a movie star, and partly because comedy writing is a real craft.

Opportunities abound to write comedy outside of film and TV, too. There's the whole entire Internet, for example, about 98 percent of which is made up of things designed to make people laugh. You can write jokes for other comedians or you can punch up copy for a local furniture commercial. There's books and magazines and, to an increasingly anemic degree, newspapers as well.

Comedy writing is everywhere—but it's not easy. If it were easy, everybody would be doing it, and our economy would collapse. It's hard not only because of its technical complexity, but also because of the toll it takes on the writer. It can be dreadfully lonely and frustrating, but if you're good and dedicated and willing to work like a dog, you can do it. And if you're not that good at first, don't worry: that will usually catch up with the second two traits.

Chapter 1

NUTS, BOLTS, AND PHILOSOPHY

Facing a blank page is akin to standing before oblivion: it is nothing but unrealized potential. Infinite possibilities must be constrained and fit into the finite shape of the page. That can be daunting. What's more, you cannot help but consider that the words that will eventually fill that blank page might not be any good. In fact, they might suck. You might suck.

Everything might suck.

I have felt within my heart the most severe hopelessness while sitting in front of a computer screen, writing. I am not overstating this, and if you've ever tried to write Something Really Great, you know that I am telling the truth. Writing is sad and it is hard, because when you set out to write, something in you has to die.

The part of you that interacts with the outside world, distracted by every little click and hiss and urge and blog, bouncing on the contours of life—that *you* has to be murdered. Your task as a writer is to siphon out what is in your brain and shape it into something that can be understood by others, and to do that you have to concentrate really, really hard. You have to conjure from thin air objects, people, and actions, make them interact, and give them form, and you have to do it all alone.

Maybe it requires a kind of narcissism, or at least ill-advised confidence, to suppose any of our inner thoughts are worthy of immortality. Any fleeting thing can be spoken and then forgotten, but committing it to paper means you want people to remember it! You want it to be read! By this very act, you are putting your own work in the same category as *Don Quixote*, *To Kill a Mockingbird*, and Chili's $9.99 Triple Dipper appetizer menu.

How We Write

The impetus to write is usually born out of a vision of the Finished Thing. It may be a clear vision or a blurry vision, or it may be an elaborate vision of a fat man falling in spaghetti. From that vision, we must extrapolate the details in order to get from a blank page to something funny.

Most of writing, then, is problem solving.

What we must do next doesn't make any sense, for it involves disassembling something that does not yet exist and putting it back together, without any instructions. The writer must describe just what it is they see in their mind's eye, and in so doing, give it a beginning, middle, and end—and, in the case of comedy, also make it funny. Which stinks, because it's really hard to write things that are funny. It requires an epic amount of creative energy, concentration, perseverance, and rebellion against reality itself. This is because nature has no sphere set aside for comedy: trees and galaxies and death and defecation just *are*, without comment or interpretation.

So, really, all you need to do to write a funny sketch about a team of spies who communicate by farting is to subvert the momentum of a thousand millennia and stake a claim for human consciousness in the vast, thoughtless plane of existence.

An Interview with **Jack Handey**

"I am motivated mostly by guilt, that I am falling into dissipation, and also by the occasional interesting idea that pops up."

Jack Handey's name has the mind-bending distinction of having become synonymous with itself: it sounds made up, though it is not, yet there is no name better suited for the kind of writing the real Jack Handey does. He is a master of absurdity and owns the cultural trademark on the phrase "Deep Thoughts" — those perfect, compact musings that first aired (and were narrated by Handey himself) on *Saturday Night Live* in the 1990s. He continues to write the occasional comedy piece for the *New Yorker*, and he released his first novel, *The Stench of Honolulu*, in 2013.

On Starting Out

I can remember my parents telling their friends to ask me where I got my pretty green eyes. I knew to say either "the milkman" or "the mailman." It always got a laugh, but I didn't know why. And when you think of it, that's probably a good lesson for writing comedy: don't worry about *why* something is funny.

The worst advice I've ever gotten was probably from my mother: "You can always go dig ditches for your Uncle Wally." I started writing a humor column in high school. It just sprang out. It was actually pretty popular. Not popular enough to get me a date with Julie McCabe, but still popular.

On Developing Characters

To me, a character who innocently and earnestly pushes stupid, even dangerous ideas is infinitely funnier than a character who speaks in wisecracks. I don't really know why. I suppose you keep

23

it "real" by not straying from the premise. I have overreached many times, as when the audience doesn't laugh.

It's funnier—and perhaps more sympathetic—if a character doesn't *know* that he's being mean. If he's oblivious and actually thinks he's nice. A friend once described my characters as "all dressed up and no place to go."

On Taking Risks
[The biggest risk I ever took was] probably moving to LA, and then New York. You want to stay in your hometown, but you can't. I would urge aspiring comedy writers to take that leap. Even if you fail, it's good to try out the big city.

On Fame
I used to think I would like my name to be famous, but not my face, so people wouldn't annoy you. But what happened was my name got some recognition, but people think it's a fake name. You can't win. The first joke I ever sold was to Steve Allen, and he said my name sounded like a product.

On Writing Novels
Don't write a novel. It's too hard. You can rewrite a novel forever. After a while, nothing in it seems funny anymore.

On Motivation
There is no better thing to make you write than a deadline. With a deadline, it's going to be 95 percent as good as it's ever going to be. That's not 100 percent, but you don't need 100 percent.

A good paycheck is also a good motivator.

Now that I am mostly freelance, I am motivated mostly by guilt, that I am falling into dissipation, and also by the occasional interesting idea that pops up.

I am very lazy. But I'm also—as a firstborn—fairly responsible. So I get it done. Beware of any writer who says he loves to write. Writers, as the saying goes, love to have written. What drives me to write is, that is what I do. Nothing more, really.

SEVEN INDISPENSABLE TIPS TO BECOMING A LESS-INSANE WRITER

Some people are able to infuse a sense of play and joy into their process and make it fun; others type each word with the weight of all their flaws and dashed hopes behind them. I am somewhere in the middle, depending on the day, as most of us probably are. As we discussed, the act of writing is at odds with the very nature of reality, so one must be willing to forgive oneself if it is at times difficult. To that end, here are my Seven Indispensable Tips to Becoming a Less-Insane Writer.

1. WRITE ALL THE TIME It doesn't have to be comedy. I keep a stupid little diary. I've started and aborted multiple Tumblrs and *New York Times* Op-Eds. Many times during the writing of this book, I've whipped off scripts for video ideas. Sometimes, whatever you are writing needs to work itself out on its own, and during that down time, it can be helpful to distract your brain with something else to push and pull on for a while.

2. DEMARCATE BRAINSTORMING AND WRITING TIME There's a time for doodling and taking notes and throwing things against the wall, and then there's Go Time, when you have to make the idea into Something. The first requires looseness and openness and play. The second requires focus and determination. The two do not mix. When it's time to switch gears, I take some extreme steps.

Use "full-screen" mode in Microsoft Word, Google Docs, or third-party software like WriteRoom, these "distraction-free" programs are very helpful for getting in the mood.

Use the software Freedom. This is the saddest, most pathetic, and also greatest invention for writers: the program turns off your Internet access for a set period of time. It is priceless. Not only can you not check Twitter every six seconds, but it also sends a message to your brain that you are serious about focusing.

Use headphones. Always wear headphones or earbuds. I personally find it difficult to listen to music while writing, but even the act of putting them into my earholes is a ritual that prepares me for some heavy concentration. If you work in an office, it also makes it clear to people that you do not wish to be disturbed—even if you secretly *do* wish to be disturbed.

3. MAKE YOUR BED This small habit reminds you, and anyone who may wander into your room for God knows what reason, that you still take pride in being a human being. It actually does make a difference when you look around in frustration and self-loathing to find one thing that's clean and orderly. Please trust me on this one.

PRO TIP! BINAURAL TONES

Have you heard of these mothers? They're supposedly capable of producing states of relaxation or concentration in the brain by playing two tones at slightly different frequencies in each ear. I have no idea if this is based in any scientific reality, but like headphones themselves, I use them when I really want to concentrate and block out external noise. The effect, whether physiological or placebic, is real enough for me, which is why I don't use them all the time—only when I require that true, deathly disengagement kind of concentration. You can purchase white noise or binaural beats apps in the goddamn app store.

> **PRO TIP!** KNOW WHEN TO STOP
>
> I usually write for about fifteen minutes after the point at which I feel "satisfied"—partly because I need time to cool down, and partly to wring any last little morsels that might turn into something in the morning. Ernest Hemingway, who didn't really specialize in comedy but was still pretty accomplished, said about quitting time: "You write until you come to a place where you still have your juice and know what will happen next and you stop and try to live through until the next day when you hit it again."

4. EXERCISE BEFORE YOU WRITE It doesn't take much. I usually do a set of thirty push-ups and some of those godforsaken body squats. Then my blood is flowing and I feel a sense of accomplishment already. Even stretching is something.

5. CHANGE LOCATIONS While habit is important to writing, so, too, is breaking it. If you're hitting a wall, go and write somewhere else. Moving the seven feet from my desk to my bed can refresh my eyeballs and downshift my brain to a more relaxed mode where new possibilities arise. It's important, however, not to change locations in the middle of a streak. This is a common impulse from some deep reptilian spiral of your psyche that would prefer to be basking on a rock than doing good mental work, and it can be devastating to momentum.

6. REWARD YOURSELF Because human beings are no more complicated than dogs who eat their own feces and only learn through

> **PRO TERM!** WRITER'S BLOCK
>
> The writer's natural state of being.

WHAT IS COMEDY?

The simplest definition for what makes something funny is "abnormality." Like a tumor, for example. In the most general sense, things become funny when they depart from what is expected; when logic takes us down a certain route, and we are suddenly detoured from that route. The jarring nature of this diversion produces a nervous reaction (laughter) as our brain hiccups and then reroutes itself to get back on course. The resulting sensation is what we call "funny."

There is, on the other side of the coin, a category of funny that is based on the familiar. Here we laugh not because we did not see it coming, but because, once it arrives, it is something we immediately recognize, and this brings us both pleasure and relief.

From time to time we also find physical discomfort or injury in others to be funny. Many believe this comes from some cruel and ancient bestial synapse, but I think it has more empathic roots: we've all been hurt before, and because we were not able to laugh at it during our own trauma, seeing it in someone else acts as a kind of sympathetic release valve. "We've been there, buddy, and while we feel sorry for you, we also can't help but be glad it's not happening to us. Ha, ha, ha."

Wit, too, can be funny, although wit usually boils down to little more than clever, but slightly annoying, observations.

Shocking things can be funny, as can disgusting things, and sometimes things that aren't funny can be funny because of the way in which they are not funny. Poop is the funniest thing in the world. Poop.

Comedy, meanwhile, is the genre of entertainment by humorous means. It is structured and purposeful. While it does not encompass everything that is funny, it can use anything that is funny to attain its means. There is black comedy, standup comedy, romantic comedy, absurdist comedy, slapstick, urban comedy, situation comedy, animal comedy, comedy of manners, screwball comedy, mimicry, gross-out comedy, family comedy, satire, parody, irony, and something known as "Adam Sandler." Comedy, then, is the organized pursuit of abnormality.*

*For money.

a simplistic work-and-reward system, you probably do this already. You have to be your own dominatrix, though, so be strict: If your goal is to write until 10 pm, then sit in front of your computer and write until 10 pm. If it's to write two thousand words, then write every one of those two thousand words, you worthless, dirty worm. Then, and only then, can you have your reward.

7. SLEEP ON IT Your brain needs a break every once in a while to run some equations while you're asleep or daydreaming. I like to email myself a pdf copy of whatever I'm working on at the end of the night and not open it till the next morning. I find reading a script eight hours later in an email adds an extra layer of distance that can help me assess it with more objective eyes.

Chapter 2

WRITING WITH A PARTNER

Perhaps because there are so many dualities inherent to the form—setup and punch line, straight man and foil—there have been a plethora of famous comedic partnerships. You can't have Abbott without Costello, Pugo without Togo,[1] Key without Peele, Et without Cetera, etcetera. When it comes to writing, it is great to have someone to bounce things off of, because so much of comedy comes down to action → reaction → action → reaction → action → bizarre, unexpected reaction. Writing comedy is a kind of ping pong, a game designed for two. By the same token, however, the writing needs to be tightly crafted, forever escalating in service of the central joke, and that requires a discipline that most large groups cannot achieve. Writing with a partner allows you to theoretically double your creative output without having to rely on the politics and second-guessing of comedy by committee.

---

1 The Laurel and Hardy of the Philippines, this duo started as a vaudeville act and made films throughout the 1940s and 1950s, including *Utos ng Hari*, *Hindi Mababali*, *Sa Lumang Simbahan*, and *Binibiro Lamang Kita*.

The Benefits of Being a Duo

TRUST Among all the comedy partners I talked to, the most important factor by far is having someone you can trust. You need someone you can rely on to tell you when your jokes are no good and to praise you when they are. You have to be able to give them your most precious possession—your imagination—and trust them to make it better.

MORALE Comedy writing brings you to the brink of self-immolation on an almost daily basis. Having someone who can talk you down from time to time and convince you that life is worth living—and that you can figure out how to make the dolphin-in-a-business-suit joke work in the morning—is a valuable asset.

VOCABULARY Working very closely with someone allows you to form a compact language for creation. This language might make absolutely no sense to anyone else, yet there's an efficiency to this kind of succinct, intuitive communication that allows concepts to be conveyed outside normal means—often nonverbally—and can sometimes generate its own comedy: inside jokes that form in the insane echo chamber between writing partners can wind up becoming their own sketches, scenes, and references.

FUEL There's an extremely practical reason to write with a partner: you don't have to do everything yourself. Writing is exhausting not only for your brain but for your fingers and eyeballs, too. It is nice to be able to hand things off to your partner every once in a while. I mean, what the fuck else have they been doing all this time?

Mike Lazzo, the head of Adult Swim, has a general rule not to develop shows by individual writers. His theory is that, in order to keep up a sustained series that will last several seasons, you have to have at least two minds working on it at all times.

POLARITIES As in marriage and other codependent relationships, good writing partnerships complement each other by representing opposite ends of a spectrum. Where one partner may always want to go to the loudest version of any joke, the other may tend toward understatement, and somewhere in the middle lies what is unique about their collaboration.

MIRACLES A strange comedic alchemy takes place when two people who have all of the things above merge their creative energy. Through a means they cannot explain, their partnership forms something that neither one could create on their own. They make a comedy baby with their shared DNA. They need each other to function creatively, and what they make by working and thinking and being together is greater than what either could ever make alone.

An Interview with **Tim Heidecker and Eric Wareheim**

"Who cares what the idea is? Let's make the idea work."

Tim Heidecker and Eric Wareheim have created a whole comedy universe by going against the grain. Their first show, *Tom Goes to the Mayor*, was a cult hit that paved the way for their genre-bending, poop-splattering *Tim & Eric Awesome Show, Great Job!* — which has inspired a generation of comedy absurdists. They've since gone on to make a feature film, *Tim and Eric's*

Billion Dollar Movie, to spin off actor John C. Reilly's character into his own show, *Check It Out! With Dr. Steve Brule*, and to start a production company that's bringing that same kind of offbeat, hard-to-define, relentlessly modern comedy into the mainstream.

On Bonding

Eric: In college, a lot of people are slackers, but I think Tim and I bonded because we were just like, "Yeah, let's work all weekend on this thing and edit it and make it cool and funny and take it seriously." Not a lot of my friends were those kinds of people *and* funny. So we latched onto each other because we had these same sensibilities and were both really enthusiastic and motivated to just make anything.

Tim: The thing that changed from the very beginning to the time that we got this order to make ten episodes [of *Tom Goes to the Mayor*] is that we had to create a lot of ideas. We had to fill a lot of holes. I don't think that either of us are the kind of people who have a ton of ideas. I know there's comedy people out there that are like, "Bam-bam-bam-bam! This-that-this-that, idea, idea, idea!" But we're like, "Oh, Eric, I have an idea for an episode." "Oh, yeah? What is it?" "Pioneer Island." "Okay, let's make *that* work." Who cares what the idea is? Let's make the idea work. Generally, the idea is just a seed.

Eric: It could just be a joke. Or a name.

On Developing Ideas

Tim: We just start making a list of these ideas and prioritizing them. Then we talk it out, and one of us goes off and writes it. But the writing is just one layer. It's not precious in any way at all. And then it's just back and forth, shaping it. There's a whole other layer that happens in the shooting of it, and the decisions about the costumes and locations. All those things are just back and forth.

Eric: An important part of our relationship, too, is that 99 percent of the time we agree on comedic and aesthetic things. The reason we became friends is because we like the same kind of shit. If one of us is passionate about something that the other doesn't agree with, we just go, "Okay, I'll let you have that one." When you make so many episodes of something, every idea is not as precious as it was when you were by yourself, writing your masterpiece.

Tim: If I have an idea, the first audience for my idea is Eric. How am I gonna sell him on the idea? If he's into it right away, it's great. It's easy. But sometimes he doesn't see it the way I see it, and it makes me rework the idea and make it better. If an idea isn't there, he pushes it. He'll say, "It seems a little too traditional" or a little too safe.

On Process

Eric: The core of our writing is the same thing we did in college when we were instant messaging each other: "I have this idea." "Ha, ha, ha." "What about if we did this?" "Ha, ha." Just back and forth, and that little paragraph turns into the kernel of a script.

Tim: Some things, like the [2013] Halloween special, *Bedtime Stories*, are written to be filmed, and that was filmed pretty accurately to how it was written. But we always know, "Okay, this script is just here to get us started." It's not the Bible. It's not some kind of David Mamet or Aaron Sorkin thing.

Eric: It's really just a tool to get our production staff working more than anything. We need a fireman's costume or we need to shoot in a mall. With *Check It Out*, it's very loose. The whole idea for an episode could be "Brule goes to a farm." That's it! We just go to a farm and walk around and see if we're inspired by a horse or anything, and then John C. Reilly will just improvise.

On Writing Movies

Eric: But then, on the other side of it, for our movie [*Tim & Eric's Billion Dollar Movie* in 2012], we had to be more locked into the script because of the amount of money that was going into each location and scene and costume.

Tim: We broke up the script into fifteen-page segments, and we wrote it more traditionally. We would meet and have lunch and sit across from each other and just be like, "All right, then what happens? What could be funny about this?"

Eric: At Adult Swim, we're writing for one man: Mike Lazzo. He trusts us. But in the movie business, you're writing for these money guys, and you have to make them laugh, and they have to see something that's got a traditional setup. So we have to be much more detailed than we're normally used to.

On Philosophy

Eric: There's this one moment in *Tom Goes to the Mayor*, where, in the mayor's office, there's this extension cord that's taped to the wall, going into the other room. That's the core of what we think is funny: just the shittiness of life. Shitty products and shitty commercials and how people are shitty to each other. And we never want to do anything that anyone's ever done before. That's always in the back of our heads. When we were doing *Awesome Show*, we didn't like the *Saturday Night Live* formula of, if a sketch works, just keep doing it. Tim and I were like, if a sketch works, let's kill that character and try to come up with another thing. We just liked that energy.

Tim: But even with *Awesome Show*, as much as that was a rule, there were certain things about that show that were like, how many times can we introduce the show and stumble on our words or make weird sounds? And that got a little creepy because the whole identity of the show is about surprising you. It's weird to now have what people consider a Tim & Eric standard that we have to live up to. But we're always gonna be throwing that shit away and trying different stuff, and it's not gonna be comfortable for fans.

Chapter 3

TASTE & SENSIBILITY, *or* HOW SOON IS TOO LATE?

An entire industry of outrage has sprung up and thrived in the incubator of the Internet. Every few weeks, someone says or writes something that a vocal segment of the population finds offensive—sometimes justifiably so—and the rest of us are dragged into an intense, hateful, demi-debate. Accusations are leveled! Apologies are demanded! Gilbert Gottfrieds are fired! And the next morning, as we peer through the haze of a self-righteousness hangover, we take stock of what we accomplished and find: just about nothing.

What does it mean to call something *off-limits*? Where are these limits set and how are they marked? If we can agree that there are some things that *do* require limits, who decides what those things are, and how did those people acquire this authority? Is it *ever* okay to make jokes about rape, child molestation, the Holocaust, sexuality, child molestation during the Holocaust, AIDS, someone with AIDS raping a Nazi after learning their child was molested during the Holocaust, or race? The deeper one explores this idea the more one sees that it is diametrically opposed to two primary functions of comedy: to push the bounds of comfort and to challenge authority. Without these two principles—and an important and universal third principle, which is to smear the edges of tragedy with a shared sense of the absurd—one does not have comedy.

Sorry. No more ha-ha.

These topics are sensitive because they exist in the dimmer corners of our culture, in places that we do not want to face. But it's our job as comedians, satirists, and wiseacres to poke at these issues, to get them to squirm around, to take their measure and expose enough surface area to allow the civilian population to judge for itself. Even the crappiest, least-subtle comics have a part to play, since it is often their unwieldy sledgehammer strikes that first crack these things open. To confront some of these off-limit topics, be they religious, moral, economic, or scatalogical, also confronts the unjust structures that prop up those in power and that keep the rest of us down.

I can't think of anything more offensive than a standup routine

THE EBERHARDT SCALE

Developed by Dr. Oskar J. Eberhardt in 1979, this highly attuned instrument is the most objective tool to date for measuring propriety in comedy. Taking into account a range of data—such as the nature of the tragedy, number of people killed, likelihood of the disease being cured, geographic location of victims, average age of children in the burning bus, year of incident, and spray radius of exploded animal—it uses a complicated internal algorithm to calculate appropriate comedy on a scale of 1 to 6. While his scale is by no means perfect, Eberhardt still boasts that it has an accuracy rate of 98.2 percent. Typical fucking German.

based on racism or misogyny—not only because this perpetuates ignorant, socially violent ideas, but because it's boring. It's mediocre, and there's nothing more dangerous than mediocrity. You do not get a pass to be an unequivocal asshole merely because you're standing onstage with a microphone. It's about context and intent. Does your joke make a broader point about sexism, or is it just using those boring old tropes for an easy laugh? Are you taking a stand against racism, or are you just being racist? The first category is noble. The second is cowardly.

Lessons in Taste from *The Onion*

CHOOSE THE RIGHT TARGET

Weirdly enough, the two most sensitive areas among readers when I was at *The Onion* (AD 2006–2012) were child molestation and the troops. That didn't mean we could never do jokes about either one; we just had to make sure that the jokes weren't at the expense of the victim. It was perfectly legitimate to make a joke about Jerry Sandusky, the Penn State football coach who was convicted in 2012 of sexually abusing dozens, maybe hundreds, of children over several decades, so long as the joke condemned him, the media, or the university cover-up. To make a joke at the expense of the children or their families would not only have been in bad taste, it would have been pointless. Likewise, I remember an occasion sometime around 2007 when we were discussing a headline that went something like, "Soldier Just Knows He'll Be 4,000th Casualty in Iraq." Then we realized that there actually *would* be a four-thousandth casualty, and when it happened, the joke would not be about some abstract idea, but about an actual person with friends and family who would be mourning them. We decided not to run it.

DON'T MAKE THE FIRST JOKE, MAKE THE BEST JOKE

One of the great things about *The Onion* was that it did not always weigh in on every topic right away. Because the editorial process took two weeks from pitch to publication, the jokes tended to have a more timeless quality, and they were often as much about the cultural response to the news as the news itself. Nowadays, *The Onion* publishes on a daily basis, but it still refrains from stories that it doesn't have a fresh angle on.

YOU WILL ALWAYS OFFEND SOMEONE

I swear there was a form letter that unhappy *Onion* readers could download and fill in with their own specifics, and it started like this: "Normally I am a big fan of *The Onion* and appreciate your humor, but this time you've gone too far." They would then enumerate the ways in which they were personally offended by the joke or jokes that they, personally, did not find funny because it was a topic they were sensitive to, personally. If *The Onion* is doing its job right, each article should offend at least a thousand people.

SOME PEOPLE WILL HATE YOU

It doesn't really matter to the offended party what your intention was and, ultimately, you cannot fault someone for being annoyed or angered by what you say. That is their right, just as it is your right to offend them. It seems like a balanced equation to me: you are allowed to attack their most sensitive issues, and they are allowed to criticize, complain, and call you names. (Also: It is fun to piss people off!)

IF YOU'RE NERVOUS, YOU'RE ON THE RIGHT TRACK

Sometimes your goal is to push the aforementioned envelope, and that means delving into areas that will make everyone, including yourself, uncomfortable. It is important to follow your gut in such matters, but to distinguishe the eternally yucky kind of gut feeling that accompanies something truly tasteless from the sort that emerges naturally from trepidation. I remember feeling this way in 2010, right before *The Onion* ran a fictional Op-Ed by Rush Limbaugh in response to his terrible remarks that Haitians deserved the recent earthquake that had devastated their country. The column, "I Don't Even Want to Be Alive Anymore," essentially called for his assassination because he was too cowardly to kill himself. I was concerned that readers would think we'd gone too far, and that Limbaugh himself might seek legal action. In fact, we got only positive feedback from fans and never heard from Limbaugh.

DON'T BACK DOWN

The Onion has remained independent and beyond reproach for so many years not only because it goes after all targets, but because it has always stayed above the fray. It almost never responds to critics[2] or comments on its own material, and when it does, it does so in an irreverent, above-it-all tone that deflects the heat back

---

2 There's only one occasion that I can think of in the history of *The Onion* when the organization officially apologized for a joke, and that was when it tweeted during the 2012 Academy Awards that nine-year-old actress Quvenzhané Wallis was a cunt. It was a joke that did not go over well in context, and out of context, it sounded monstrous. Many thousands of people, including LeVar Burton and Maya Angelou, were up in arms on social media and the blogosphere (is that still a term people use?). *The Onion* almost immediately deleted the tweet, and the next day, CEO Steve Hannah printed a full apology on the front page, where the satire and jokes are supposed to go. I disagreed with the decision because his response only added fuel to the fire and, moreover, *The Onion* is one place where nothing is supposed to be off-limits. With the writing of that letter, the limits were set in stone.

on the questioner. This approach takes strength of will borne out of *The Onion*'s editorial voice and anonymity and not many individuals can pull this off. However, if you've checked off all your boxes above, built up a reputation for falling on the right side of things, believe in the joke and stand by it, you should have nothing to apologize for.

Chapter 4

WRITING FOR THE WEB

It has been said that there are more jokes written in one minute on the web today than were written in all of the twentieth century.[3] It's also been said that someone else would say, "Yes, but only three of them are funny."[4] The Internet seems to have an insatiable desire for more and more content, but historically it has not cared as much about quality. Most writing for the web is disposable; it often feels like putting a little sailboat on a river and watching it go over a waterfall, never to be seen again.

Still, in the Internet's vast breadth are innumerable opportunities to write comedy, in almost any form, length, or style you can imagine. Since every conceivable audience is currently online, there is something for everyone, which means that someone's got to write it—*sometimes even for money*.

---

3 By me, just now.
4 Me again, literally thirty seconds later.

What Works Online

There's no formula for successful online content, despite new scams for getting clicks coming out every six months or so. Yet reading habits *have* taken shape.

SHORTNESS Don't expect people to read anything online for more than one minute. Maybe less. There's a place for longer pieces (they're called "longreads"!), but just remember that everything online is competing with *everything else that is online*—not just comedy, but everything. The Internet is synonymous with overstimulation and too much information. To stand a chance of being read, you've got to stay short.[5]

SHAREABILITY This and shortness go hand in hand. People are infinitely more likely to share something they've actually read (at least half of), and they'll only read something online if it's very short (see "Shortness," above). After brevity, shareability is enhanced by several essential qualities. Writing should be:

Entertaining. It doesn't have to be the funniest thing in the world every time. Just be funny enough to hold someone's attention for ten seconds to a minute.

Simple. People should instantly get the joke. Do not make people work to understand your "concept." Your concept should be the part that's funny.

---

5 Good comedy writing should always be as long as it needs to be: long, detailed TV show recaps, for instance, are some of the most popular humor pieces online. But it takes time to build that audience and, in the case of recaps, they are based on something that a vast swath of readers are already interested in.

Relatable. People like cats, and they share pictures of cats online because lots of other people like cats, too. If you write about medieval military philosophy, don't expect people to post it on Facebook. Unless it involves cats in suits of armor.

Positive. Believe it or not, people are less likely to associate themselves with anything negative, hateful, hurtful, or mean. Nasty jokes can get you noticed, but they won't be shared as much, because that's not how people want to be seen by others.

Surprising. "Whoa!" and "Hahaha," and "That was surprising!" are things that people enjoy saying to their friends and colleagues. Surprise people, and they will want to tell their network of friends about it.

Cool. People like thinking they're cool. They also like being the first to find something cool and tell their friends. What makes something cool? Mix the qualities above and add style.

TOPICALITY What is everyone talking about? Write about that. If you prefer, make fun of what everyone is talking about or try to destroy it. You stand a better chance of getting noticed if you're having the same conversation as everyone else.

MASH-UPS It is a sign of our postmodern times that we like to see two or more things that do not belong together combined for comedic effect, be it unlikely animal friends or old Shakespearean actors reading YouTube comments.

Where to Write Online

BLOGS

In the latter part of the first decade of the twenty-first century, comedy blogs began popping up all across the Internet to serve the growing number of people who consider themselves not only comedy fans, but comedy *nerds*. There are now enough blogs that dedicated writers and followers of comedy can find opportunities to write for one of these existing entities (if they don't start their own blogs). There are comedy aggregators, like BuzzFeed or HuffPost Comedy, that "curate" content from around the web and occasionally comment on it—usually positively. There's quite a bit of original content, too, from lists to interviews to infographics. Another fairly recent phenomenon, and a viable genre all its own, is the comedy news blog. Sites like Laughspin and Splitsider offer gossip, interviews, reviews of live shows, and coverage of events, like the several thousand awards banquets and festivals that take place each year.

HUMOR SITES

The ever-growing number of humor sites online has created an incredibly competitive business. Some provide original content, some specialize in low-cost user-generated content, and some do both. Like anything worth pursuing, few offer paying jobs. But it's a growing industry, and as the demand for entertainment grows, so will comedy site jobs, at least until our society collapses under the weight of its own sloth and arrogance.

FUNNYORDIE.COM What started as an experiment in user-generated content has grown into a massive comedy brand with extensions in film, television, and music, as well as an extremely vibrant branded-entertainment unit. Funny Or Die (FOD) built its reputation on the celebrity of its cofounder, Will Ferrell, and high-profile cameos are still its stock-in-trade. Yet the staff churns out tons of great sketches and videos on a daily basis.

Submissions guidelines: All users are permitted to submit videos. Full-time staff are hired based on work and reputation.

Based: Los Angeles.

Pros: You get to work for one of the most highly visible comedy websites in the world, writing and producing sketches that may feature international superstars and be seen by millions.

Cons: The creative process can be chaotic and confusing, and the editorial mission of the site is not always clear.

ONION.COM *The Onion* is a difficult place to get a job. Typically, you have to know someone who knows someone and then hope for an opportunity. Recently, however, *The Onion* has expanded into video production and adopted a different model that relies on a smaller full-time staff and more freelance writers. Still, it is difficult to get a job without some personal entrée.

Submissions guidelines: Does not accept submissions.

Based: Chicago.

Pros: You get to work for one of the most prestigious comedy institutions in America with almost total creative freedom.

Cons: The hours are long, the work is intense, and the pay is not high, especially when starting out.

CRACKED.COM The magazine that was launched as a direct competitor to Alfred E. Neuman and *Mad* way back in 1958 is today one of the most popular comedy websites in the world. It has rejiggered its editorial focus several times over the past few years; the current, successful formula includes very interesting and funny lists, Photoshop, and short videos.

> **Submissions guidelines:** *Cracked* probably has the most liberal and permissive guidelines of all, and they have a decent development system.
>
> **Based:** Los Angeles.
>
> **Pros:** Very well-trafficked articles and features and a chance to write with little oversight.
>
> **Cons:** Freelance pay is not always great, and the voice is fairly limited.

PRO TERM! BRANDED ENTERTAINMENT

A modern form of the medieval patronage system whereby one rich entity pays another, usually smaller entity to produce something that feels like content but glorifies the generous patron and clearly communicates its overall brand message in an engaging, entertaining way.

COLLEGEHUMOR.COM This website is exactly what its name purports to be, and it is very good at it. With a combination of curated videos, lists, articles, and original series, CollegeHumor covers a lot of ground and updates frequently.

> **Submissions guidelines:** You can submit videos, articles, and photos that may be featured on the site through your user account.
>
> **Based:** Los Angeles.
>
> **Pros:** It is a very popular website, and your material will surely be seen by millions of people per month.
>
> **Cons:** Not as open to outside pitches as Funny Or Die and if pop-culture parody isn't your thing, your options are limited.

SOMEECARDS.COM Wildly successful, funny greeting cards that everyone likes and you don't have to pay for—why didn't we all think of that? While many websites produce ecards, Someecards's content is topical, visually distinct, crude, and very popular.

> **Submissions guidelines:** There's a small staff of writers and a large base of contributors and user-generated cards.
> **Based:** New York, but you can work from anywhere.
> **Pros:** Great way to start getting material published regularly.
> **Cons:** The format is fairly limited, and there is not much in the way of pay.

MCSWEENEYS.COM If you are a comedy writer, you've probably submitted *something* to *McSweeney's*. Internet Tendency is the digital, and much more accessible, extension of the quarterly literary magazine founded by author Dave Eggers back in 1998. It's slightly less cutting-edge cool than it was then, but it remains a consistently funny place to write and read comedy in a simple, unadorned web environment.

> **Submissions guidelines:** The site features extensive, clever guidelines, but in short: keep all pieces under one thousand words, avoid attachments, and send original, unpublished work only.
> **Based:** San Francisco.
> **Pros:** Great way to have material published alongside well-known humorists and comedy writers.
> **Cons:** There is no pay for anything ever.

CULTURE SITES

This is a broadly defined category that includes anything that is not strictly news and contains content other than comedy, including Slate, Gawker, Boing Boing, Salon, Deadspin, io9, and others. Culture sites will generally have a house voice that ranges from irreverent to hip to snarky to hyperpolitical, and they proliferate across the web. These sites tend to have a defined editorial structure, so the content feels more like it belongs in one place and has a reason for existing. Thought is put into how and why things are published, and the good sites have established trust with their readership—a trust that allows some written pieces to be longer than a hundred words and probe deeper than the first observation that any casual cultural observer would come up with. Hopefully, moreover, it is relevant.

For these sites, you will most likely be required, from time to time, to write about things that might not contribute to the betterment of our society or our spiritual evolution as a species, and so long as you are okay with that, and with encouraging readers to "sound off" in the comments section below, you will probably be okay.

An Interview with **Brook Lundy**

"Some ideas take a while to get right, and some go from copy to being live on the site in about fifteen minutes."

Brook Lundy cofounded Someecards when he had the brilliant realization that Someecards didn't yet exist. Several years later, he runs one of the most popular humor sites on the web, with a dozen full-time staffers and a core of thirty contributors.

We try to go for sentiments that feel as honest and unexpected as possible rather than one-liners that are basically jokes without much of an insight to them. We always suggest to the writers that they start with the idea rather than the joke. All cards need to be one sentence, no question marks, no exclamation points. We established those rules at the beginning to make the cards as stripped down and simple as they can be: one image, one sentence.

Two senior editors and I send out a daily assignment to our contributor list. It could include anything from "backhanded holiday cards to send your boss" to "we need ideas about the new place Miley Cyrus fondled herself." Then we write ideas on our own and see what comes in throughout the day. The biggest indicator that an idea is right is if the three of us laugh, or at least feel something. Some ideas take a while to get right, and some go from copy to being live on the site in about fifteen minutes.

Someecards was an experiment that, best-case scenario, could lead to the job we really wanted: having our own thing. So we used all our free time on it. I woke up a lot at 3 am with my laptop on my belly and hundreds of ecard lines on it that needed to somehow be turned into cards the next day. But it was fun and absolutely worth it.

Writing Scripts

Whether or not you wind up on staff at an Internet comedy concern, you should be writing and producing videos of your own as often as you can. Why? Because you love comedy, and it is easy to do. Don't make me tell you why, jerk.

In my first year at Thing X, which would later become AdultSwim .com, we made two hundred videos. Some of them worked, a lot of them didn't, and almost all of them were too long. In time, we started to figure stuff out. The rules are generally the same for web as they are for film, except on the web you've got to do everything quicker and with 1/150,000,000 of the budget.

MAKE IT VISUAL Your videos have to look interesting from the very beginning and create an environment that viewers can immediately understand. (Unless your goal is to confuse them, in which case, do that in a visual way.) You don't have a lot of time to get your joke across, so you have to give us as much visual information as possible in the first five seconds.[6] In that short time, your script should answer the following questions:

What is the genre or context? If you are spoofing an action movie, say so right away with low-angle shots of a sweaty heroine tied to a chair or a close-up of a Russian terrorist talking into a walkie-talkie with a subtitle that says, "CAIRO—04:39." If it is a fake laundry detergent commercial, soften that focus and show us a dog running through a white sheet hanging from a clothesline. If it is a porno, people should be having anal sex. By setting a familiar context right away, you give your audience expectations that you can very shortly subvert.

Who is your main character? Whether they are fat, skinny, white, black, a car salesman, a doctor coming out of surgery, a divorced amputee, a gay Mongol, or a washed-up game show host, communicate this very quickly with powerful, specific details: Cover that doctor's face in blood and gore. Have that divorcée smoke Menthol Ultra 100s with a prosthetic hook. Give your Mongol a cashmere sweater. Allow your audience to make an immediate judgment about who this character is and what they want.

Where are we? Setting can tell a story right away, so be very clear from the opening shot. It makes a difference if the washed-up game show host is getting drunk at an elementary school talent show or has been kidnapped by al-Qaeda to star in their recruitment videos.

---

6 As soon as Vine came onto the mobile app scene with its six-second video limit, I knew right then that that was the new attention span. Not because Vine became the dominant content-delivery system, but because its users immediately started proving that videos can be entertaining and engaging while telling a story in under ten seconds. What's more, Vine is most popular with teenage and younger kids, meaning they'll be expecting their comedy to come in ultra-short form when they get out of college and have more money to spend. For Vine videos themselves, the attention span is actually a bit shorter: I have gotten bored of Vines after one or two seconds, meaning *YOU NOW HAVE ONE SECOND TO ENTERTAIN ME*.

Is anything ever going to happen? Right away, someone should answer a phone, get hit by a car, or wrestle a squid in a tuxedo. Nobody wants to watch two people talk to each other in a white room unless those two people are extremely famous or nude, and if they are nude, you can't show it on most websites. Action gives your characters something to react to and your audience something to be interested in.

DON'T OVERDO DESCRIPTIONS I have a terrible habit of skimming over description in scripts. People write too much of it and I get bored. You should never get bored with description. For example, you don't need to tell people exactly how many cubicles are in the office, but you *do* need to tell them that it's rapidly filling with smoke. Also keep these incredibly important tidbits in mind:

Be clear and forceful. People and objects shouldn't "seem" or "appear" to be anything. They are or are not. We're not doing magic tricks in Victorian England; we're writing web video scripts.

Let the reader fill in the gaps. Everyone knows what an emergency room looks like. They don't know that everyone in it is an Elvis impersonator.

Write like a caveperson. Subject—verb. That's it. "He falls." "She laughs." "Clown explodes." Boom.

MAKE IT SHORT Everyone should know this, but you would be amazed by how many first drafts still come in at three or four or— *Jesus Christ, no*—even five pages. Five pages equals five minutes in script time, and five minutes in Internet time is literally an eternity.[7] Your scripts should not be longer than two pages. If they are, they

---

7 Have you ever sat through a five-minute video online that was not either instructional, personal, or pornographic? It is impossible, because the video lasts for all eternity, and eternity is a concept the human mind is incapable of understanding.

had better be incredible: fast-paced, surprising, and mind-blowingly funny.

MAKE IT FUNNY Your script should make you laugh. If it doesn't make you laugh, then what's the point of writing it?

MAKE IT MAKEABLE The point of a script is to be produced, so, unless you are going for something highly stylized, everything in your video should look and feel as real as possible. Here are some guidelines. (However, since a script should always include whatever is necessary for the comedy, these aren't immutable laws.)

Limit your locations. The more locations you have, the more time it takes to shoot, the more lighting setups you have to endure, and the harder it will be to keep everything looking real. If your video *has* to be on a spaceship, then set it in the break room and make liberal use of aluminum foil.

Limit your characters. Good actors are hard to find, and every character you put in a script, no matter how small the part, needs a good actor. Can your spoof of *12 Angry Men* become *3 Dyspeptic Jurors?*

Limit your elaborate action sequences. Most fights are not funny if they don't look realistic, and it's very hard to make them look realistic. The same goes for jumping out of cars or getting attacked by a dog. There are, of course, exceptions, but the comedy is usually in how fake they look—why do that again?

Avoid children and animals. The old saying is true: "Children and animals are dumb and they ruin everything, so don't use them, ever." Even most adult humans don't take direction well, so don't push your luck with a kid or a python unless it's absolutely necessary.

Curb your special effects. There is so much amazing stuff that can be done with After Effects etc., but unless you can do it

AVOIDING "COMEDY IDEAS"

Did you know there's a difference between something that's *funny* and a *Comedy Idea?* It's true! A Comedy Idea is a concept or conceit manufactured by a comedy writer that gives the appearance of being funny but that lacks any real joy or inspiration. All of its components meet the criteria for comedy, but when taken as a whole, it falls apart. Why? Because the comedy writer created it scientifically in the hopes that the end result would resemble comedy enough to be funny. If you were to ask the comedy writer if they *actually find it funny*, however, the writer would have to say no. If they say yes, they probably should not be a comedy writer.

IDENTIFYING A COMEDY IDEA

- The setting is unnecessarily extreme, crude, or bizarre. The comedy writer is trying to force a laugh right away without establishing any kind of reality that the viewer can relate to.
- A lot of dialogue. Because it lacks inherent inspiration, the writer needs his characters to explain to the viewer why this idea is funny and to move things forward by talking.
- Violence. It can be used in plenty of truly funny ways, but one of the hallmarks of a comedy idea is to just start shooting or maiming and hope that the shock of violence will cause a few laughs.
- Familiarity. If you cannot shake the feeling that you've seen this idea before, neither could the comedy writer. A comedy idea without substance will naturally start filling itself in with details and jokes from previous comedy pieces that do have substance.

yourself—and do it well—limit how much you put in your script. Don't let exploding heads and ghosts become a crutch for comedy. That special effect should be a great, unexpected payoff, not a limping laugh line.

WRITE FOUR MILLION OF THEM Yes, four million scripts. Write them in your downtime and in your uptime. Give yourself restrictions: Use no dialogue. Use only two characters. Use only female characters. Keep the script to one page. Use no green screen. Use only green screen. When you have written four million scripts, then, and only then, will you be a comedy master who is also dead.

Chapter 5

WRITING SKETCH COMEDY

Sketch may well be the purest form of comedy, but like that game Othello and probably a bunch of other stuff, it can take a lifetime to master. Sketches are short, tight, packed full of jokes (or one incredibly well-earned joke), and often grouped together as part of a larger show. Some sketches are absurd, some are parodies, and some are musical, but all sketches are essentially one premise, explored and stretched and taken to the farthest degree possible—in the shortest possible time.

In the great arc of human history, there's only been a handful of successful sketch comedy shows: *Monty Python's Flying Circus, The State, The Kids in the Hall, A Bit of Fry & Laurie, Mr. Show with Bob and David, Saturday Night Live, Chappelle's Show, Key & Peele, The Tracey Ullman Show.* Sketch comedy is a noble pursuit but very difficult to pull off with any regularity. Even the cast and writers of *Saturday Night Live* only have to do it twenty times a year, and it's hard for them to maintain a decent batting average. Each sketch needs to exist as a complete piece all on its own, and it has to do so in three to five minutes, and in such a way that it is unlike any other sketch in that particular show. Moreover, in the case of *SNL*, most of the sketches need to be accessible to a national audience, incorporating recognizable personages, events, and trends—and all of it should be, you know, funny.

Where to Write Sketch Comedy

There are very few jobs dedicated to writing sketch comedy, but most comedy writers have written sketches at some point or another, usually while in college or as part of a sketch team at a local comedy theater. It's a great way to start out, since it teaches you about economy and structure, and it offers opportunities to explore many different genres, from fake commercials to period pieces. Naturally, most of the sketch comedy writing that happens on college campuses and in local comedy theaters is unpaid.

TELEVISION

The best way—although not the easiest way—to get work on a TV sketch show is to write and produce your own sketch show. The Kids in the Hall were discovered by *Saturday Night Live* producer Lorne Michaels this way, and The State was picked up by MTV based on their live performances. The Whitest Kids U' Know sold their show to Fuse after winning awards at a comedy festival. The few sketch shows that do exist will accept submissions in the same way as any other show (see chapter 6). Usually you need an agent, though it never hurts to contact a producer (just watch the credits!) and inquire about the show's policy.

RADIO

England has a legacy of radio sketch comedy that doesn't exist to the same degree in America (at least not since the 1970s). In Britain, the League of Gentlemen got their start on radio, as did Peter Serafinowicz (see page 58) and Robert Popper of *Look Around You* fame. Plus, the BCC's Radio 4 continues to produce sketch comedy shows. In America, there's not much more than a handful of NPR programs. Sketch comedy podcasts, however, are a growing genre, where you have creative freedom and a forum for attracting attention. For instance, *Comedy Bang! Bang!* started as a podcast before it was developed into a TV show on IFC.

LIVE

Surprisingly, you can make money performing live sketch comedy! Some clubs feature sketch nights, and there are paying gigs if you wind up on a sketch team at Second City or another prominent theater's touring company. Likewise, successful local sketch shows are not unheard of: the group Kasper Hauser has been doing shows for years in the San Francisco area, and *The Thrilling Adventure Hour*—a monthly staged reading in the style of an old-timey radio play—has consistently sold out in Los Angeles.

An Interview with **Seth Reiss**

"I hate laziness, and I hate when people lack passion."

Seth Reiss has written for *The Onion*, *Comedy Bang! Bang!*, and *Late Night with Seth Meyers*. He was also a member of the New York–based sketch group Pangea 3000, and he is one of the most focused and intense people I've ever had the pleasure of knowing. He's a lunatic, honestly, but a funny one.

A good sketch needs a good, solid, interesting concept. A great idea. And the sketch executes that idea perfectly. That's not to say the idea can't be simple. Even better when it's interesting *and* simple.

I really dislike when one person is acting crazy and the joke is other people commenting on how crazy that person is acting. People acting weird is great, but not when everyone else is completely sane. Then I wonder why the weird person isn't in a mental institution or why the sane people don't just say, "Yeah, I gotta go," when the weird person comes onstage.

I don't like when jokes come from conflict or arguing. I like when everyone is on the same page, carrying out the concept of the sketch together. Conflict-free sketch comedy.

I also don't like anything that feels like this: "An intervention, but instead of alcohol, it's for..." Shit like that is the worst. Any writer who comes up with that idea needs to say, "No, this is not funny or original. It mathematically works as a sketch, but it's not worth my time."

I hate laziness, and I hate when people lack passion. It translates when the group is onstage. The performance lacks energy. And, by the way, passion comes in all forms. Some people are quietly passionate, and that's equally as effective, if not more so, than being loudly passionate. I also always think I am an inch away from being the laziest person in the world.

Questions to Ask About Your Sketch

WHAT'S FUNNY ABOUT IT? You should be able to describe in one sentence what it is that you—*you*—find funny about your sketch, and then strive never to veer too far from that. Your sketch needs a strong central premise, but to me, that is secondary to the thing about it that makes you laugh. The premise may be that there's a scientist who doesn't know math, but what you may find *funny* is the way in which the scientist overcompensates by loudly identifying math whenever he sees it.

IS IT GROUNDED IN REALITY? Most great sketches, no matter how bizarre, have at least some connection to a relatable situation. It can be a small detail (an alien bounty hunter who needs coffee in the morning) or the framing context (a wedding for dolphins), but without something to relate to, the audience has no subvertable expectations. There's no real reason for anything to happen, which creates a general lack of reality. The sketch may be funny, but it will leave everyone feeling a little cold.

DOES IT HAVE A BEGINNING, MIDDLE, AND END? Who cares? A sketch doesn't need to follow traditional storytelling structures. All it needs to do is get something funny across in a surprising, committed way. The more it breaks structural conventions and lives in a territory just beyond description, the more memorable it will be.

CAN IT BE SHORTER? Antoine de Saint-Exupéry, the French aristocrat, writer, and founding member of the sketch comedy troupe the Horny Rhinos, wrote that perfection is only achieved, not when there is nothing left to add, but when there is nothing left to take away. It has never been said that a comedy sketch was too short. As you write, strip away anything that is not in the immediate service of the main joke or that does not propel us toward the end. Anything that you can do in four pages is twice as funny in two pages. That's just good math!

HOW DOES IT SOUND OUT LOUD? Read your sketches out loud, preferably as you write them, to experience them as your future audience will. Untold oodles of comedy are discovered through the rhythm and pace of the spoken word, and lots of jokes that sound funny and natural inside your head do not translate outside of it.

WHAT IS THE BIGGEST JOKE? This may not be the biggest laugh. The biggest joke is the moment the whole sketch builds toward. Locate that joke and you've found your ending. At that point, it doesn't matter how you get out, just do it fast. Your audience will appreciate an abrupt but perfectly timed ending more than a logical one that stretches the sketch beyond its big joke.

IS YOUR SKETCH A SKETCH? Sometimes what you're creating is better served by another format. If you've written seven pages and could keep going, you might actually be writing a screenplay. Or you might find that you don't know how the main character should act. This one might be a one-panel comic. Sometimes, that great idea might actually just not be very good. Let it slip into a coma in your notebook, and when you are famous, you can publish all that shit and sell it to the fans who have come to love and admire you for work that was good enough to finish.

An Interview with **Neal Brennan**

"Look at how crazy the world is if you're not white."

The cocreator and cowriter of *Chappelle's Show*, Neal Brennan is a director, voice artist, and standup comedian. Neal met Dave Chappelle while working at a comedy club, where he'd offer Chappelle and other comedians ideas for taglines to use in their acts. He talked about that and having a moral compass in sketch comedy.

On Influences

I started arguing with adults when I was six, and they weren't pulling punches. They were like, "You're a faggot! You're an idiot!" You know? There were no holds barred. It was full-contact, Irish, angry-male adult standard. I'm argumentative as hell as a result. People say, "Stop yelling!" And I go, "I'm not even yelling at all. What are you talking about? That's just my tone."

Being raised Catholic and going to Catholic school is a real primer for hypocrisy. It's like, "Oh, this is just constant bullshit—you're all full of shit! You're a molester. You're going to church, but meanwhile you're a horrible person." So I feel like I strive for social justice, and that was the special sauce of *Chappelle's Show*. It was this deep sense of, hey, look at the world from someone else's point of view for once. Dave Chappelle just happens to be one of the smartest dudes on earth who also happens to be black, but still, just look at how crazy the world is if you're not white.

On *Chappelle's Show*

It was the first personal sketch show. That was the magic of *Chappelle's Show*. There was Tracey Ullman's show, but Tracey Ullman was never actually Tracey Ullman. *Chappelle's Show* was sketches from the point

63

of view of one person. I mean, there were two of us, and sometimes we'd take outside ideas, but the filter was one guy. It wasn't a troupe.

We talked about "real" a lot. The difference between what's advertised versus what real life is really like. A lot of our formula was, "We're gonna do the real version of (blank)." The real movies. Like, *Pretty Woman* for real. It's taking the bullshit and going, "No, no, no. You're glossing over something here. Like, really, are all gangs interracial, moviemakers? Is there always a shifty-eyed white guy in a ski hat? Stop insulting our intelligence."

There's a sketch where Dave is playing George Bush, and he doesn't do anything different. I fought him on this, saying, "You're not doing an impression of anything. It's like a school play." And he was like, "It'll be funny." So he was just him. And it was like, you think George Bush looks crazy? Imagine how he would look if you were *black* looking at him. Here's how it would look, white people, if someone who wasn't white said, in the middle of the Gulf War, that we need to go to Mars. It's insane.

On Collaborating

I like writing with people. It's the difference between fishing alone or fishing with somebody. It can be really fucking lonely fishing by yourself. I like it because it's social. I'm a talker. I think that there's a big element of feeding off each other.

Dave once described he and me as thrill-killers. Where he'd stab somebody, and I'd be like, "Chop his fucking head off, Dave!" Then he'd be like, "You think so? You think I should chop his fucking head off?" And then he'd chop his head off, and he'd be like, "You should eat his fucking head!" And I'd be like, "Yeah, I should eat his head!" He'd write, and I'd write, and we'd turn to each other and try to entertain or impress the other person. That's part of writing with somebody: you don't have to imagine an audience. They're just right there.

On Dave Chappelle

It was one of those freaky things where Dave and I just have similar aesthetics. Even cinematically, it's like—the Rick James character *is* an Errol Morris movie. No one knows that, but that's what it is. Chappelle can do all of [former Defense Secretary] Bob McNamara's monologues from *The Fog of War* because he's just watched it over and over again. He can do a really good Bob McNamara, too. It's weird.

Dave was a guy who grew up around white people and black people. His dad was the first black student at Brown University. That's fairly significant. So when you look at that, it starts to make sense. All these guys, Kevin Hart, Kanye, Dave: their parents were all academics. There's something to that. I don't know what. They were coming out of the 1970s black power movement and civil rights; these guys are all an extension of that. So we couldn't really espouse bullshit. Me and Dave are both seekers in a way. We give a shit. I try to be moral. Don't get me wrong, I have tons of fucking moral failings—but at least I'll preach morality. Or espouse it in sketch comedy. That's the best I can do.

Chapter 6

WRITING FOR TV

Working in TV is the comedy-writing equivalent of being a lawyer: the pay is good, the hours are long, everyone thinks you're smarter than you really are, and most of the job is just sitting around. Even though there are fewer jobs in TV than there are in, say, HVAC repair or microbiology, it is an actual industry that offers comedy writers real opportunities to make a career. TV writing is not for everyone and is rarely as glamorous as the Instagram feeds or Emmy broadcasts would have you believe. Once you are in, though, it's easier and easier to get more work, and the more experience you have, the more money you make. And what is comedy writing about if it's not about getting those motherfucking Benjamins?

Getting Staffed

In TV, getting a job is called "getting staffed," and staffs can change from season to season depending on any number of things, from job performance to ratings. Most comedy writers work on a bunch of different staffs throughout their career, though some find one they like and manage to stay there for years.

WHERE

Like Washington, DC, Cupertino, and Nashville, Los Angeles is an industry town, and most TV writing jobs in the world are located there. One can find a TV job in New York on a talk show or the occasional network sitcom, and there are a few other cities with small TV industries, like Atlanta and Boston, but the vast majority of jobs are found on the West Coast. This is why so many New York comedians have trekked across the continent like Dust Bowl migrant workers, wearing hoodies instead of porkpie caps, in search of a steady paycheck.

WHEN

Most shows operate on the networks' programming schedule, and they hire writers depending on what gets renewed or canceled for the coming season. This usually takes place during the six-week period from mid-April to late May known as "staffing season." It's a bit of a feeding frenzy, with agents and managers pressing their writing clients to finish their goddamn writing packets (see page 78) and spec scripts (see page 86) so they can be considered for a position on staff. It's exciting and stressful and, like most things in TV, completely insane.

There are exceptions: If a show is picked up or a staff writer leaves midseason, positions will be filled then. Cable programs and those produced for Netflix, Amazon, Xbox, and the like operate on their own schedules and staff up as needed.

HOW

Show runners, producers, and head writers make the hiring decisions. They'll have a few people whom they know they want, and after that they'll go to their most trusted agents and managers and ask them for recommendations. Prospective writers will be asked for a writing sample, usually in the form of a packet or a spec script. Many places also want to see your Twitter feed, whatever videos you've written or produced, and of course, any other TV writing you've done.

> **PRO TERM!** SHOW RUNNER
>
> Part head writer, part producer, and part despot, the show runner is the most important person on any TV production. Depending on the person and the production, the show runner is responsible for the overall creative direction of the series, as well as hiring and firing writers and crew, fighting with network executives, and developing story lines. A good show runner is as comfortable in a writers' room as in an accountant's office, and they will often be the first person hired by a network or brought on to repair a struggling show.

WHO

First of all, producers and show runners want experience. TV shows are ticking time bombs waiting to blow up and get canceled, so producers are looking to reduce their risk by staffing people with a proven track record. Head writers always say that they're just looking for the funniest people, and they usually are, but they're also looking for people whom they know can hack the long hours, deliver scripts on time, and actually do the job that millions of people think they can do but never possibly could. So the first thing you need to do is obtain some experience, and the only way you can do that is by working, and the way to get work is to get noticed, so do standup, make videos, and contribute wherever you can. *That's* why you should be writing scripts all the time.

The Writers' Room

The writers' room is TV's inner sanctum, where ideas are born, changed, debated, and murdered. These are legendary places that very few people are ever allowed to see—special places that embody a weird alchemy of creativity, competition, camaraderie, and whiteboards. Each one is different.

The first writers' room I ever worked in was at *The Onion*, and from the moment I walked in, I felt an immediate sense of hierarchy and decorum. I wasn't even allowed to sit with everyone else and was relegated to one of the shitty chairs off to the side. It was only after several almost-silent months that I was permitted a seat at the table itself.

Like at *The Onion*, most writers' rooms are a complex topography to navigate: they are the one time and place when the whole writing staff must come to consensus—or something resembling consensus—where style and substance can be discussed and brought to life, and when the force of will can overpower the strength of written words.

Each writers' room works differently, depending on the chemistry of the group, the leader's style, and organizational traditions. But all of them will (usually) include these three parts: the pitch, the brainstorm, and the table read.

THE PITCH

When writers pitch, they bring their ideas for episodes, storylines, character arcs, and scenes and try them out before the whole staff. This affords a great opportunity to gauge first reactions, cut bad material, and identify potential. There is a performance aspect to pitching as well, whereby you attempt to bring your idea to life in the room and convince a group of skeptics that it can work on the screen.

SOME TIPS FOR PITCHING[8]

Be confident. Nothing undersells an idea like a yawn or a mumble in the middle of your pitch. Don't say things like, "This is dumb, but . . ." because the first thing people will think is "This idea is dumb." Confidence inspires others to take the idea seriously and gives them permission to riff on it, and a riffed pitch is a healthy pitch.

If you aren't confident, fake it. You should already be doing this.

Let go. If your pitch doesn't go anywhere, put it in a deep freeze and say good-bye. Give yourself one chance to clarify or elaborate, but spending time defending something that doesn't inspire enthusiasm will wind up making everyone hate you and your idea and your next idea. You will look much better if you improve it on your own time and repitch a better version later (where it will probably die again).

Focus on what is funny. Don't bury your pitch in details and caveats, but emphasize immediately what makes *you* laugh. I often hear, long after the pitch has lost the room, "I just think it would be funny to see [blank]." Describe what you think *is actually funny* about your idea right off the bat.

---

8 Please note that these are general tips, gleaned from my own experience working in, observing, and talking about writers' rooms. These do not apply to all rooms and circumstances, and following them can sometimes get you ridiculed or fired.

Bring backup. A good idea sparks other good ideas, so be ready with some jokes and brainstorms of where your pitch could go. Don't lead with hilarious options, but offer them as fuel for the creative fire or as a defense against detractors.

THE BRAINSTORM

This is usually the funnest part of the process, because it's a chance to joke around and build on each other's ideas before anyone has to go off and actually turn them into scripts to be judged and befouled by the monsters you work with. Brainstorming happens at different times depending on the show, be it during the pitch or table read, or as a separate meeting.

THE TABLE READ

The staff comes together to read aloud whatever scripts were written that week. It's often the first time anyone has read this material. Scripts are torn apart, punched up, lauded, made better, or sometimes ruined. This is where new writers learn the most about how to improve their work and get the opportunity to perfect one of the most important parts of the job: taking notes.

SOME TIPS FOR TAKING NOTES

Listen. You worked very hard on your script, and you really want to impress everyone, but at first you are going to suck,[9] so the best thing you can do is just listen. Over time, you will be able to pick out the notes that really matter, and you'll identify trends in the kinds of notes you're receiving.

---

9 There are only two people I've ever worked with who never sucked: Mike DiCenzo, who was one of the first people hired at *Late Night with Jimmy Fallon*, and Megan Ganz, who has worked at *Community* and *Modern Family*. Everyone else was terrible over and over and over again until one day they suddenly weren't. Myself included.

Assume people want to help. It's very easy to feel that you are under attack (because you are) during the notes phase, but you will get more out of it if you understand that everyone is just trying to make the show better. Of course, this isn't actually the case, since there will always be people who only want to hear themselves talk, but treating them with respect will force them to do the same for you. (Or not. But don't worry: everyone on staff knows they're an asshole.)

Don't look defensive. Even if you feel defensive, just look down at your script, nod, and write something—anything—in your notes. But never smile! You will look like an insane person.

Ask questions sparingly. If you legitimately need clarity on a note, ask for it, but don't do it just to be contrary. This isn't to say you should be silent, either, which can come off as disengaged. Just pay attention and ask questions when you really need to, but only then, okay?

Don't take every note literally. It's hard to know which notes to implement and which not to, but as a general rule, the only ones you need to leave the room and go write down verbatim are the ones given by your boss. The rest of the time, you should do your best to pick and choose from the funniest suggestions and try to put your own spin on them.

Beware the big laugh. One of the gravest mistakes you can make is to take a brainstormed joke that was very popular and try to wedge it in somewhere it doesn't belong. The danger here is that you will become so distracted trying to chase that one moment in the room that you lose sight of larger, more important notes. You should always try, though, so you will have an answer for the inevitable question: "Hey, what happened to that joke about the overweight raccoon that I came up with?"

An Interview with **Danny Zuker**

*"I've seen more writers fired for not shutting
up than just about any other crime."*

Danny Zuker has been working in television since 1848, starting
off at *The Arsenio Hall Show*, where he learned to write topical
jokes, day after day, on deadline. Eventually he wound up at
Modern Family, one of the best, most popular sitcoms of the
2000s. He talked about what he thinks makes a good writers'
room and how they work.

On Starting Out

My first sitcom room was *Evening Shade*. I spent the first half of that
season really listening to the more seasoned writers. Learning about
story. And of course pitching to a room. It's a delicate balance for a
new writer. It's about picking your spots. I learned that there. Also I
learned that sometimes the cast of a show isn't your friend. I guess
what I'm saying is Burt Reynolds is evil. This lesson was important
because I would then go on to work with Roseanne and then Brett
Butler. It wasn't until I got to *Just Shoot Me* that I dealt with great
actors who were also great people and great collaborators.

On the Process

At *Modern Family,* we come up with the stories in a group. These
often come from our own lives or people we know or sometimes
out of thin air. As we talk, the stories take shape, and we write out
very general beats on a whiteboard as a writers' assistant takes notes.
One of us will then go off and turn those notes into a detailed
outline. The outline will then come back to the group, and we will
pitch on that, often throwing out stories and coming up with new
ones or at least modifying them significantly. Then with the revised

outline in hand, a writer will hole up for a week and write a draft. The draft then comes back to the room, where we tear into it yet again. Even a great first draft will change significantly through this process. Then the actors read this table draft around, yes, a table. Based on the read we will make changes yet again and get it ready for shooting the following week.

On Collaborating

I personally have scripts with my name on them that as much as 60 or 70 percent came from other writers in the room. Conversely, there are scripts I'm not credited on where I've written whole acts. You learn quickly not to become too precious with your material or you don't last long.

The writer or writers of the draft are very involved in the shoot—on the stage or location for all of it. Often doing more punch up or bigger changes on the fly. Working with the director and the actors. After all, no one is more intimately familiar with the material than the writer. It always boggles my mind that in features the writer is frequently barred from the set. I honestly believe this is why movie comedies are never or rarely funnier than the funniest TV shows. You want writers there to pitch when things don't work.

Getting By in the Room

I think the best rooms are supportive but demanding. There needs to be a benevolent dictator at the head of the table who sets the ground rules, who determines when the discussion is over and it's time to move on to the next thing. And to call people out who are either talking too much, not enough, or pitching hacky stuff. It's up to the writer to have a thick skin, to be shot down and come back and pitch something else.

I've seen more writers fired for not shutting up than just about any other crime. That said, you're only talking too much if your ideas or jokes aren't great. As long as good stuff is coming out, by

75

all means keep on talking. Best thing a new writer can do is listen to the room. Get a feel for the direction the room is going. Many times I've seen the room decide on a path through a story after much deliberation, and as we go down that path a new writer begins pitching again on something we've already locked onto. When I'm running a show, I'm really looking for jokes from new writers. It's great if they have story pitches. I mean, we need them, but a great way to contribute is to really listen to what the room and show runner want and pitch within that framework.

The worst thing any writer can do is get married to their ideas. Write a book if you want final say, but in TV it's collaborative. And don't take a rejection of your jokes or stories as a rejection of you. You really need to take it with a smile and keep pitching.

The Shows

Up to this point, we've mainly been looking at the sitcom model of TV comedy writing. But other types of shows require staffs of comedy writers to write them. Here's a very brief overview of said types.

THE TALK SHOW Popular and relatively inexpensive to produce, the talk show has provided work for comedy writers for millennia. From *Conan* to *The Daily Show*, talk shows offer a number of advantages for writers:

Reliability. Once established, they run much longer than the average sitcom. You can almost always rely on the fact that they will be hiring and that there will be new positions each year.

Good hours. Because these shows are daily, they tend not to break your back *quite* as much as programs that have more time (which means more time to fill with work) to write each episode.

Longer contracts. These shows are usually on air forty weeks a year, four or five days a week, which is much more airtime than a ten- or twenty-episode sitcom season.

Other opportunities. Even if you don't get on staff, you can usually submit ideas or bits on a regular basis. Most talk shows also have writers dedicated solely to the monologues, which is another way to get your jokes on air.

THE SKETCH SHOW At the time of this book's writing, the sketch comedy show was enjoying a veritable renaissance on American television, with at least four on Comedy Central, as well as *Portlandia, The Eric André Show,* and the perennial *Saturday Night Live.* Each show does things in a different way and relies heavily on writing (for more, see chapter 5).

THE REALITY TV SHOW Lots of writers got their start writing for cable reality shows like those on Spike or MTV. This doesn't mean all of the participants' lines are written, but things like scenarios, interview questions, and little pop-up commentaries are. They do not pay extraordinarily well, nor are they the most elevated version of the comedic form, but they offer a great experience and a chance to experiment with weird and tasteless comedy without a ton of oversight.

THE PANEL SHOW Programs like *Chelsea Lately, Best Week Ever,* and *Girl Code* offer a sumptuous buffet upon which the world's comedians may feast. Their format is designed for joke writing and allows for a wide variety of voices and styles.

THE KIDS' SHOW There will never, ever, ever be a shortage of programming for children, and almost all of it, even on the most educational shows, is comedic in nature. Programs like *Adventure Time* and *Regular Show* offer smart comedy that can be written and consumed by adults without shame.

The Packet

Since comedy is designed to be an endlessly cruel enterprise of disappointment and agony, the profession has devised the one thing more horrible than a cover letter: the packet. This can take any number of forms but is ultimately a representation of what you, as a comedy writer, are capable of. A packet can be a thirty-minute spec script, a pile of sketches, an original teleplay, or some combination of the above. If it is for one of the late-night talk shows, it will often consist of monologue jokes, sketches in the host's voice, jokes for recurring segments, or ideas for new segments that fit into their milieu.

Except for a very few born writers—those lucky psychopaths who take pleasure in crafting jokes and structuring entire humor pieces—writing a packet will be a difficult and trying experience. This is on purpose: most shows want only the best writers, and they want those writers to jump in and start producing material right away. The first few times you submit a packet, the only reward will likely be the satisfaction of a job well done. That is, the position will go to someone else.

Your packet should be something you are proud of, something you are always updating and improving, because openings will come up unexpectedly—and so you, the unwitting potential comedy writer, will be asked to submit one with little or no notice.

CREATING A PACKET

Long before you have a specific show to submit to, you can start compiling your best sketches, prose pieces, scripts, and monologue jokes. Then be brutal: throw them away, and write new stuff. If you want to write for a particular show, start coming up with episode ideas for that show and, slowly but surely, plug away at a twenty-two-page script. Then throw that away and start all over again. Show your work to people you trust, and if you can gain the access (e.g., via Twitter or by being related to a head writer), show it to someone in a position to hire comedy writers while there *isn't* an opening. That way, you'll get their honest feedback. Pressure is great, but so is the opposite of that.

SUBMITTING A PACKET

GET AN OPINION If you have one, an agent or manager is the first person you should show your packet to (see chapter 21). They should be your first and last critic, because they have a vested interest in you and the people they are bringing you to. They know what the shows want, and they know what goes into a good packet. So listen to them. Feel free to ask trusted friends and acquaintances for their opinions as well. But it's your manager's opinion that really matters. He or she is the only one who gets paid if you get hired.

KNOW WHAT YOU'RE WRITING FOR Watch the show you're submitting to and get your hands on some scripts. This seems boring, and is boring, but this is work, after all, and if you turn in something that doesn't match the tone of the show, you will look like an idiot.

EDIT IT Cut anything that you wouldn't read aloud in front of the people you hope will hire you. Then go through and do it again. And again, and again. I know that less than 1 percent of comedy writers actually do this, but I also know that 97 percent of that 1 percent are currently working on a show somewhere.

DON'T TAKE REJECTION PERSONALLY Yes, you are pouring your heart and soul into your packet, and yes, it's the very best you can do, but it doesn't mean you're not funny if (when) you get rejected. Everyone gets rejected, and shows are looking for different kinds of writers at different times.

INSIDE THE PACKET

Here's what a handful of shows have asked for in their packets.

The Daily Show
- Sample correspondent piece
- Headlines
- Ten to fifteen monologue jokes

The Nightly Show with Larry Wilmore
- A two-minute rant for Larry on a current event
- 15–20 monologue jokes
- Two ideas for field pieces
- Two ideas for studio segments

Modern Family
- Half-hour sitcom spec script
- Your personal Twitter account
- Any other personal writing

Saturday Night Live
- Three to five sketches, including at least one commercial parody, one topical/pop culture sketch, and one other
- Any other writing
- Links to produced videos

SAMPLE PACKET

Reproduced below, for your consideration and my humiliation, are packet submissions that did not get me jobs at *Late Night with Jimmy Fallon* or *The Daily Show with Jon Stewart*. These were not only great practice and a lot of fun to write (hahaha, just kidding! They were horrible for me), but they also taught me a very important lesson about the Business of Comedy: No matter how good, bad, or mediocre your style of writing may be, if it's not a fit for the particular show you're trying for, you probably will not get the job. It says nothing about your sense of humor, your work ethic, or the quality of your formative childhood trauma—it is just the way it is. For this book, I've amended these submissions with notes from my older, wiser self.

THE DAILY SHOW

Analysis of SCOTUS Ruling: Free Speech Should Not Be Limited

Jon Stewart: The Supreme Court reversed nearly a century of progress today, ruling that corporations should be allowed to spend as much money as they want on political campaigns, because it is their first amendment right to do so, since they are technically considered people. Massive, extremely rich people who live forever, throw really awkward Christmas parties, and never go to the bathroom.

Here now to give us a little insight is our own Joe Randazzo.

Joe Randazzo: Thanks, Jon.

Jon: Joe, what's your take on this whole "corporations are people" thing?

Joe: Well, I'm a people-person, Jon, so I'm all for it. Look, life will not change for the majority of Americans with this new ruling. The only thing that's going to be different is you'll have to send Exxon/Mobil a birthday card once a year as well as totally bend to its will when it comes to politics, rule of law, and how this very country is run.

> I read this and think, "You obviously used to work for *The Onion*, Joe Randazzo," because this last part feels very much like one of their joke constructions. —JR

Jon: Don't you think corporations are already well represented, what with lobbyists and the sheer amounts of money they possess?

Joe: Not at all, Jon. If anything, this is a chance to get closer to our corporations. For instance, did you know that Raytheon, the weapons manufacturer based out of Massachusetts, prefers to go by "Jim" and he's extremely sensitive about his dandruff? This is why he's going to buy out Selson Blue in a hostile corporate takeover and donate $50 million next fall to a Republican candidate for Congress who will draft a law making it illegal to wear black turtlenecks.

> Hey, this concept isn't half bad: give these big companies the traits, flaws, and foibles of ordinary people, making the whole idea of corporations as people seem ridiculous. Nice job, Past Joe! —JR

Likewise, few are aware that McDonald's is their brother-in-law, and now he'll pretty much be able to crash at their place whenever he wants, driving them and their families crazy because he smells like grease and won't stop singing that "I'm Lovin' It" song. Viciously slaughtering cows in the bathroom will also really start to wear on people's patience.

> This is not how people talk, Joe. Reads like something written by a comedy writer. —JR

In the coming weeks, we'll learn so much more about Nike, who has plans to adopt more than 30,000 Indonesian children, and KFC, who's lovable but definitely has crabs, and L.L.Bean, who's pretty much the annoying, stuck-up prick you'd expect him to be.

Jon: What about Volkswagen?

Joe: *(whispering)* Gay.

Jon: Really? Who else?

Joe: Heineken.

Jon: Who else, who else?

Joe: *(Mimics the action of loading and firing a gun)*

Jon: A gun company?

Joe: All of them.

Jon: I knew it!

Joe: Oh, and Avon? *(mimes drinking and stumbling around drunk)*

Jon: Isn't there a larger concern here, Joe? For years Congress has sought to limit the influence of corporations on politics, and now the Supreme Court says, "The person with the most money gets the loudest voice," which in many ways undermines the very foundations of democracy, doesn't it?

Joe: No.

Jon: WHY NOT?!

Joe (delivered as impassioned soliloquy): Because, Jon, I deserve a break today. The best part of waking up is everyday low prices, and there are some things money can't buy. For everything else, there's MasterCard. You know, Jon, if you really think about it, I betcha can't eat just one. R-O-L-A-I-D-S, because you're worth it, they're grrrrrrrrreat, and raise your hand, raise your hand if you're sure. Kills bugs dead. Look, maybe she's born with it, but *maybe* it's *Maybelline*. Let your fingers do the walking. You've come a long way, baby. Fly the friendly skies, Jon. We love to fly and it shows. So see what Brown can do for you! Snap into a Slim Jim, Jon. Think different. Be all you can be. Sometimes you feel like a nut, sometimes you don't. Taste it again, for the first time, but most of all: Why ask why? Try Bud Dry.

> Pretty funny idea! Too long, though, you jerk. Not sure the audience would sit through this… —JR

Jon: Is that really your response?

Joe: (humming the Intel jingle) Do do do dooooo!

Jon: Joe Randazzo everyone.

LATE NIGHT WITH JIMMY FALLON

Thank-You Notes

Thank you, airplanes, for being mankind's greatest technological achievement that I can pee in.

> Thank-you notes was an existing bit on the show. —JR

Thank you, people who reply to emails all in lowercase, which is basically like saying, "I think you're important, but not important enough to hold down the shift button three times."

> I like this joke, but maybe it's not clear enough in its construction to be immediately gettable. —JR

Thank you, lady who stood in front of the ATM checking her receipt for forty-five seconds even though there were, like, eleven people waiting in line behind her…for saving me from that ATM fire the other day.

> What? I wrote this, and I have no idea what it means. —JR

Thank you, people who say, "To be honest with you," which is basically like saying, "I have never been honest with you."

Thank you, crippling case of Tourette's Syndrome, for never flaring up in the middle of a nationally televised [*PAUSE as Jimmy struggles to stifle a torrent of swearwords*] let's move on to the next one.

> Probably better not to make jokes about conditions that are truly nightmarish and debilitating for some people, right, Past Joe? Maybe you should read chapter 3. —JR

Thank you, birds, for being the only member of the animal kingdom that can sing, fly, and be made into a nugget.

Thank you, Standard & Poor's, for downgrading America's credit rating but not repossessing the Grand Canyon.

> Please stop trying to write topical jokes now. —JR

> This was a bit I conceived for the packet —JR

Proposed Desk Piece: Know Your Fads

Jimmy keeps up-to-date to the ever-changing fads today's young people are getting into.

We've all heard of sexting, but do you know about "Tex-Mexting"? It's when two people share mouthwatering recipes for fajitas, chili con carne, and margarita chicken over a mobile phone, and then have oral sex.

> Proposed Desk Piece just made me laugh, which means that I hate myself more now than I did when I wrote this. —JR

There's another one that's really catching on in Florida right now called smorkeling, which is smoking cigarettes while snorkeling.

And of course, one of the latest and hottest new fads, "doodling," when teens absentmindedly draw random pictures on a piece of paper during class or a meeting…and then have oral sex.

> You have to know what's appropriate for your audience. Oral sex jokes on network television need to be a little more indirect than this. Even if it's a funny concept (which is debatable), if it can't be aired, it's useless. Come on, Past Joe, Alex Baze explains this on the next page. —JR

An Interview with **Alex Baze**

"Most people's packets aren't that great."

Alex Baze has worked as head writer on *Late Night with Seth Meyers* and as producer of Weekend Update on *Saturday Night Live*. As the guardian of some of comedy's most respected voices, he's had occasion to look at hundreds of submissions and think about what makes a good one and what makes a bad one.

Be Original

Most people's packets aren't that great. It's hard to do. It's not even so much that we're looking for something as it is we're looking *past* something, to be honest. You get a lot of the same shit. For Weekend Update, we asked people to send in ten jokes, and I had people asking if we want more. No. You can tell after three jokes, so believe me, it's an act of generosity that anyone's allowed ten.

You read down the list and think, "I've seen that. Leno did that Tuesday. There's nothing new here." So I'm just looking for anything new—a voice I haven't really heard, or a version of a voice that I haven't really heard. If it's original and it's funny, then it will get swept up and incorporated into the Update voice. I want people who can write stuff that sounds like Update, but I don't want it to sound like Update from three years ago. I want it to be able to fit but be new.

Do Your Homework

There are people who send in jokes that are filled with curse words, and I think, "Oh, you don't even understand what the job is." Gone. Or racist stuff, or super sexist stuff, and I think, "You don't even understand that this is television. This is a network. We can't do that." Listen, I love racism, but this is a network and we can't do that.

85

Do they understand what the show is? Do they understand who the host is and what he or she can do? And do they have some original bite of some kind, whether it's structure, subject matter, or something we haven't seen. It's rare.

Deal with Drudgery

It's really hard to write setup/punch line jokes. You're starting from scratch twelve times. If the first joke eats it, all right, start again. If one joke does great, that has nothing to do with the next joke. Start from scratch again. It isn't like a sketch, which builds and ebbs and flows. You're starting from zero every time. I've been doing it for ten years now, and I'll go in on Monday and look at the setups and think, "I have no idea how to do this. No idea."

At Weekend Update, they have to cover the same jokes that every other late-night TV show, and all the blogs and prominent Twitter users, have already had five days to warm over. So, when covering something that has already been through every conceivable iteration, what you want is for the audience to hear your Anthony Weiner joke and think, "Wow, they fucking found a new one. After all the shit I've listened to this week, they found a different take. Cool."

PRO TERM! SPEC SCRIPT

An unsolicited, unproduced episode of an existing television show written for a prospective employer. You will almost always be asked to submit a spec script for a show other than the one you're applying for. This is done for two reasons: to get a demonstration of your range, and to make sure that writers who don't get hired will not later accuse producers of stealing anything from their submission.

Chapter 7

WRITING BOOKS

Though the printed word was officially pronounced dead in 2009 at the age of 560, a small number of humorous books are still published each year. In fact, book writing remains an important part of the Comedy Person's portfolio, be it in the form of memoirs, essays, instructional manuals, or plain old silliness.

This is not to say that selling (or writing) a book is easy. Nowadays, it's hard to get a publisher to invest in anything that isn't already a proven commodity. This means that prospective authors usually have to demonstrate a built-in audience through a popular blog or Twitter account or, even better, be famous. The best way around this remains the oldest: write something incredible.

There are other options besides being a genius. Many people today are self-publishing with growing success. The publishing industry itself is undergoing incredible change now that people carry powerful computers with access to all the information in the galaxy in their jacket pocket. The old business models are dying, but until they are replaced, book publishers remain the best way to reach a wide audience, get a nice-looking book, and earn some walking-around money.

How to Get a Book Deal

When I first thought of writing a book, I wanted to do a parody of a writing instructional manual that would "accurately" portray the abject horror and pain of the writing process, with suicide tips, a masturbation schedule, drinking program, and any number of hilarious comedic constructs. My agent suggested that I broaden the scope of the book to the whole comedy industry with interviews and useful information and not as much about masturbation. The reason he suggested this, besides it being a good idea, was that he knew a specific publisher that wanted a book just like that. It took us a while to come up with an idea that I was excited about and that we both thought would work, and then I started writing a proposal. When that was done, we presented it to the publisher, and they passed. They weren't interested in the idea anymore. I committed suicide, and my agent retired from representation forever and ever.

Then the real strength of having an agent came in: he took the proposal (which was over twenty pages long, and quite humorous, thank you) to several other publishers and held what is called an open auction for the rights to the book. We met with four houses, talked about the book and how many celebrities I was going to beg to do interviews for it, and three of them put in a bid. I chose Chronicle, and then, all of a sudden, the book was written, designed, laid out, marketed, and published, just like that!

Here is that process again in seven easy steps:

STEP 1. HAVE AN IDEA

This part is pretty important, guys. A lot of the book business—indeed, the entire content-creation business—depends on the originality of the idea. Unless you are a celebrity or have lived an incredibly weird and accomplished life pockmarked by bizarre sexual encounters with celebrities, start by exploring an established publishing niche. Remember, we are talking now about *conceptualizing* your topic, not necessarily *writing* a book. The topic, the idea, is what you'll sell the publisher on, and what you'll eventually sell readers on, so think in simple terms that are easily blurbable. You can worry about being funny later.

The possibilities are infinite, but let's make them finite for a moment with a list of all the categories under "humor" on the popular e-commerce site Amazon.com:

Business & Professional; Cats, Dogs & Animals; Comedy; Computers & Internet; Cooking; Doctors & Medicine; Essays; Hunting & Fishing; Jokes & Riddles; Lawyers & Criminals; Limericks & Humorous Verse; Love, Sex & Marriage; Parenting & Families; Parodies; Political; Puns & Wordplay; Religion; Rural Life Satire; Science & Scientists; Self-Help & Psychology; Sports; Theories of Humor; Urban Legends

While this may seem like an exhaustive list of the whole of human experience, one should be able to skim it and identify gaps. For instance: Every household has a bookshelf full of "Limericks & Humorous Verse," but do they own a limerick book that deals exclusively with the well-endowed cast of *Mad Men?* Or, mine your own experience for inspiration: maybe you grew up in a fundamentalist religious household and know how useful it would be to have a how-to book for people like yourself who want to reenter society. It's not enough to be funny. Your idea needs to be both immediately identifiable yet original in ways that hook the public, the publisher, and an agent. Here are some comedy genres to consider.

PARODY One of the most recognizable and best-selling forms of written comedy is parody. Readers have an immediate entrée to the subject matter and format, meaning that the book doesn't have to rely on *you*, the goddamn *author*, as its sole selling point. (Great for noncelebs!) There is almost no limit to the kinds of books that can be parodied: in-flight catalogs, children's books, encyclopedias, true crime, best sellers, historical memoirs, survival manuals, and AP style guides, to name but a few.

ESSAYS/MEMOIR It helps when writing a memoir or personal essay if people are already interested in your life, but this genre also allows comedians not necessarily known for their literary talents a chance to expand their range. Other memoirists began their careers as journalists or freelance writers. Another thing you can do is be one of the people from *Duck Dynasty*, a wildly popular reality show from the 2010s that no one I know ever actually saw.

SHORT STORIES In general, short stories do not sell as well as other genres, but they also represent some of the best comedy writing ever. Think: George Saunders, Donald Barthelme, and James Thurber. This is not, however, a way to make your millions. For those who want to write fourteen funny short stories, self-publishing is a great option.

IMPULSE HUMOR This probably accounts for the bulk of the humor books printed these days: simple, funny concepts that can sustain themselves over a short book. Talking dinosaurs, life advice from cats, life advice from dogs, robot porn, etcetera. These sell well because they're broad and gettable and their concepts can be proven on blogs or Tumblr.

ZOMBIES Fucking books about zombies.

CURATED These are collections of funny things, which can range from humorous autocorrected text messages to funny sayings by famous dead people to the brilliantly inane letters, and their equally inane responses, of British comedian Robert Popper's alter ego, Robin Cooper, in *The Timewaster Letters*, and its sequels.

POLITICAL HUMOR The only thing people love more than being told they are right is seeing their enemies humiliated. Hence, political humor. This genre achieves the rare comedy double whammy of making readers feel that they are part of an inside joke while also disparaging an entire group of people. There are endless angles and styles, encompassing parody, satire, commentary, and memoir; the only criterion is that you say something mean about the other side in the book's title.

STEP 2. GET AN AGENT

Though there are occasional tales about wildly talented first-time writers signing deals based on the strength of a manuscript that found its way through some serpentine miracle to the desk of the right editor at the right time, the reality is that writers need representatives to navigate the publishing world. Agents understand trends, can help shape your proposal, and most importantly, know the people who make books. Their job is to know the things you can't know (and shouldn't have to worry about) and to make you look better than you actually are—and you're already pretty damn good.

Most Comedy People get noticed for their blogs, freelance writing, or work they've done in another forum, like standup or acting. It is certainly possible to cold call a talent agency and let them know you exist, but it helps if you have some reason for them to think you might be interesting to a wider audience.

Start by scouring the acknowledgments and thank-you sections of your favorite humor books for agents or their agencies. Make a list of these names and then compose what is called a query letter: a three-paragraph letter or email explaining your idea, who you are, and why you are contacting them. Most agents will accept query letters but are under no obligation to read or reply to them. If you haven't heard back in a month or so, you can write a brief follow-up reminding them who you are (easily achieved by replying to the original email that you sent a month before), but don't push it beyond that. It just won't accomplish anything.

PRO TIP! CHOOSE YOUR AGENT WISELY

Never work with agents who try to charge you a fee for reading your material or meeting with you. Most agents will ask you to sign an agreement outlining your obligations to each other and their fee structure, but an honest agent will never charge you anything until you start earning money yourself.

An Interview with **Daniel Greenberg**

"The Internet has become the proving ground for book ideas."

Daniel Greenberg has been an agent since the early 1990s and represents some of the biggest names in comedy, including Marc Maron, Patton Oswalt, Demetri Martin, Kristen Schaal, Mindy Kaling, Chuck Klosterman, Anthony Jeselnik, and *The Onion.* In fact, it was his work selling *The Onion*'s first original book that helped launch his career selling humor and comedy books.

On Starting Out

I called the editor-in-chief (of *The Onion*), Scott Dikkers, and asked if they'd ever thought about doing a book, and that became *Our Dumb Century.* So that was suddenly my niche. I developed an eye for it and got a reputation for working in comedy. I did always like comedy and humor, and it was nice to realize that I could follow my passions into my job.

On What Publishers Want

If you're not a well-known person, the Internet has become the proving ground for book ideas. It's very hard to predict what the next successful humor book is going to be, and publishers would prefer to sign somebody up who already has some sort of following online. They are aware that, just because something is big online, it doesn't mean it's going to be successful as a book. But the thinking is, why not go to somebody that people are already looking at and enjoying? That said, I still look for fresh ideas from people that are just funny—it just really needs to be spectacularly funny now to sell it to a publisher. It's doable. It just needs to be great.

On Comedy Essays

We see comedic essay collections all the time because of the success of Chelsea Handler, Tina Fey, David Sedaris, and Mindy Kaling. It's proven to be a category of book that people want to read. It's a high bar, but if you have an organizing principle for your book and the essays are laugh-out-loud funny, it would be my responsibility to call a publisher and say, "You haven't heard of this person, but you need to read these pages."

We'd want to see thirty to sixty pages of writing—enough to get a real sense of the voice—and an outline of what else would be in the book. It's almost always sold off a proposal, rather than a finished manuscript.

On Good Proposals

One of the most important things for a comedy proposal is a great title. It's nice to get a laugh right off the bat, and it also shows that you have an idea that's easily gettable. You have very little time to explain to people what the book is, and a good title is able to do that. You also need a real sense of the marketplace so that you can say, "This is for the readers of X, Y, and Z." And don't use the obvious ones: at this point, you can't use David Sedaris or Chelsea Handler. That's not a good thing to do because everyone uses them. You want to show that you're thoughtful about what else is out there and how you're going to help the publisher market the book. Use specifics. People who can help you support the book, concrete ways to get the book out there, and creative ideas. Come across as someone who realizes that the book is not going to sell itself and that you're going to be involved in that process.

On Finding an Agent

You're going to want to look at what other books they've represented, and you should ask them specific questions about how the process worked with other writers at your level. Big names are nice, but if you're not a big name, you shouldn't be overly impressed with an agent who has famous clients. It's a different process selling somebody who's trying to break through. You also need to like your agent and get a sense of trust. You want them to be realistic and not promise too much. You'll want to ask them for specific ideas: if you have some general ideas, see if they seem to be pointing you in the right direction for the kinds of books you can write. That's always a good sign.

On Choosing a Publisher

You really want to make sure you and the editor are on the same page. The worst thing you can do is agree with everything they have to say about your proposal just to get the deal, and then find that you really don't see eye to eye. You'll want to give your contract a very close read and have someone walk you through exactly what you're responsible for and what happens if you deliver something late or different from what you'd promised. And you want to look at the exclusivity—if you're going to be funny professionally, you'll want to make sure you don't have to wait a long time after publishing this book to start contemplating new ideas that you can take to other publishers.

On Self-Publishing

As for ebooks, you can upload your book to the major online sellers, and if you already have a platform—audiences who follow you and like you—you can direct them to the retailers, and they can buy your book directly. You can make a lot more money per book that way, but you won't get an advance, so if you need money to write your book, you're not going to get it that way. And there are a lot of people doing this and a lot of clutter, and you'll be fighting to be seen. Doing print distribution on your own is a lot more challenging. The other thing is, the media and publicity outlets that you'll want to write about your book are still mainly going through traditional publishing houses to decide what to cover.

STEP 3. WRITE A PROPOSAL

Once you have your great idea, and you've gotten an agent and put them on speed dial, which is not even a thing anymore, I don't think—what would it be called now? Favorites? Friends and family? Laser dial?—you need to write a proposal. This is a condensed version of your book that acts as both a sales pitch and a proof of concept. It should take a lot of time and effort and leave anyone who reads it with a tangible sense of what the book will be and how passionate you are for the subject. It should articulate the following:

- Who the book is for
- What will be in it
- What readers will do with it
- What you will deliver to achieve it

Be thorough: include a table of contents, a summary of each chapter, and any resources you may have access to. Give anyone who reads your proposal the sense that a lot of the work has already been done and this is just one step toward its inevitable completion and place atop the best-seller list for novelty car manuals. Your proposal doesn't need to be ninety pages long, or even fifty pages

PRO TIP! BE PROFESSIONAL

Your query letter should be extremely well written but approachable and in your own voice. Don't be overly clever or stiff. Just be a person; a clear, concise, professional person. We're not trying to impress our creative writing professors.

long. It needs to be long enough to give a good sense of your voice and include a representative portion of the kind of material you'll include in the book. Roughly ten to twenty pages, on average. Respect the people who will be reading it enough not to presume that they have the ability, or the inclination, to spend a lot of time reading something that isn't even really anything yet.

STEP 4. SHOP IT AROUND

Now you've got to find a publisher to buy your book idea. At this point, your agent will get in touch with their contacts at the various publishing houses. The ideal situation is to get multiple parties interested enough to spark an auction or, even more sexy, a bidding war. This usually only happens in one of two scenarios: you are already something of a hot commodity (e.g., you recently ate nothing but human flesh every day for a year), or you and your agent have managed to create that elusive "buzz" (e.g., "This is the next [fill in the blank], and if you don't get your hands on it, someone else will!").

If you don't have an agent, you can submit directly to publishers. However, this approach will surely fail if you don't do meticulous research about the editor you are targeting. Like locating an agent, scan the acknowledgement pages of comparable books for the editor, then send a short, charming email to that editor saying, "I loved what you did with X title. Check out mine." But many publishers don't accept unsolicited submissions, so this may be a tough road to hoe.

STEP 5. SIGN THE DEAL

This is the best part because you will probably be getting some money, you feel great because you have accomplished the impossible, no work has to be done yet, and you get to sign your name on a legal document, something I very much love to do. But don't forget to read the contract first: what are the terms of the deal and what do they mean? Here, too, is where an agent is extraordinarily helpful. Agents understand not only what is standard but how to get you what you want out of a contract. Here's a brief survey of some common contract terms and what they mean.

ACCEPTANCE OF MANUSCRIPT Publishers always have specific criteria that their authors must meet before their finished manuscript will be accepted. Then, and only then, will you receive the remainder of your advance.

ADVANCE The "advance" is the money paid by a publisher to a writer before the book is published and starts earning royalties. The advance is literally an advance on those royalty earnings and is intended to supplement a writer's income while he or she works on the book. It is usually broken into two or three payments, such as at the execution of the contract and the delivery of the final manuscript.

ROYALTIES The author's percentage of sales *after* the publisher gets back its advance. Royalty payments can come in units ranging from $0.08 to $0.11 to $63,495.22.

ADVERTISING AND PROMOTION These are the publisher's commitments to get the word out for your book, including publicity strategy, possible book tour, marketing budget, social media campaign, foreign sales, and so on. From my experience, publishers are not always great at this part. While most have great enthusiasm and intentions, they rarely have the budgets to mount a legitimate offensive, nor is the publishing industry celebrated far and wide for its cutting-edge approach to digital media.

AUTHOR APPROVALS This specifies when you will be consulted, and when your approval is required, before any final decisions are made on edits, cover design, layout, art, copy, and your likeness.

SUBRIGHTS This specifies who has the right, you or the publisher, to sell the book, or the main idea behind the book, to other entities for foreign editions, book clubs, movies, TV shows, and so on.

REVISIONS What, when, and how many revisions will take place and with whose approval.

An Interview with **Kelly Oxford**

"The Internet gave me an audience without me having to go anywhere."

Kelly Oxford is the author of the book *Everything Is Perfect When You're a Liar*, two screenplays, and a handful of TV pilots. She's also one of the funniest, and most popular, people on Twitter.

I'd filled four diaries about nothing by the time I was in the second grade. I've always written about my life. When I quit working my diner and coffee shop jobs to stay at home, take creative writing classes at night, and raise kids, I just kept doing what I'd always done, but the Internet gave me an audience without me having to go anywhere.

When I was shopping my book proposal around, some people had heard of me and others had not. When the bids came in, the highest offers were from the people who had followed my Tumblr and Twitter.

The "getting started" part is the hardest part. Once I'm in the zone and writing I can go for hours, but getting into my own head and blocking immediate life and emotions out can take a while. I always say, at first you love what you're writing, and then you hate it . . . and when you hate it, that's when you know you're probably halfway through.

MANAGING THE WRITING PROCESS

I've participated in the writing, editing, or note-giving of five books of vastly different scopes in my short career, and there are some habits and strategies I've picked up in that time.

Plan. At *The Onion* I worked on parodies of an atlas and an encyclopedia, both of which were massive in breadth and daunting in different ways: with the former, the question was, how do we say something funny about every country on earth? With the latter, the issue was deciding what to cover when we had to choose from everything that's ever happened or existed in the history of the universe. So we spent the first six months planning, and planning ,and planning some more.

Take notes. Anything that you think at any point, no matter how stupid, should go in your notebook or note-taking app. Most notes will never be used, but it is important to maintain this creative compost pile; I am always surprised when going through old notes, not by the quality of my ideas, but by how remote and distant they seem. Notes represent a different you from a different time, and just having access to that can give you insights to your work.

Outline. An outline is a necessity with almost any book, and it's the best way to organize the major topics while still covering a fair amount of detail. Outlining also provides peace of mind, knowing that everything you need to write is all there in one place. And it is a good tool against writer's block: if you are stuck on one area, you can scan your outline for something else to write about.

Be willing to throw plans away. Your book is going to evolve. Usually it will evolve for the better because you are a creative person who is influenced by the world around you and creativity is a process. Sometimes I spend so much time planning that I lose sight of the actual writing. Be thorough but flexible.

Set deadlines. Sticking to deadlines is hard, but most of us find them indispensable for finishing anything. The key is to find a balance between positive inertia (hit your first few deadlines, and you build up the confidence to hit your next few) and shame (do your work on time or else admit that you're a complete failure as a human being).

Get on a schedule. Writing a book is a war of attrition, and to win that war you need to build good habits. Pick, say, an hour a day to work on your book, and try like hell to stick to it. You can spend that hour taking notes, drawing designs, brainstorming jokes, contacting contributors, interviewing people, or writing—anything that will add to the final product. The key is not to write a certain amount of words each day, but to commit to spending some dedicated percentage of your waking life working on this creative project until it's done.

Do one thing at a time. You won't finish your book by worrying about how you're never going to finish your book. You'll finish it little by little. If you have a great outline, lots of notes, and a relatively consistent schedule, you will get your book done. Just make sure you work on one thing at time, and before you know it, things will begin to take shape.

Don't revise as you go. This is a great way to get mired in abstraction and lose focus on the big picture. Ernest Hemingway liked to spend the first hour or two of each day reading over what he'd written the night before, but most of us don't have that much time and we're not Ernest Hemingway. Take time once a week or month to revise things, if you must, but it's usually better to wait until you've reached a milestone or completed a first draft.

Trust your editor. A good editor will offer concrete criticism and help point you at the right target. He or she will be approachable and hands-on, will understand your working style and offer suggestions that complement rather than negate it, and will have a great sense of timing: your editor will offer assistance at just the right moment.

STEP 6. WRITE THE THING

Depending on the kind of book, this part will either be moderately easy, easy, or extremely easy. Just kidding. Are you nuts? Writing a book will be one of the hardest things you will ever do, including having to choose which of your children will be killed by a totalitarian regime. It will drain you emotionally and intellectually and test your faith in yourself and your ability. Even the smallest book requires an intense amount of planning and detail if you want it to be funny, thorough, and high quality. But most of that energy is expended in the early stages, when you're trying to build up momentum, narrow your focus, and give your Big Idea some structure. Once you've established a rhythm and built something to work from, you may even begin to enjoy the process. Chilling! And there is no feeling more glorious than completing that manuscript.

STEP 7. PROMOTE THE THING

Finishing your book only opens up the door to a whole other process: somehow convincing people to buy it. Your publisher will be able to help (a lot or a little, depending on their size and ability), but they'll still rely on you to contribute all of your best PR contacts and marketing ideas. The good news is that there are a million ways to reach people through the power of the Internet, and those who excel at this are able to see the writing of their book in parallel to the promotion of their book. They see opportunities for a year in the future (as they arise during the writing process), and they remember them and follow through. Making a book and selling a book go hand in hand. No need to be cynical or coy about that. Here are some good habits:

START EARLY Begin developing your marketing plan right away. Think about how to get your audience excited about your book before it even comes out. Start writing blog entries, identify friends and fans on Twitter and Facebook—but don't get so carried away with the fun of poster design and possible speaking tour locations that you lose focus on the actual task of writing.

IDENTIFY YOUR NICHE What's special about your book and, moreover, what is special about you? Write an author bio that reflects who you are in a way your audience might identify with.

PROMOTE OTHERS A great way to foster goodwill and help create a community around yourself and authors you like is to promote others. It's also a good cosmic practice. Help people out when they need it and good things come back to you—assuming your book doesn't absolutely suck.

An Interview with **Baratunde Thurston**

"You can build a movement around anything."

Baratunde Thurston is a personality in technology, politics, comedy, race, whiskey, and literature, and he is the CEO of the creative agency Cultivated Wit. He approached the marketing strategy for his 2012 book *How to Be Black* like a political campaign, and it debuted at number twenty-one on the *New York Times* bestseller list.

On Getting a Head Start

I signed the deal with Harper in March 2010, and we started planning promotion right then. I knew the name of the book, and I was on a panel at SXSW Interactive talking about black people and the Internet. I titled my short presentation "How to Be Black (online)." That was probably the formal launch of the marketing campaign. I wanted to socialize the title, so I would use the hashtag when engaged in activity related to the book, for example, traveling to interview people.

I took specific political campaign structures to heart in designing the marketing campaign. Our field operation was a virtual street team. Our high-value donors were individuals who had potentially significant influence in terms of spreading the word. Our media team was mostly the publicist at Harper. We didn't go so far as to have an opposition research group.

On Participation

You can build a movement around anything. The question is how large and effective that movement will be. Create an element of the campaign that allows people to add their own voice or version to the story. This could be as simple as posting questions publicly for readers at large to answer. It could mean soliciting images or short posts to round out the extra content on the book's website. It could be a short poll or survey. The specific tool doesn't matter so much as having an avenue for people to join in.

Consider the where and when of release. Is there a location or time that makes more sense than others? It was obvious to launch *How to Be Black* during Black History Month. Use that to your advantage, and don't ignore opportunities to reach people self-identified with the topic of your book, especially if someone else has already done the work of gathering them.

On Outreach

Make a list of everyone you know who might care about the fact that you have a book out. Put it in a spreadsheet. Be methodical. High school friends. Former teachers. Fellow writers. Bookers. Editors. Everyone. Rank them in order of likelihood of caring/ability to help. Then reach out to the most interesting or valuable ones one at a time. When you do, tell them exactly how they can help. You have to look at your relationships through the eyes of your book and figure out who would care, and for whom your book offers some assistance, even if it's just a distracting bit of entertainment.

You spend your time doing the above, and it will pay off.

Self-Publishing

If you want to skip most of that other stuff, and you have the freedom to write and edit and promote a book in the exact way you want, without compromise, or if you can't get a book deal, there are more opportunities than ever to publish on your own. Amazon has changed the publishing landscape, for good or ill, and streamlined the process for writers to get their work directly to readers. One major drawback is that most print retailers and e-marketplaces will not sell Amazon-published books, since they are seen as "the competition" and "evil."

Other companies, sometimes known as vanity presses, include CafePress, AuthorHouse, Lightning Source, Blurb, and iUniverse. Most offer more favorable royalty rates than traditional publishers. But with that extra freedom comes extra work, as you are solely responsible for the writing, editing, design, marketing, administration, and promotion of your own book.

Magazines, Newspapers & Other Types of Print

Though the print industry may be fading, human beings still exist at least partially in the physical world, and they enjoy holding things in their hands. Some newspapers employ humor columnists, as do a handful of comedy publications and general-interest magazines, but not much exists anymore on any significant scale. Even *The Onion*, whose newspaper kiosks could once be found on every college town street corner, ceased its print publication in 2013. And it was free.

That said, there is a certain prestige in having your work published in print. It confers permanence and legitimacy at a time when anyone can broadcast anything they want, without an editor, from their phone, anytime they want. Further, you may want to join the proud tradition of humor columnists, which extends from Dave Barry, who got his start as a general-interest reporter; to Erma Bombeck, who started as a newspaper "copy girl," was a housewife for ten years, and then wrote her first humor columns for three bucks apiece; to Patrick McManus, who writes about hunting and fishing for *Field & Stream* and *Outdoor Life*.

WHERE TO FIND PRINT WORK

The majority of comedy writing for magazines and newspapers today is published on the local level, in town newspapers or the ever-present college campus humor magazines. These are the first places to contact about submitting work. Smaller opportunities can also be found everywhere, from small-town weekly flyers to office newsletters. Here, though, are a few of the high-profile print magazines that still employ comedy writers; they also all have websites with separate, additional content.

THE NEW YORKER The *New Yorker*'s weekly "Shouts and Murmurs" feature is probably the most coveted humor space in America, consciously highbrow though it may be. It's fairly vaunted, however, and does not generally publish work by anonymous civilians. Still, you can always track down their articles editor, send a friendly but brief email and a submission, and cross your fingers.

MCSWEENEY'S This quarterly humor and literary magazine has featured humor pieces from some of the best writers around. Its cousin periodical, *Believer*, also prints funny articles. Both accept submissions and offer some pay for printed work.

MAD MAGAZINE Since 1952, the home of Alfred E. Neuman has printed pop culture parodies, sendups, comics, and features with an emphasis on blecch. They do accept original submissions—especially visual pitches—through their website, though they will not consider any film or TV parodies or rewrites of existing features.

ANNALS OF IMPROBABLE RESEARCH This bimonthly humor publishes satirical science articles and diagrams and also gives out the Ig Nobel Prize, an annual award for the most asinine achievements in science. They accept submissions through their website.

MODERN DRUNKARD Its six annual issues are dedicated to the celebration of inebriation. They accept submissions (through their website) of articles, poems, and short fiction that are deeply positive about drinking and drunkenness.

NEWSPAPER SYNDICATION The fastest way to get your work published in multiple places at once is through newspaper syndication, and there are a number of syndicates to which you can submit.

- King Features: The biggest syndicate, they ask for five pieces of six hundred words. Be aware that it is very competitive: only 1 percent of the 2,500 annual submissions are selected each year.
- Tribune Content Agency: Accepts submissions, but asks that they be sent through an agent. Tribune is also extremely selective.
- Creators.com: Works with multiple regional newspapers and ask for four to six samples of six hundred words each.
- Universal Uclick: Specializes mainly in cartoons, but does accept text submission—six to ten pieces of five to six hundred words each.

SPECIALTY PUBLICATIONS

Magazines and books will exist for as long as there are trees, but publications dedicated solely to humor will remain niche items: rare objects for those who like the smell of ink and the overpowering, enveloping intimacy of a density of words. A whole genre of beautifully designed, high-quality journals and magazines began to emerge in the late 2000s, covering everything from art to food to film. These are not mass-produced pieces—even by today's anemic industry standards—but limited edition labors of love. My friend and colleague John Harris has created one for humor with his zine *Pendulous Breasts Quarterly,* a self-published, crowd-funded journal, with writers handpicked by John, in the style of George Meyer's legendary magazine *Army Man.* While it is certainly a lot of work (and printing costs are only increasing each year), there is something to be said for creating a tangible item to last the ages, or at least until something is spilled on it.

Chapter 8

WRITING
FOR FILM

I wish I could tell you that I have all the answers, kid. That there's some magic, secret recipe for making it big in Hollywood. That all you need to do is rub the right lamp or suck the right peace pipe or have sex with the right metaphor and then, boom, you're a successful comedy screenwriter with awards, money, respect, and a decent commute. But I can't. That kind of thing doesn't exist, and if it did, I wouldn't give it away in an $18 book. I'd make you pay $1,299 for a two-day seminar at a Radisson in New Jersey.

The truth is, only a handful of people have managed to make a career out of writing comedy screenplays—maybe three handfuls, give or take, depending on the size of the hand. It's a competitive market, and comedies, especially, are difficult for unknown writers to sell if they do not have a known commodity attached to them. Comedy trends change from decade to decade: the slobs vs. snobs paradigm of the 1970s gave way to buddy cop movies in the 1980s; gross-outs and spoofs dominated the 1990s; while the 2000s ushered in the man-child–with-a-big-heart comedy. The next wave is being written and conceived right now, and *you can be part of it.*

Writing the Screenplay

There are giant, flaming container ships full of books about the craft of screenwriting, so I won't attempt to teach you how to write one here. Instead, we'll just cover some of the basics and how they apply to a comedy.

THE THREE-ACT STRUCTURE

Screenplays, as you probably know, almost always follow the same basic three-act structure. There is nothing inherently different about a comedy screenplay except that (1) the plot or situation can, and usually should, be humorous in and of itself, (2) the protagonist's path from A to B is peppered with funny incidents, and (3) it will tend to be on the shorter side.

This structure was made mainstream by Syd Field in his book *Screenplay* in 1979. Ever since, screenwriters, studio executives, professors, and critics have devoted themselves with almost religious fervor to this idea. It makes a lot of sense: our simplest, most intuitive

> **PRO TIP!** WRITING MOVIES
> FOR FUN AND PROFIT
>
> One of the best, most entertaining, and practical books I've ever read on writing screenplays is *Writing Movies for Fun and Profit* by Robert Ben Garant and Thomas Lennon. This duo helped create *The State* and *Reno 911!* on TV, and they cowrote the movies *Night at the Museum* (and sequels), *Herbie: Fully Loaded*, *Reno 911!: Miami*, and *Balls of Fury*. While their book is not this book, you should still consider buying it.

conception of reality is that all things have a beginning, middle, and end. This ancient formula, along with some of the principles of the hero's journey,[10] form the basis of the three-act structure.

All of this is just a framework to hang your story on, and inside that framework are countless possibilities to Do Funny Things. How does the conflict unfold? By what circumstances does your hero experience a second-act fall from grace? Who is the funniest, least-expected antagonist you can think of? This structure is not supposed to be a strict set of rules from which you can never deviate, but it is helpful to have guidelines for getting the plot mechanics down, especially when starting out. This will make your comedy better. Don't be wary of having a traditional structure; use it as an opportunity to make surprising choices.

ACT 1: THE SETUP We meet our hero, see their world, and find out what the "big problem" is. Near the end of act one, the protagonist makes a decision that puts them on an irreversible path into action, setting our plot in motion. Here are examples from two actual comedy movies:

The Jerk. Navin Johnson, so moved by hearing the whitest music imaginable on the radio, decides to leave his all-black family in search of more music like it.

Knocked Up. Career-minded Alison calls up stoner Ben to tell him that their one-night stand two months ago got her pregnant. He decides to stick with her through the pregnancy.

ACT 2: THE CONFLICT Things are moving along, and this is where the bulk of the action takes place. Our hero reacts to forces or to

---

10 This is the mythic structure set forth by Joseph Campbell that encapsulates the archetypal pattern found in stories from around the world. It's pretty famous. Look it up! Also, Christopher Vogler's *The Writer's Journey* uses the hero's journey as a template for breaking down the screenplay structure.

an antagonist working against them, gets to the point at which all seems lost, and then starts becoming proactive.

The Jerk. Navin gets a series of ridiculous jobs, meets his soul mate, Marie, loses her, makes millions with a ridiculous invention (the OptiGrab), gets Marie back, becomes cocky, and loses everything after a class-action lawsuit.

Knocked Up. After the completely mismatched Alison and Ben attempt to make it as a couple, they have a huge fight, and Alison kicks Ben out in the middle of the road.

ACT 3: THE RESOLUTION The hero defeats the antagonist (either a literal or metaphorical villain), overcomes the "big problem," and changes in some way. All the loose ends are tied up, and the credits roll.

The Jerk. Destitute and at the end of his story, Navin is saved when Marie and Navin's family roll up in a limousine to take him home, having made their own fortune from investing the money he sent home every week.

Knocked Up. After separating from Ben, Alison goes into labor, but when she cannot reach her doctor—she calls Ben for help. The two reconcile in the hospital and decide to raise their new baby together. THE END!

OTHER PLOT STRUCTURES

LIMITLESS ACTS One of the best and smartest writers out there, Film Crit Hulk, says that the three-act structure is a myth. In his book *Screenwriting 101,* he argues that films rarely have any hard act breaks—and they should certainly not be limited to three. Instead, a series of decisions made by the characters move the plot forward. A film, he says, can be full of action and suspense and Things Happening, but if the protagonist isn't making choices that Mean Something, the movie will ultimately feel empty and flat.

SKETCH Some comedies are structured like an anthology, with a series of sketches or vignettes. While there may be a thematic throughline, no single protagonist makes a hero's journey over ninety minutes. These were especially popular in the 1970s and 1980s with such inimitable classics as *Airplane, Amazon Women on the Moon*, *Kentucky Fried Movie, The Boob Tube,* and Monty Python's *And Now for Something Completely Different* and *The Meaning of Life*. These are difficult to pull off because of the difference in style and tone across sketches, the need (usually) for a large cast, and the difficulty of making eight or ten separate little movies equally funny. Not to say it's impossible, but they've been most successful when made by a group that already works together (Monty Python) or by a master (John Landis).

REALITY These are movies that pit some character or situation against real-world people and environments for yuks and ha-ha. These include the Sacha Baron Cohen's vehicles *Borat, Ali G Indahouse*, and *The Dictator*, and the Jackass movies and their spinoffs.

OUTLINING YOUR MOVIE

Very few screenwriters don't outline their stories, and many believe outlining is where the bulk of the work is actually done. This is where you get your story right, where you take care of the core mechanics—what happens when to whom and in what order—so that you can then concentrate on the details that bring it to life, like dialogue, jokes, ellipses . . . A good outline will map out each scene (defined by a change in location) with a brief description of the action and a piece of essential dialogue. There are usually between forty and eighty scenes in a screenplay. The outline will include all the essential information you need to tell your story and show how and where the narrative advances. Writers sometimes spend months and months working on their outlines before writing a word of the script, and there are a number of tools and techniques you can implement to fit your working, and thinking, style.

INDEX CARDS In the days before the microchip, the best way to organize a screenplay was by writing each scene on an index card. This provides a great visual depiction of your story, allowing you to add, throw away, or move scenes around as needed. The software Final Draft automatically creates digital index cards of each scene, but a lot of writers still use the dead-tree objects.

SOFTWARE I often write the first draft of my outline in Word or Text Edit, then move it to a program like Tree. Using "Scene View" on Final Draft will also give you something approximating an outline form. There are programs designed specifically for outlining, too. Movie Outline is the most prominent. Some people also use task-organizing apps to do their outlining. You've got a lot of options, okay?

CHARACTERS

Great characters are the key to a great comedy. Their actions, decisions, and point of view drive the story and give the audience a filter for their own emotions. A strong character can make even the most formulaic structure interesting. If you tend to start with a concept, like I do, you absolutely must find a compelling character to put in that situation. Otherwise, the whole thing will fall flat.[11] You need to get to know your main characters, figure out who they are, and then start subjecting them to scenarios that challenge those ideas in every way possible. Keep doing this over and over. Go back over your script repeatedly to make sure that your characters are acting

---

11 One noteworthy exception is *Airplane*, where most of the characters are talking tropes playing straight man to the movie's relentless onslaught of jokes and gags of any kind. A character who reacted to that world in any other way would have made *Airplane* something less than the FUNNIEST MOVIE EVER.

in ways that are consistent with their desires and worldview—unless they have a truly compelling reason not to—and then keep going back again to make sure they are surprising you, and you will have yourself a comedy, bud.

CHARACTER DEVELOPMENT EXERCISES As hard as I find it to expend any energy on any writing that is NOT THE FINAL PRODUCT, it can be very helpful to delve into your characters with some simple exercises. Like these!

Pros and cons. Pretend that you're someone considering dating your protagonist. What would you write down as their best and worst traits?

Wikipedia page. Write a few paragraphs for a character's Wikipedia entry, focusing on the whens, wheres, and hows, and highlighting the most important moments of their life—including the details of their death.

Job application. Download an online job application and fill it out as your character would. Include a cover letter and resume.

Therapy session. Imagine that your protagonist is talking to their therapist the day before the events of your script take place. Write out everything the character says. You can also try having your character talk about their childhood, parents, school life, and so on. This is a nice way to get to know your character's voice, too, and you'll discover things you didn't know about them before.

Selling the Screenplay

Writing the funniest screenplay of the last ten years is great, but selling it is even more greater because you get to make money. For instance, the WGA (Writers Guild of America) minimum payment for an original screenplay ranges from $70,000 to $130,000. It's also relatively cool to see your ideas and hard work come to life on the silver screen.

> **PRO TERM!** COVERAGE
>
> *Coverage* is the term for how studios assess screenplays based on their marketability, scope, budget, and overall quality. This is usually done by a junior employee who grades the screenplay based on a rubric determined by each studio: a typical one will rate the premise, plot, characters, and dialogue on a scale from poor to excellent, as well as a summary of the script followed by notes and analysis. There are also people who, for a fee, will assess your screenplay in the studio style. If you are just starting out, this can be a helpful hundred dollars to spend to get an impartial opinion.

SEVEN THINGS YOU NEED TO SELL YOUR SCREENPLAY

Most screenplays, especially those bought by a studio, are sold through an agent. Agents have the most connections, understand the value of a script, and are familiar with the changing texture of the marketplace. Scripts can also be sold to producers and production companies, who will try to get funding or make them on their own. Whether you're seeking representation, or taking your work to studios or producers directly, you should compile these seven elements first.

A title. You need a great title. It should be short, descriptive, and evocative. *Meet the Parents, Blazing Saddles, Anchorman, Dumb and Dumber, Ghostbusters, Ace Ventura: Pet Detective*—these are great titles, people! Give whoever's reading it the subconscious impression that your screenplay can, and will, be a real movie.

A logline. A one-sentence description of your story. Not only is this a fundamental marketing material, it's also necessary for the writer to distill the story into simple terms.

A synopsis. This little guy breaks down the major plot points of your story and adds a little more detail and color than the logline.

A treatment. A treatment combines all of the first three things and acts as a kind of top sheet for your script. It can be used to get your foot in the door with a studio, producer, or agent.

A query letter. A formal inquiry through which you can introduce yourself to prospective agents and buyers and see if they accept unsolicited submissions. It should be short and professional and give a sense of who you are and what your script is about. Take the time to print out a letter and send it by mail, rather than just zapping off a mass email. Rejection, or no response, is very common.

More scripts. The odds are long that your first script will find a buyer. But it may intrigue one or two people, and if they ask to see more, you should have options. It's a great idea to have multiple scripts ready to go before you go out trying to sell even one.

CONTESTS, FESTIVALS, AND DATABASES

There are a number of contests and festivals that give unknown writers the opportunity to win representation, money, or the right to pitch their ideas to studios and producers. Likewise, winning a contest like this can be a nice boost for your morale and expose your work to Real Professional Hollywood-type People. You can also sign up for services that send out regular emails listing screenplay requests by production companies and agencies. I do not know how many careers have been launched by these means, but a simple Google search will turn up plenty of results.

PRO TIP! WORK IN PUNCH UP

Since nothing is ever perfect, especially in Hollywood, a lot of comedians and writers make a little extra scratch on the side by working on other people's scripts to make them funnier, smoother, or just, you know, better (see chapter 22, Development). This is called a punch up. Sometimes this is done with multiple comedians sitting around a table, all pitching jokes to the director, and sometimes it's done by one writer sitting alone in an apartment gritting their teeth. This work is usually acquired through agents or one's reputation, and once you do a few of them, the opportunities come up more often.

An Interview with **Terry Jones**

"When we started writing Monty Python and the Holy Grail, *the only thing we had at first was the bit about the coconuts."*

Though he's written books, documentaries, cartoons, and operas, Terry Jones is best known as one of the founding members of the sketch comedy group Monty Python, along with Graham Chapman, John Cleese, Terry Gilliam, Eric Idle, and Michael Palin. Jones co-wrote and directed their features *Monty Python and the Holy Grail, Life of Brian,* and *The Meaning of Life,* and was the driving force behind the troupe's flowing,

118

stream-of-consciousness style. He also penned the original screenplay for the David Bowie–Muppet adventure *Labyrinth* and wrote and directed *Absolutely Anything,* which he'd been working on for almost twenty years.

On His Writing Process

I don't outline or anything. I sit at my typewriter and write, really. I just make it up as I go along. I am a morning person. I can't work at night, so I really have to start at 8 o'clock and just work through till lunch. Other than that—it's a bit like being a shopkeeper. You show up and just wait for the customers to come around. The customers are the sketches and the comedy. That's what it feels like.

On Writing with Partners

The advantage to writing with someone is you get an immediate reaction. When Mike Palin and I were writing for Python, we'd go off for a couple days on our own, bring a few sketches back, and see what the other thought of it. When we started writing *Monty Python and the Holy Grail,* the only thing we had at first was the bit about the coconuts. We expanded from there.

On Never-Ending Sketches

I'd seen Spike Milligan's sketch comedy series *Q4,* and I realized that he didn't finish sketches! He just went off on a tangent of some kind. I rang up Python members Mike Palin and Terry Gilliam, and I said, "Why don't we not finish sketches? We can move on to the next one, or Terry can fill in the gap with his animations." And so that's what we did.

On Writing The Meaning of Life.

For *Life of Brian,* we went on holiday to Jamaica for two uninterrupted weeks, and so that's what we did for *The Meaning of Life.* We went to Barbados, I think. On the plane going over I read the script and it was just dreadful, going round in circles. Like we'd lifted it from Buñuel, *The Discreet Charm of the Bourgeoisie*.

I woke up Wednesday morning and I had a sinking feeling in my stomach, and I thought, "It's not going to work." We met and Mike's suggestion was to go home and turn it into a TV series. I had the script girl's timings, which were 90 minutes. And I said, we had a lot of wonderful bits and sketches which are A quality, and we can abandon the structure and just do that for 90 minutes. That breakfast, we really got going and said, "Let's do it," and it engendered enthusiasm for the project. And everybody around the table said, "We can call it The Meaning of Life!"

On Writing *Labyrinth*

I'd almost forgotten about that! I rang Jim Henson's office about a project I was working on and his secretary said, "He was just going to ring you about writing *Labyrinth*!" So I wrote the first draft, but he wasn't happy with it. He said he wanted to get to the Labyrinth sooner in the film, whereas I thought it'd be more like *The Wizard of Oz*, in which an incompetent person had been at the center of the labyrinth. Jim was also talking about Michael Jackson at the time. He wanted him to play Jareth. So the script went away from me for a year, and then it came back to me, and Jim said, "Could you put all the jokes back in?" And I sort of drew it back to the original draft, but put them in the labyrinth a little bit sooner. Jim insisted on that.

On Stopping the Interview

May I stop now? I'm sorry, but I've got to take my dog Nancy out for a walk.

Part 2

PERFORMING COMEDY

like begging the universe to confirm that you exist, again and again, until you die

I've spent nearly my entire life closely observing, and often participating in, the performance of the comedic arts. I've seen and done it all, from standing-up comedy to storytelling to teeny little videos with sixty-four views, and I've determined that there are five essential building blocks of great comedy performance.

Look upon these traits. Feel their power. Find them in the work of those you enjoy and apply them to your own performances to master this most delicate, yet hilarious, of arts. Then, and only then, can you begin your eternal journey toward Getting Paid for This Shit.

RELATABILITY The audience needs to be able to feel for the character in the same breath as they laugh at the character; to like as easily as loathe. In comedy, having some essential humanity makes everything you do easier to laugh at—nay, laugh *with*. (And at.)

TIMING This is a huge "no duh," but it cannot be overstated. Sometimes bad timing is good timing because timing is completely dependent on the element of surprise. If the audience is *expecting* a joke or a line or a look to come at an exact moment, that is not necessarily good timing; that is more like good training. Unfortunately, true comedic timing cannot be taught. Though it can be edited (see "Editing," page 224, in chapter 15).

SHAMELESSNESS The only dignity in comedy is in one's willingness to forego all dignity whatsoever. Self-consciousness in any form will completely sabotage comedy. The job of the comedy performer is to be able to expose the raw inner animal of the human being at a moment's notice—to look like a fool. If there's even a hint of worry or concern about how one will look, the spell is broken and the comedy is dead. *Dead, I say.*

YELLING Any comedic actor's greatest ambition should be to yell as well as Gene Wilder. (Bob Odenkirk is also an upper-echelon yeller, and other honorees include Chris Rock, Lou Costello, and Roseanne.) A good primal yell is equal to thirty-seven solid spit takes or nine pratfalls. It represents the deepest, least-eloquent form of communication, the bottom rung of emotion, hopelessness, the last straw. In other words: comedy itself.

VULNERABILITY In the end, comedy performance is just like any other performance: we have to believe it is real. Even the most hyperstylized comedy must feel as though it is emanating from a human being, or else comedy could just be contained in a series of punch cards and bar codes. Being vulnerable opens up a world of comedic possibility and is an act of generosity to your audience. An act they will pay back.

Chapter 9

STANDUP COMEDY

For generations, standup comedians have been defined by a kind of tragic, star-crossed relationship with fame and their chosen career: grizzled, jaded, cynical, and unable to exist in a society that has no convenient place for them. From this agitated state of outsiderness comes their material, raw and real and penetrating. They're maladjusted, sleep-deprived, emotionally damaged. They're beer and cigarettes and restlessness. They are a little bit insane.

Over time, however, the belief that standup comics must torture themselves onstage has softened and, to some degree, abated. It is perhaps not so romantic, in the age of the Paleo Diet and self-actualization, to live like an animal for the sake of a good set. Standup has grown diverse, both in style and in the kinds of people who do it.

It is also one of the best routes for the aspiring Comedy Person to take. Standup is a showcase of one's stage presence, writing ability, and acting skills. It gives confidence, instills an almost unparalleled work ethic, and connects with other comedians. It also builds character, thickens the skin, and if done well, can create some of the best moments humankind is capable of. It can illuminate and shock and entertain and change points of view. Standup comedy can rejuvenate the spirit, or inspire, or remind you not to give so many shits. It can be hilarious and sad and everything in between.

It can be art.

Getting Started at Standup

THE OPEN MIC

The first thing you have to do before you can speak profound truths about the human condition and own your own boat is go to an open mic—these are low-pressure shows where you can try out material in front of a largely sympathetic crowd composed mostly of other comedians who are also trying out new material. Everyone has to do this. Even the most seasoned comedians still attend open mics from time to time. It is possible to skip doing open mics in some extreme cases, like if W.C. Fields were to suddenly rise from the dead, or if you know someone who hosts a regular comedy show.

> **PRO TIP!**
> The term "open mic" is actually short for "open-form micro-phone-amplified comedy performance," but you should never say the whole name to fellow comedians or you will come off like a know-it-all!

At open mics, you arrive early, sign up for a slot, and usually get five to seven minutes onstage. Sometimes you can sign up ahead of time online or in person for a future show. It depends on how the show is run. The host will bring you up, or maybe just read your name from a list, then pat you on the shoulder and maybe remind you not to go over on your time because there are a bunch of other people waiting to get on.

Now the stage is yours. Here are a few things to keep in mind:

DON'T GO OVER YOUR TIME A bunch of other people are waiting to get on after you. When you see the host or producer hold up the Light (which is usually a cell phone), that means you have one minute left. Finish on time and be courteous to the other animals in the room.

NOTICE HOW THE JOKES FEEL COMING OUT OF YOUR MOUTH This may seem obvious, but talking onstage is different than talking in real life. Getting acquainted with that is one of the first things you should be working on at an open mic.

RELAX (OR DON'T) Similarly, your body language is magnified when you step onstage. Maybe you will start prowling back and forth like Richard Pryor or projecting outward from one infinitesimally small spot, like Todd Barry. Move around. Stand still. Notice the difference. You'll settle into a physical presence over time.

DON'T WORRY ABOUT THE LAUGHS It's actually more important at first to learn how to deal with rejection than with wild success. If you're desperate to manufacture laughter, the audience—especially if they're comedians—will pick up on that immediately, and it will suck the generosity right out of the room. If you get up on stage with a spirit of what-the-hell, the laughs will come. Probably.

BEWARE THE BRINGER These are shows that will only allow you stage time if you bring X number of paying guests along with you. Bringers are inevitably run by boneheaded bar owners who will not make any effort to foster a supportive environment for young comedians. Fuck bringers. If you live in a medium-size city, there should be enough legitimate open mics that you should be able to avoid these altogether, but if not, just have them call me, and I will berate them verbally and spiritually.

DON'T QUIT The vast majority of new comedians quit after the first open mic, so following this tip already puts you well ahead of most of humanity. Good job! On the other side of the coin, you will almost certainly come across people who probably *should have* quit after their first open mic, and you don't want to become them either. But you won't get there for a few years, at least. For now, Just Keep Doing It.

COMEDY SHOWS

Now that you've begun to get your stage knees, which is a real term and not one that I literally *just* made up for this sentence, the next step is to start getting booked at comedy shows. A lot of shows when you're first starting out might not be much different than open mics, except that they will have fewer performers and there will almost always be a headliner.

Try to pick a show that you find enjoyable and that seems accessible. If you live in some place like Coeur d'Alene, Idaho, find the one show that there is, get to know the people who run it, and ask them if you might be able to fill in a slot sometime. If you are doing open mics regularly and feel that you've got five minutes' worth of solid material, it shouldn't be a problem to find a show that'll give you a shot. Be upfront about the fact that you're just starting out.

At first, all you'll get is five minutes. Later you'll get seven minutes, and then ten, and right after that you get your own sitcom on CBS. Just kidding! You have to do a parody Twitter account about your elderly dad to get one of those. Other comics will start noticing you and asking you to come do their shows, and the next thing you know, You Are Getting Booked!

THE CLUB When you think of standup comedy, you think of clubs: the brick wall, the two-drink minimum, the overenthusiastic host whose jokes never quite seem to land, and a crowd who is still amazed by the subtle differences between men and women. The club

OPEN MICS ARE KIND OF AWESOME

Besides the opportunity they offer to hone your craft, open mics also feature diverse, weird, and uninhibited performers less likely to get stage time at paid shows. On a given night in New York City you might come across the lisping, five-foot-one Gary, whose self-deprecating humor churns out such gems as, "The last time I was in a woman, it was the Statue of Liberty!" and his catchphrase "unbe-fucking-bewievable!" Or the sixty-something woman who went on for fifteen minutes in graphic detail about a guy she met on Craigslist who wanted her to shit on his dick, and who was either doing one of the most sophisticated meta-comedy bits in history or was profoundly clueless. There are acts of every imaginable shade of horrible, and real flashes of brilliance, too. You can see the unbridled arrogance of the meathead whose friends all tell him he's funny, alongside the humble poetry of the comic book fan girl just trying things out. It's a genuine parade of humanity, and it is absolutely free!

OPEN MICS IN YOUR AREA

Here is an extensive list of local venues that hold open mics:

- Google.com
- Bing.com
- If you own an iPhone, hold down the Home button until you hear two quick beeps, then say, "Please do a web search for comedy open mics in my area, thank you!" Then, when you locate an open mic in your area, you can do a joke about the lady who lives inside your iPhone who helped you find the place

is designed to appeal to the broadest audience with the most credit cards possible. I am, of course, Generalizing for Comedic Effect, but clubs do tend to prefer more conventional acts that won't alienate

COMEDY AT SEA

Cruise ships regularly employ comedians as part of their on-ship entertainment, and plenty of skilled comedians pay the bills with these gigs. On the one hand, it's a well-paid job with access to an array of amenities, and you get to work in showrooms that are often superior to those on dry land. On the other hand, you are on a cruise ship.

In many cases, the main act is a singer or a magician, and you'll perform a few nights a week. The rest of your time may be spent wandering around the ship, avoiding children who seem to have eczema, and marveling at the vast infinity of the sea, its overwhelming majesty and loneliness, and wondering what will happen to you and everyone you know after death.

There's usually a buffet, too.

Because cruises are huge, floating, family-friendly corporations, a lot of cruise shows have strict language and content guidelines. You might not be able to swear at all in the early show, and you will be allowed only two shits and an asshole in late night. More than anything, cruises are looking for consistency, professionalism, and a predictable comedy product, night after night, with very few surprises or causes for concern. It's not a place to try out your new chunk on Hitler-themed kiddie porn.

To get booked, contact the cruiseline's entertainment department, being sure to include a resume, head shot, and a video of two twenty-five-minute, PG-rated sets. Some lines book and produce all entertainment themselves; some lines use an outside production company.

or confuse uninitiated crowds—at least until you've reached a level of recognition with your style to attract a wide enough audience.

SHOWCASES These are events hosted by beneficent club owners whereby young performers get a chance to do their best act in front of the people who regularly book shows. A lot of comics get their first major club gigs after performing in showcases. If club

THE COMEDY SHOW PERFORMANCE HIERARCHY

OPENER The first comedian to go up. Sometimes this is a very strong comedian who will get the audience going. Other times it is the comic with the least experience or name recognition. On very rare occasions, it is a talking dog or a puppet.

MIDDLE The performer in the middle. Okay, next thing.

FEATURE Usually the second-to-last act, this is someone with a fair amount of exposure and experience. The Feature's sets will usually run fifteen to twenty minutes. A comic might spend a few years in this spot before moving up to . . .

HEADLINER This is the main act on a bill and usually the person whom the audience is there to see. In downtown or alt-comedy shows, this is the comic who has been on *Conan* and done a few commercials. Many headliners make their living touring the country, while others use the exposure to open the next chapter of their career, like starring in a movie with the talking dog from the show's opener.

HOST Also known as the emcee, this person introduces comedians and keeps the energy level high throughout the show. He or she usually does a set before the opener, goes on between all the acts, and says good-bye before reminding audience members about the email list signup sheet at the back of the room.

owners or bookers like you, they'll ask you to come back, either for another showcase or for a paid slot in a comedy show at some ungodly hour like 12:45 am or 4 in the afternoon. If they don't like you, they won't!

While the scenario in the TV show *Studio 60 on the Sunset Strip*— in which a struggling comic is offered a job writing on TV's most prestigious sketch comedy show based solely on three minutes of mediocre material—will never, *ever* happen in real life, it's entirely possible that the showcase audience will include agents, managers, bookers, and local comedy writers.

PRO TIP! THE PROXIMITY METHOD

Myriad are the tales of comedians, writers, and managers alike who got their start in comedy merely by hanging out. They had no real plan other than a primordial notion: *I like comedy; this is a place where comedy happens; being around a place where comedy happens will put me closer to comedy; if I am close enough to comedy, I might become part of comedy.* In other words, if you get to know the people who form the local comedy community, you might, through an unpredictable sequence of events, find yourself onstage or in a writers' room.

An Interview with **Rob Delaney**

"The day to day is like any career; you get out what you put into it."

Rob Delaney is one of the hardest working and hairiest men in show business, and he's done a little of everything: written a book, perfected feminist raunch on Twitter, starred in a British sitcom, and even created his own board game. But standup is his first love, and he spends a good portion of the year on tour.

I limit the amount of time I'm away. After four days there's no sanity for me, so I generally try to keep my trips shorter than that. I tend to not exercise much and eat total garbage on the road. It's also good for me to socialize with people during normal daylight hours on the road so I feel human and not like a night-dwelling C.H.U.D., which is a constant danger on the road.

The biggest thing I've learned in dealing with clubs is that I'm the boss. It is very important—to them—that I am happy, whether they know that or not. Because what's most important to everyone is that I do an excellent show. Nobody's ego is as important as that fact. So I try to be a nice guy and easy to work with, and I expect the same of others. The bulk of people are pretty cool.

For me, making a living in comedy also coincided with my becoming a father, so my comedy lifestyle isn't really "glamorous" unless I'm on a TV set or something or onstage at a big theater, both of which are exciting and cool. But my day to day is pretty normal-seeming, like that of a work-at-home tech guy or journalist or something. While comedy and entertainment have cool frills, the day to day is like any career; you get out what you put into it.

Priceless Wisdom for the Neophyte

SUPPORT OTHER COMICS Community in standup comedy is huge. Comics rely on one another for more than just support: they are friends, colleagues, rivals, and sometimes spouses. While jealousy is natural—and, at least among humans, largely unavoidable—its negative effects can be mitigated by offering aid and succor to those around you. It's also good practice not to start your career off by being a jerk. The writer Liana Maeby said something great on Twitter: "In some ways, the best career advice might be to figure out how to get to a place where you can be happy for other people's success."

> **PRO TIP!** HOW JOAN DID IT
>
> Whenever Joan Rivers went up at a smaller room with new material, she brought all her notes from the previous week, scribbled on scraps of paper and old receipts, and layed them out before her. She worked her way through the new jokes, trying to get laughs. She tape recorded every show, then went home and reviewed the audio, and took note of what worked and what didn't. She then finessed the writing and tried it again. If a joke worked three times, she put it in her act.

PRACTICE Stand in front of a mirror and do your routine. You will find things there, and it will be embarrassing.

DISCOVER WHO YOU ARE They say it takes ten years to find your comedic voice, and while that seems like a long time, it is. But if you just accept that that's how long it will take, and put that in the back of your head and leave it there, you won't have to worry about it on a weekly basis. In the meantime, strive to figure out not what you want to talk about, but what you need to talk about. (See also "Crafting a Persona," page 144.)

SEEK INSPIRATION There will be moments of intense disappointment, desperation, exhaustion, and anxiety. You'll spend half your time worrying about your upcoming set, and the other half overanalyzing the set you just did. The best thing you can do is continually seek inspiration. It doesn't have to be from other comedy. Go to museums, read comic books, watch the faces babies make when they take a shit, see a movie. Comedy encompasses all, and shaping your perception to reflect, and be enriched by, that can be an incredibly powerful tool.

HAVE FRIENDS Most comedians have a group of friends they grow and change with. Gossip and decompression are key, but so are people you trust who will tell you what they think, good or bad, and who you know are going through the same things you are. Standup comedy PTSD bonds can last a lifetime. Also, it's good to care about how someone else is doing. Narcissism is exhausting!

GIVE YOURSELF A BREAK I used to get so bogged down trying to write the best standup routine of all time, which is impossible, that it led to creative paralysis, and then I became too precious about what I did manage to write. Don't do that! Be willing to do things that will not work, and don't kill yourself if they don't. Your odds of revolutionizing comedy in your first couple years are fairly slim, anyway, so cut yourself a little slack.

An Interview with **Pete Holmes**

"Comedy is the pleasure business. Once you get the opposite of those feelings, you see what you're fighting for."

Pete Holmes is a comedian, writer, podcaster, host, and *New Yorker*-published cartoonist. But before that, he was, by his own accounting, one of several million tall, blonde, gregarious male standups. It wasn't until he was turned down for representation by a prominent manager that he began to see who he was as a comedian.

I wanted to know why he didn't sign me, and he said, "When I watch you, you're funny, but I have *no idea who you are*." He was like, "What do you care about, what makes you angry, what gets you passionate?" And as he was saying that, I remember being a little bit haunted because I knew that I didn't know the answer to any of those things. At that point *nothing* worked me up because I was a two-dimensional guy.

I spent a lot of my life trying to do comedy that I thought would please the broadest group of people, trying to do a show that your grandmother and your teenage son could both enjoy—and there's virtue in that. But at a certain point, you find yourself at twenty-eight, and your wife leaves you for another guy, and they get married, and that kind of throws you off the rails. The next thing you know, you're onstage, and there's urgency. You've gotten a taste of pain, you've gotten a taste of loss, and you see what you're fighting for. Comedy is the joy business, the release business, the pleasure business. Once you get the opposite of those feelings, you see what you're fighting for.

At the end of the day, you have to have an awareness of who you are—that's your job as a comedian: Who am I? What am I doing onstage? How do I come across onstage, and what am I presenting onstage? What are the things that are important to me? After you start putting that out there consistently, there's a certain expectation to keep being that. And that's a good thing, when you get to the point that the audience expects that from you. So the bits that I do that I'm known for and that get great responses—and that also come from my heart—tend to be a little bit more positive or uplifting. That's my job. I look like a youth pastor. I should be a youth pastor. That's who I am, that's who I like being, and that's who I want to keep being.

Stage Fright

It is a mystery at the center of standup that the very thing that defines the comedian can also cause such anxiety and terror. Perhaps this paradox is present in any kind of public creative act: you take something private and present it to an audience to be judged, and you never know if it will hold up under the weight of scrutiny.

Every time you go out there, you might fail. And if you fail that one time, you might fail again. And if you keep failing, then maybe you aren't as good as you thought you were. And if you aren't as good as you thought, then perhaps you oughtn't be doing this. And if you oughtn't be doing this, then maybe you are an imposter—or worse, a fool. And what could be worse than that?

There's no cure for stage fright, but there doesn't need to be. Feeling scared and worried that you are a fake and have no reason to be there, that everyone is going to *hate you,* that you will never be as good as you want to be, and then stepping in front of the microphone and performing anyway is enough. Actually, that might be the whole point.

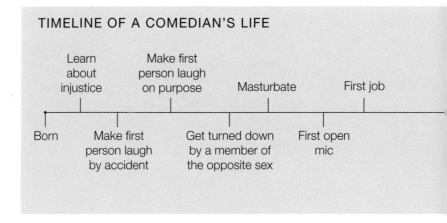

TIMELINE OF A COMEDIAN'S LIFE

Learn about injustice — Make first person laugh on purpose — Masturbate — First job

Born — Make first person laugh by accident — Get turned down by a member of the opposite sex — First open mic

---

An Interview with **Joan Rivers**

"My first year, I got fired from every job after the first night."

There are few comedians who've done as many shows, told as many dirty jokes, or left as big a mark as Joan Rivers. She was a legend who got her big break on *The Tonight Show* in the early 1960s and never stopped performing, or getting stage fright. She passed away in September of 2014, not long after talking with me.

I get stage fright all the time. Before I walk on, absolutely! Do not come and visit me in the dressing room before. I just don't want to talk to you. I'm too nervous and I'm very snippy.

The comedians that don't have stage fright are losing something. The minute you think you know it, and the minute you think you're secure—"I know what's funny and they don't"—you're finished. You're done. Your good years are done.

My first year, I got fired from every job after the first night. But every once in a while, you would have an audience that got you,

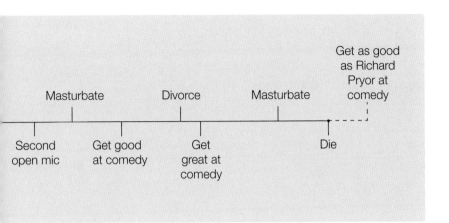

and you realize, "I am all right." And also, I knew that this is what I really want to do. So the drive is extraordinary. I don't know anyone who has really made it, and stayed, who has not had this incredible drive and strength just to do it. I'm talking about Sarah Silverman: What do you do in your off nights? "I go into a club and I try out new material." Whitney Cummings: "I'm going to a club when I leave here from dinner." Howie Mandel told me he's on the road three hundred nights a year! So we all have this tremendous drive.

I fight to the end. Bill Cosby told me once that he works seven to ten minutes and then he goes on automatic if they don't like him. I will jump through hoops. I will bark. I will do cat impressions. I want you to have a good time to the very end. I punch my way home.

Whether I'm performing for a room of a hundred people, or I'm on the road performing for five thousand people, it's the same. You're being judged again. You want those strangers to walk out loving you. But the joy never leaves you. When you're with an audience, and they're laughing, and you're laughing with them—I mean, just the fun of that. The joy never leaves you.

Microphone Grips and Their Uses

THE CLUTCH

The clutch conveys a sense of danger and desperation to the audience. If this doesn't go well, everything around us will fall apart and we will all disappear into oblivion. Why can't you all see that!

THE LEAN

The lean is used to evoke relaxation and utter control on the part of the comic, even though what they're really thinking is that if this doesn't go well, everything around us will fall apart and we will all disappear into oblivion. Why can't you all see that!

THE MOST VALUABLE OBJECT

This grip immediately tells the audience that the comedy they are about to hear is rare and precious. Shh—be careful or the comedy might break.

NO GRIP

This comedian doesn't have the time or desire to remove the microphone from its stand, giving off an unmistakable air of fuck-you-ness.

THE LOADED GUN

This comic is sick of the bullshit! They are gonna tell it like it is and lay some goddamn truth on everyone in this motherfucker. They also never had a strong female role model.

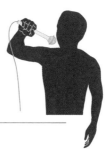

THE HUNGRY CONFESSOR

The hungry confessor is used when the material comes from such a deeply personal place that the comic wants to put the entire audience inside his or her body. Also great for fart noises.

THE STRANGLER

This comedian is a strangler.

THE HEADSET

This comedian is *too busy to hold a microphone* and has probably already figure out some way to *hack into your checking account and take you for EVERYTHING YOU'VE GOT,* thank you, good night!

Crafting a Persona

Even if you are the most naturalistic comedian in the world, just being onstage and presenting prepared material means that you are, to some degree, occupying a persona. It's a big part of what you offer an audience beyond just the jokes. Are you the everyman? The girl next door? A chain-smoking misogynist in a leather jacket? Your persona allows your audience to identify with you, to feel they already know you, which gives you a lot of ways to surprise them. The alpha male persona can get big laughs by talking sensitively about how he pampers his parakeet, just like the sweet little thing can by talking graphically about anal sex.

For some comics, their stage persona is a modified extension of themselves, like Louis CK or Tig Notaro. Some embody a character who might only be distantly related to who they are in real life, such as Gregg Turkington's Neil Hamburger. Other comedians are somewhere in the middle. Even though Gilbert Gottfried didn't break character during his hour-long interview on *WTF with Marc Maron*, I have it on good authority that he doesn't really talk like that every moment of his life. (I met him once at an event, and he was decidedly unshrill.)

You may find that your most natural stage persona emerges when you confess your darkest secrets in front of an audience. Or, you might settle into a hyper-exaggerated version of your most manic self, far removed from your typical way of being. Your style can fall anywhere on this spectrum, but the only way to find it is to perform as much as possible and notice what works best for you.

Here are the some of the main standup styles:

OBSERVATIONAL Typified by Jerry Seinfeld, this comedian's main approach is to notice everyday things and point out to an audience what they have overlooked about those things. If the comedian is good, they will do this in such a way that the audience's worldview will shift, however imperceptibly, for a brief moment in time, either pertaining to our society or to missing socks.

ENERGETIC Embodied by Dane Cook, these comics are full physical performers, marching up and down the stage inventing new gestures. The energetic comedian's main approach is to overwhelm the crowd with Sheer Presence, sometimes because it's a part of their genetic makeup, and sometimes because it makes for a more dynamic show. (And sometimes because they are stronger squatters than they are writers.)

PROP While it rarely seeks the Deep Human Truths that comedians prefer today, but prop comedy is nonetheless a style of visual humor and wordplay that requires skill and dedication. Most prop comics—a dying breed, to be sure—are not only clever with puns but are skilled craftsmen and carpenters, often building or augmenting all their own props. Past devotees include Steve Martin, Gallagher, Carrot Top, and Joel Hodgson.

SCHTICK. Larry the Cable Guy.

ONE-LINER-ERS There are not many comedians today who rely solely on the one-liner. It is a writer's enterprise that allows little room for performance tricks or gimmicks. If Henny Youngman ("Take my wife. Please.") is considered the king of the one-liner, Steven Wright is the prince, Mitch Hedberg is the vice-admiral, and Demetri Martin the West Coast operations manager.

SURREAL. Spaghetti and meatballs. Also see: Brent Weinbach.

POLITICAL Political comedians range from the old-school stylings of Lewis Black to Baratunde Thurston and Jamie Kilstein. Their stock-in-trade is pointing out the insanity of our various broken cultural and political institutions, thereby in some small way perhaps opening a wayward soul's eyes to the proper political path. In reality, much like politicians, they tend to attract likeminded fans, but there are some who can walk the line between opposing views by sticking to jokes about the one thing everyone can agree to hate: the finale of *Lost*. I mean, Congress!

An Interview with **Justin Willman**

> *"Do as many shows as you can. Even seemingly shitty, nonpaying ones."*

Comedy has long played a part in magic, a unique craft with broad appeal to audiences of all ages. One magician who blurs the line between standup and magic is Justin Willman. He's been the host of *Cupcake Wars* and *Win, Lose, or Draw*, and he has appeared on *Ellen*, most morning talk shows, and approximately four thousand podcasts. He's even performed for Barack and Michelle Obama.

How do you develop a new trick?
It starts with a premise that I hone at home and with friends. I always have ten to twenty magic premises or routines on deck that I want to get around to. Different routines can take different amounts of prep time—a week, a month, five years. But it's not until a piece has been in my show for at least six months does it really begin to shine and take shape.

You used to work as a children's magician before moving into more cor-porate stuff. What was the best and worst part of each?
Best part of children's shows is that it's usually super fun and you get to really develop a comedic persona. And there's plenty of work

146

if you know how to get it, and plenty of work means plenty of stage time to hone the act. The only negative part of children's shows is the stigma that comes along with it . . . that you're somehow lower on the show-biz hierarchy. But that's all bullshit, of course.

Corporate shows are great because they're obviously more lucrative, but you often end up having to entertain drunk businesspeople who'd rather be flirting in the hotel bar than watching the act their boss hired.

A lot of the stuff you do now incorporates modern technology. Are these essentially the same illusions but with different trappings?
It's exactly that. It's taking one-hundred-year-old ideas and figuring out a way to do it with a modern premise and object. For example, I took the classic cut-and-restored-rope trick and used earbuds instead of rope. Same method, but now it seems fresh and topical because the prop is something we all have in our pockets.

What first attracted you to magic?
When I was twelve, I was riding my bike while wearing rollerblades in some sort of idiotic attempt to impress girls. I ended up flying over the handlebars and breaking both arms. I was in casts for six months. My orthopedic surgeon randomly recommended I learn some card tricks to get my dexterity back, and that's what got me hooked into magic. I've been obsessed ever since.

What advice would you give to someone just starting out in magic?
Do as many shows as you can. Even seemingly shitty, nonpaying ones. Get a gig at a restaurant doing table-to-table magic, do kids shows, volunteer at a hospital. Find a way to practice your stuff for real people in the real world. It's the only way to get great.

And don't copy other people's material. It will stunt your growth.

Dealing with Bombing

Most people fear bombing more than death itself, but for comedians, failing in front of a crowd is actually worse than death because, after it's over, you are still alive. Bombing is a terrible feeling: Confusion followed by dread, and then panic as the reality sets in. Time stretches out like a silent desert before you, with no shelter in sight. In fact, cottonmouth is a common side effect. Your hands shake, your voice echoes in your head, and you are no longer able to differentiate between reality and nightmare. Sometimes it's so bad that it suddenly strikes you as unbelievably hilarious. At that moment, you are standing on the threshold of insanity.

Bombing is going to happen to you. It happens to everybody because an audience is involved. Most of the time, the audience wants to be happy and laugh and for you to succeed, but not always. Sometimes they want to be angry. Sometimes they want to be impatient. And sometimes they're fighting with their girlfriends and Mercury is in retrograde and it's just a little too warm in the club and there's this dead space between the stage and the audience through which no connection may pass. And sometimes you just suck. Whatever the reason, there is *absolutely nothing you can do to stop it.* When you find yourself bombing, there are some options:

PERFORM FOR THE BACK OF THE ROOM The worst time I ever bombed was during a midnight tryout show for the Just For Laughs festival (see page 198). The comic before me was a rotund black woman whose whole act was about getting a bikini wax from a group of stereotypical Korean women. There was a lot of chopsticking and facial hamming and references to pubic hair that looked

148

like Dr. J's afro, and she absolutely murdered it. She destroyed. She committed genocide on that room, and then I went up. I wasn't as good. In fact, a group of sympathetic women were audibly gasping and saying, "Oh no." The biggest laugh of the night came from a guy who said, "You're not funny!" But after my set, the comedians at the back of the room complimented me on the quality of the writing and assured me that this just wasn't my crowd.

OWN IT No matter how or why the bombing has occurred, you are the one who chose to be onstage. Own the moment and take responsibility for it. If you can handle being onstage at its worst, then you are even better prepared to enjoy it at its best. Remember: Standup comedy is insane. Here are two ways to acknowledge a bombing:

Don't blame the audience. Yes, audiences are sniveling dog people who barely deserve to live, but they did not force you onstage and beg them to laugh at you. (That's your aloof father's fault!) Don't comment on the lack of laughter after every single failed joke or complain about how well this set usually does. It will always feel better to finish a set with some human dignity if at all possible—not only for yourself and the audience but, more importantly, for the other comics in the room.

Do the opposite of that. Or, bail early and tell the audience to go fuck themselves. This might happen sometimes.

TRY SOMETHING NEW Use this as a chance to try new material that you aren't sure of. Why not? Of course, this may be a terrible thing to do if you want an accurate audience response to gauge the new material. However, the nothing-to-lose attitude can lead to some interesting discoveries.

YE OLDE CROWD WORK Sometimes you just need to shift the attention away from what's happening onstage and disperse that negative energy. Sometimes this can spark something new and shift

MANAGING HECKLERS

Wherever there are crowds, there will be hecklers. Most of the time, they are drunk. Other times, they come to the show with a grievance or bone to pick. Sometimes, they are just evil, evil people. How you deal with them helps define the kind of comedian you are. The most skillful heckler-handling that I've seen live was by Paul F. Tompkins (see interview below). He turned one man's drunken chattiness into an impromptu routine on the relationship between audience and performer and the dangers of alcoholism. The heckler was respectfully silenced, the audience was entertained, and Tompkins came off smelling like roses. That goddamn Paul F. Tompkins! Here are some other ways to deal with hecklers:

Maintain dominance. No matter how annoying the heckler may be, you are still the one standing onstage with a noise amplification device. If you keep your composure and remember that you are the one in charge of the room, you'll probably be fine.

Acknowledge them and move on. Sometimes hecklers will be satisfied with a simple acknowledgment that they exist. Look at them, address their stupid little comment or concern, thank them for their time, and then continue with the show.

Acknowledge them and then destroy them. Another tack is to do the same as above but, rather than continuing on with the show, viciously berate and insult them for their rudeness, their manner of dress, and their upbringing. Offer them no quarter and send a clear warning to any other would-be hecklers in the room: they will be killed.

Let them destroy themselves. If you grant a heckler their wish and make them the center of attention, they will more often than not wind up humiliating themselves. That flame will burn out under the pressure of an impatient audience. NOTE: Occasionally hecklers will actually be funny when given this opportunity, and they might even throw an effective insult or two your way. If you don't have the time or energy to go toe to toe, just applaud them and change subjects. (Then get in the last word after they've shut up.)

Play along. If the heckler is acting like they are an expert on something, go along with that. Ask them for clarity on their point. Enthusiastically agree with everything they say. Then, when they have their guard down, you can berate them for their rudeness and manner of dress.

Repeat everything they say. This classic techniques works with younger siblings, so why not with impetuous a-holes who insist on ruining things for everyone else? Whatever they say, just repeat it back to them. This is so fun that sometimes I hope for hecklers!

the momentum. It could also fail miserably, at which point an audience can switch from indifferent to hostile. If that happens, it may be time for desperate measures. Try this: Sigh deeply and tell the audience you need to level with them. See, tomorrow is your daughter's birthday, and you wanted more than anything to be there with her, but you're on the road, and you won't get to see her for another three weeks. She's the love of your life, and she'd love it if they'd all join in singing "Happy Birthday" to your little "Maggie girl," so you can send her a special message. See if *that* bullshit doesn't turn those suckers around.

GET IMMEDIATELY BACK ONSTAGE This is the advice I heard most. It is absolutely vital that you not allow one incident to infect you like a disease, and the only way to avoid that is to obliterate it with a good set as soon as possible. Or, as Patton Oswalt told me, nothing about bombing matters except to realize that it's not the end of the world.

PRO TERM! BOMBING

The act of failing to induce laughter in a crowd of paying customers, the one thing in the entire world a comedian is supposed to do. Synonyms include eating it, eating shit, dying, sucking, dying a slow death, sucking shit, choking, choking on shit, slurping shit, ordering an extra-large shit pizza and devouring the whole thing, faring poorly.

An Interview with **Paul F. Tompkins**

"I didn't want to just get by in the clubs. I wanted to be an artist."

Paul F. Tompkins is one of the best, and best-dressed, comedians working today. He's been on *Mr. Show with Bob and David,* *Weeds,* and *Key & Peele*, hosted *Best Week Ever* and a number of podcasts, worked in film (including a teeny role in *There Will Be Blood*), and regularly does voices for animated shows all over your television. He can command a small room as easily as a large theater, and he can do it with grace and wit and a mustache and a bowtie.

On Starting Out

I started out as part of a team. I don't know when or how I would have gotten into it, otherwise. But when my comedy partner and I got on each other's nerves and split up as a team, I took a month to put together a solo set and eventually went onstage by myself for the first time. I can still remember how that felt, to be up there all alone—it was huge. It went well enough that I knew that I was really, truly someone who should be doing this.

The best thing and the worst thing about performing are the same: being up there all by yourself. It's the best when you're feeling that connection with the audience and you achieve transcendence. It's the worst when it's just not happening for you—even if you're able to draw on your professional experience and abilities to still do well—and you don't feel that connection. It's lonely.

On Bad Advice

When I was still pretty new, I was emceeing this show at a bar. I went up first and bombed. The next guy after me was this boring, hacky guy. The headliner was this super-energetic, likeable guy, but his material was just nothing. Unimaginative, all personality-driven, just not interesting to me at all. He was just killing with the crowd. The boring, hacky guy turned to me and said, "You could learn a lot from watching him." And I just knew that I couldn't. I knew that I wanted to do something else. I didn't want to just get by in the clubs. I wanted to be an artist.

Both of my parents are dead now, and they never, ever got it. My mother went to her grave asking me when I was going to figure out what I wanted to do with my life. I had been working on a television show for two years when my mother encouraged me to take piano-tuning lessons from my uncle so I'd have a trade to fall back on.

On Perseverance

For someone who's been doing it as long as I have, the most important/difficult thing you can do is keep things in perspective. It's hard to know, sometimes, that where you are is good. You get so used to trying to reach "the next level" that you sometimes have to make yourself realize that the place you are is actually pretty good.

Distributing Your Comedy

You've made your bones. You've spent your ten years discovering who you are. You've conquered all your inner demons and signed up for a great rewards program with the Sheraton family of hotels. You even have one of those neck pillows. You've developed a fan base and people know your name. So you think, "I am ready to distribute my comedy on multiple platforms, world!" Let's explore the various ways in which this can happen.

YOUTUBE

This is by now so obvious as to perhaps not even warrant its own little subsection, but the fact is, I find it very satisfying to type those little headers up there in bold and then fill in the space below with words like these. It brings me a sense of accomplishment. Also, YouTube is an incredibly powerful distribution tool with an unparalleled ability to engage viewers and introduce your work to new fans. Intrigued? Wait till you see chapter 18!

ALBUMS

For a period of time before cable TV, from the 1950s to the 1970s, comedy albums were extremely popular. Every household had a copy of *Bill Cosby: Himself* or *The 2000 Year Old Man*. Today, they don't sell quite so well. What record does? Still, it's a real accomplishment to put one out. If critics and other comics like your album, it can lead to more exposure, which can lead to new work and opportunities. Plus you get to put a cool photo of yourself on the cover (see "An Interview with Dan Schlissel," below, and chapter 11).

STANDUP COMEDY IN OTHER CULTURES

Britain The British have an extraordinarily rich tradition of dynamic, erudite standup comedians who often seamlessly mix music, philosophy, drag, and observational humor. England seems to be more accepting of experimental comics, or maybe they're just too snobby to admit that they don't get it?

Australia This continent has produced some notable standup comics, including Tim Minchin (the great, weird performance artist), Eric Bana (who is now a very handsome actor), and someone named King Billy Cokebottle, who apparently puts on blackface and tells jokes as his trademark Aborigine character. By the same token, there are a number of prominent standup comedians of color, including Nazeem Hussain, Akmal Saleh, and Anh Do.

Japan There is a form of two-person standup comedy in Japan called *manzai* that actually predates American standup by about a thousand years. *Manzai* acts usually comprise a straight man, known as a *tsukkomi*, and the funny man, called a *boke*. Think Abbot and Costello, but if Abbot was Japanese and hit Costello on the head with a folding fan all the time. And if Costello was also Japanese. One of my very favorite actors, Beat Takeshi, started out as one-half of a *manzai* act.

Nigeria This African nation has a celebrated trio of comedians, nicknamed Papalolo, Jacob, and Aderupoku, who essentially invented the country's standup tradition in the 1970s and 1980s. The three were huge TV stars and released wildly popular albums of standup and sketch.

China The Chinese enjoy a form of comedic performance called "crosstalk" or *xiangsheng,* which is made up of wordplay, puns, imitations, and song. It usually involves two people, but a popular form of solo crosstalk has emerged that is similar to standup comedy. A performer named Zhou Libo is credited with inventing Shanghai-style standup comedy that is more formalized than in the West: the performer stands in front of a music stand and delivers material, occasionally breaking into song or dramatic interpretation. Difficult to imagine this act doing well in Indiana.

Norway In Norway, the most famous comedian is Jonas Rønnig, and he is known for delivering his act through a megaphone. But there are many others in the Land of Endless Night, including political monologist and actor Otto Jespersen, whom American audiences might recognize from his role in the weird and wonderful action movie *Trollhunter*.

Saudi Arabia Even one of the world's most restrictive nations, Saudi Arabia, has seen a recent explosion in the popularity of standup comedians. One of the most popular Saudi comics is Fahad Albutairi, the very handsome, very hip host of a popular YouTube channel called La Yekthar. He's one of a growing number of comedians and social commentators in the Gulf and Mideast to gain a following on YouTube and other social media platforms.

SELF-DISTRIBUTION

Also known as the Louis CK Model, this increasingly popular direct relationship with consumers would not have been possible before the digital age. The idea of cutting out the middle man and making entire albums available to anyone with Internet access and five dollars really resonates with comics. All the tools—from the production to compression to streaming—can be easily acquired. The only thing holding the average comedian back from fully embracing this exciting new paradigm is that the average comedian is not Louis CK. As accessible and democratizing as the Internet is, you need to have fans, and you need to have a platform for communicating with those fans, and you need to have fans who will buy your material for money. Once these things are in place, however, it becomes a very attractive venture.

NACA

Almost all of the shows, lectures, and performances at colleges throughout the country are booked through one organization, once or twice a year: the National Association for Campus Activities, or NACA. Each college has its own chapter, with regional and national conferences, during which the bulk of the coming year's shows and activities will be selected. It is a fun, frantic atmosphere, with hundreds of college kids wandering around looking for something to be impressed by. You can submit an application to perform at a NACA showcase, and host your own booth on the convention floor, through their website, naca.org. Throughout the day, performers and lecturers get onstage and do five- to fifteen-minute abbreviated versions of their act for potential bookers. If you do a good job, chatter spreads through the conference like wildfire, and curious NACA kids will stop by your booth to get booking information. It's insane, but it's how the college circuit sausage gets made.

An Interview with **Dan Schlissel**

*"I am good at finding talent and helping them along
with their development as recording artists."*

Dan Schlissel is the founder of the Minneapolis-based comedy label Stand Up! Records. Since 1999, he's put out dozens of albums with such comedians as David Cross, Judy Gold, Marc Maron, Patton Oswalt, Hannibal Buress, Maria Bamford, and Eddie Pepitone. The first comedian Schlissel signed was Lewis Black, whom he met after a show and successfully convinced to put out an album on his label.

What do you look for in the comedians you work with?
People who make me laugh. I prefer to hear a comedian's honest point of view of how they see life. I find comics through travel, going to festivals, that sort of thing. I also get recommendations from folks on the label and club owners and members of the comedy industry that I am friendly with.

What can a new comedian who signs a deal with Stand Up! Records expect?
We work out the points of the deal, figure out where to record, they get some guidance on the process from me, then we record. After recording, we review the material through a couple rounds of notes back and forth. We work on a title and the art concept and get it to manufacturing. We then pick a release date and start notifying distribution and the press. It can take anywhere from four months to a year from the recording date to get the record out and on the market.

What do you offer a comedian that they can't get with another label, or if they put it out themselves?
Most comics don't want to focus on all the things that it takes to run

the business of their recordings. It really does take you out of a creative headspace to have to put on the visor and run a calculator and push papers around a lot. Sometimes you need a producer involved just to make decisions. Chances are I can make the recording better and make it sound better as well. I have contacts on all levels of the business and can get it in front of more faces than an individual artist can on their own. Some folks want to do it on their own, and that is fine. There's really room enough for everyone in that regard.

Could somebody start a comedy record label today?
I think the answer to that is always yes. It takes a certain amount of naiveté to jump into any entrepreneurial activity. I don't know how keen I'd be to do it if I knew all the steps that I would need to be on top of in order to run a business, but I am glad I accidentally backed into this as my livelihood.

Chapter 10

IMPROV

A lot of Comedy Cool Kids roll their roll eyes at improv, and not completely without warrant. Improv's positive exuberance can border on cultishness, and there is something insular and insulated about improv troupes that can feel separated from reality. From a performer's perspective, it is intense, it is intimate (improv must have the third-highest incidence of marriage behind the Peace Corps and plane-crash survivors), and all of these traits can be hard to swallow if you're not fully committed to improv comedy. More so than any of that, I suspect, is the fact that most comedians have been invited to too many Level 1 class shows to ever want to see another scene that ends with the President of the United States in a penis factory again.

That's understandable.

But improv offers things that no other training, comedy or otherwise, offers. It forces you to cultivate what is happening onstage without prejudice, meaning that you can't steer the conversation into a certain direction or avoid awkwardness, as you would in real life. It's great acting training, too, because you have to be open to each moment and react accordingly. Improv rewards those who understand the rules and can still make unexpected moves within those rules. But it also takes practice, like basketball, and when you don't practice for a while, you are not as good, like a basketball player who is not as good. What is more, the most prominent improv theaters are great places to tap into the network of successful comedians and performers who were also trained there.

How Improv Works

Improv first took shape in Chicago in the 1950s, and its influence can today be seen everywhere, from the influx of Second City and Upright Citizens Brigade (UCB) alumni like Bill Murray, Tina Fey, Stephen Colbert, and Amy Poehler to the improvised style of Judd Apatow's films and Larry David's *Curb Your Enthusiasm*.

The improv concept is very simple: performers make up everything on the spot. The audience is usually asked to provide suggestions to inspire the scene. Someone will shout out a place, time, or type of factory (penis), one performer uses that suggestion to initiate a situation, another responds, and it goes from there.

One of the key improv principles is "Yes, and." That is to say, you must accept what the other performers create and add to it. By following this principle, so the theory goes, everyone involved fully supports everyone else and accepts as absolute reality whatever is collectively created, without denying any contribution.[1] This is not to say that no one can ever disagree onstage, or that there cannot be misunderstanding or conflict or insane points of view. Rather, this principle trains performers to overcome the most basic human need to control everything in their environment in order to feel safe.

---

1 Of course, all rules can be broken at a high enough level, and especially experienced performers will sometimes seek to playfully sabotage one another onstage all the time. For fun!

Improv, at its heart, is about throwing safety into a roiling chemical fire, accepting whatever happens, and reacting to it. Without this most basic tenet, nothing worth watching can ever really happen. Within these boundaries, however, anything is possible.

GLOSSARY

Improv is all about terminology, theory, and technique, almost to the point of being an academic discipline, so there are a lot of terms to know. This brief list represents about 1 percent.

Back line. The area at the back of the stage where those who aren't currently in a scene wait, watch, and listen. It's always interesting to look at those on the back line and see the moment of inspiration on their faces right before they jump into a scene.

Opening. A semi-formalized scene or exercise that starts the show. The opening sets the tone, establishes themes, and provides information and details to use throughout.

Initiation. A declaration, action, or combination therein that starts a new scene.

Pimping. Purposely, and playfully, setting up another person in the scene to do something unpleasant. E.g., setting up a scenario where a scene partner has to dance, or sing, or squat for long periods of time, or repeatedly say, "I'm a big, greasy monkey boy."

Game. The pattern of interactions or rules, established on the fly, that everyone follows for the duration of that scene. The game changes all the time and can sometimes be hard to determine: indeed "finding the game" is usually the first thing that people in a scene will do, and the more quickly and firmly this is established, the better.

Beat. One discrete scene in a series of related scenes (see "The Harold," below).

Denying. The biggest no-no in improv is when you flat-out reject what someone else has established in the scene. A classic example would be this: Player A: "Come on, honey, we're going to be late for dinner with the Andersons." Player B: "What are you talking about? We're not married." In skillful and experienced hands, denying can occasionally be effective, even playful—but even then one can still feel some of the life being sucked from the scene.

Information. Details that help fill out the world and give other players something to build off. Every time you speak, there should be information about the setting, your past, who you are, what you want, or your relationship to the others onstage. The trick is finding funny, nonintrusive ways to do this.

Object work. Since there are no props in an improv show, this is the term for how well you mime shoveling, putting things on shelves, and serving people dinner.

WORST AUDIENCE SUGGESTIONS IN THE WORLD

It has been said that every audience suggestion is a gift and that great improvisers can make anything work. But still. Stay away from these:

- Puke
- Orgy
- Butt
- Muppet rape
- Dildo
- Double-sided dildo
- Gynecologist
- Hodor
- Penis Factory
- Miley Cyrus's vagina

- Mayonnaise factory
- Black people
- Jesus Christ's bris*
- Ninja doctor
- Child molester
- Colostomy bag
- Horse dick
- Holocaust
- Poop factory

*This might actually be a good suggestion.

Writing. The tendency to describe too much detail, motivation, past events, or future expectations. For instance, someone initiates with, "I miss dad," and another player replies: "Yes, you were always a lot closer to him than I was, which is why I killed him and you covered for me, and now we're both in prison, and I'm really enjoying it but you resent me." This might well be a fantastic scenario, but if you don't get there organically, you lose the surprise, inspiration, and fun of improv.

Status. The relationship between characters in a given scene. This is a great thing to establish immediately; it sets expectations, which can then be heightened or destroyed in surprising ways. It's also fun to boss people around onstage.

Warm-ups. The stuff improv teams do before a show to get themselves feeling loose and on the same wavelength. Usually warm-ups involve tossing invisible things around or chanting.

Editing. Ending a scene at just the right moment, either on a big laugh or when a scene really needs someone to come out and kill it. This is usually done by running in front of the action, as if to wipe the slate clean.

Talking heads. A scene devoid of action. This is when people just stand there talking to each other about what has, will, or might happen. (Boring.)

Forms & Styles

There are two major styles of improv: long form and short form. The first centers around building scenes, developing characters, and bringing it all together in a satisfying way. The latter is typified by short scenes and games, more in line with what you might see on *Whose Line Is It Anyway?* Short form is characterized by more immediate, frenetic, explosive improv "games." Over the years, people have developed dozens of variations on these two styles, some of which are listed here, for your pleasure. Right now.

LONG FORM

THE HAROLD This classic long-form style follows a three-act structure. A Harold begins with a free-form opening, followed by the first beats of three separate scenes that establish themes and flood the stage with information; next there is an unrelated group game, designed to be a palate cleanser; then the second beats of the next three scenes (these can be connected literally, thematically, or something in between); then another unrelated group game; and finally, the third beats, which will hopefully be full of callbacks and references and seek to cinch everything up in a beautiful comedy bow.

THE MONOSCENE One scene in one location with no edits. Performers can play one character or many characters, and it usually takes place in real time, without flashing forward or backward. It is my favorite form because it gives you so much time and space. I've done monoscenes in which the first three minutes were completely silent, and that is a crazy, scary, exhilarating experience.

THE ARMANDO Technically known as a monologue deconstruction, this form starts with an improvised monologue, followed by a series of scenes exploring and expanding that monologue. An Armando is usually broken into two halves, both with one longer and one shorter monologue. It ends similarly to a Harold, with a mad dash to connect everything together. (This is what is performed at UCB's famous "Asssscat 3000" shows in New York City and LA.)

LA RONDE A series of two-person scenes. Every performer rotates in and out, and each person maintains whatever character he or she first establishes. It's a good team exercise.

MONTAGE A loose form that paints a picture with seemingly unrelated scenes that are somehow bound together thematically or tonally. There are usually two or three beats. This one takes discipline and experience because it is up to the performers to impose structure.

EVENTÉ A series of scenes around one specific event, which could be a preschool graduation or a meteor strike or anything in between. The show is built around flashbacks, interviews, time dashes, and whatever else serves.

THE MOVIE An improvised movie! This starts with a series of stage directions and descriptions setting the scene, followed by a declaration of the title, and then the movie itself—usually a spoof of popular genres—is performed.

SHORT FORM

ALPHABET The team must create a scene, or tell a story, with each new line of dialogue beginning with the next letter of the alphabet.

FIRST AND LAST Players are given the first and last lines of a scene and must make up everything in the middle.

FREEZE A two-person scene takes place. Someone on the back line claps, freezing both players, and replaces one of them, taking over their physical position. The new player then initiates a new, totally different, scene.

HALF LIFE The team creates a thirty-second scene, then repeats the scene in fifteen seconds, seven seconds, and thirty seconds again. So funny!

TIME WARP At various points throughout a scene, the MC or host or chosen player will yell, "Freeze!" and move the scene somewhere in time, e.g., ten years later or twenty minutes earlier, etcetera.

Some Insightful Tips from Me, Joe, About Improv

As improv has become more popular, the notion of non-Comedy People (civilians) taking improv classes to help in some other, more important realm of their life seems to have become de rigueur for writers and corporate middle-manager types. The truth, however, is that I don't know anyone for whom improv really, truly opened any great creative portals in their writing, public-speaking prowess, or management techniques. My belief is that improv should not be treated as a means to an end. It's just improv.

That said, someday you'll be vaporized with the rest of us when an asteroid the size of Baltimore strikes the planet, so you should definitely try improv. Chances are, you'll be pretty good. Because here's the secret about improv: Everyone is pretty good at it. Once you get over yourself and unlearn some of the schtick you've grown accustomed to using in your everyday life, you're actually a fairly interesting person capable of legitimate insight, emotion, and creativity. Just like everyone else.

When you do, keep these tips in mind:

DON'T TRY TOO HARD Be willing to let things happen on their own. Without being blasé, don't work to get a reaction or force your character into a scene. Improv is very much a metaphor for life: you cannot predict how or when things are going to change; all you can do is go along and make the best of what happens with a bunch of invisible objects.

COMMIT There is nothing worse than bailing on a scene or leaving one of your scene partners hanging because you want to play it emotionally cool. Believe me, you look much, *much* dumber doing that than leaving everything you have on the stage. Being fully committed to everything you do is an important performance ethic in general, and it's inspiring to your fellow improvisers and is the fastest way to build trust.

PLAY HONEST One of my improv teachers, Rachel Hamilton, always used to say that good improv equals good acting. They cannot be separated. So play it real and don't go for laughs. Of course, sometimes you will go for laughs (and, honestly, there are a million jillion billion trillion and thirty-eight times when you probably should), but you'll get more out of a scene—and more unexpected laughs—if you play it as straight as possible.

MAKE STRONG CHOICES Have an undeniable point of view, desire, or problem right off the bat, and don't let anything distract you from it. Avoid entering a scene only to make one joke, which disrupts the flow of the scene and leaves everyone confused about what to do next. If you find you've made a weak or dead-end choice, just *do anything*. Action propels the scene forward.

DON'T RUSH When establishing yourself in a scene, it's much more powerful to take in what's already happening, look it up and down—and then react to it with conviction. Be in control, know who you are, why you're there, and what you want. The worst thing—*the absolute nightmare scenario*—is to get in your own head in the middle of a scene. Just react and add something. React and add something else. You'll surprise yourself and your audience.

WARMING UP IS DUMB Any respectable improviser will think I'm crazy, but this is my book and I can say whatever I want. Most teams do elaborate warm-ups and spend a ton of time getting on the same page before a show, but I've always found this to be contrived. I prefer the terror and immediacy of jumping onstage having no idea what's going to happen. If you can get to a place of trust with your teammates, then you shouldn't have to sing a silly rap song to be ready and willing to go onstage and die for the other people up there with you. YES, DIE FOR THEM.

DON'T KILL PEOPLE It's a rare improv scene in which killing someone works out well. For one thing, it almost never feels earned. For another, it creates the very awkward situation of having a person who must lie on the floor for the remainder of the scene.

JUST EDIT THE SCENE PLEASE. Don't hesitate. The window for a perfect edit is very brief, so you've got to follow your gut. It's painful to watch someone edge off the back wall to edit and then stop midstep. If you feel like the scene has run its course (e.g., established a tone, introduced lots of detail and memorable characters, and gotten a big laugh), just go for it.

WHEN ALL ELSE FAILS, GRAB SOMETHING OFF A SHELF This is the oldest trick in the object-work book, but I always preferred it to shoveling, which is the second oldest trick. If you don't know what else to do, reach up high, down low, or in the middle, and find something new on an invisible shelf. Feel it, play with it, and allow whatever the fuck it is to dictate what you say next.

Chapter 11

MUSIC

When I was a kid, I had a bootleg cassette tape of Dr. Demento's top songs of 1987, and I played that goddamn thing into the dirt. It was a mix of parody, goofiness, and straight up original weird I'd never heard before. It felt like a rare and special prize. Decades later, audiences have found that same joy in the work of people like the Lonely Island or Tobuscus, who make music that parodies web and video game culture and who do it mostly from the comfort of their own homes.

Comedic music has a long tradition, extending back to court jesters in medieval times. Today, it is such a staple of the entertainment industry that it almost defies categorization. *The Howard Stern Show* and morning drive-time radio prominently feature song spoofs. Flight of the Conchords, New Zealand's self-proclaimed "fourth most popular guitar-based digi-bongo a capella-rap-funk-comedy folk duo," had their own TV show and won a Grammy. Reggie Watts feels equally at home doing art shows in Paris or Bud Light commercials. Heavy metal comedy gods Tenacious D sell out whole stadiums, and Weird Al Yankovic, the king of parody pop, has had a Top 10 hit in three decades.

Define Your Style

When thinking about making a career in comedy, one of the most important considerations is style, and this is perhaps even more important when it comes to comedic music. Nobody wants to make a bad deal or to fall into the wrong line of work or, even more bluntly put, to look like an idiot. But while independent artists in the twenty-first century need to be fluent and creative in so many more fields than their chosen area of creativity, the most important thing they can do is figure out who they are. As an artist. As a creator. As a comedy musician or musical comedian. Whatever. It will take some time to determine which one you are, but it's worth pondering and, occasionally, writing down or saying out loud to yourself.

Is music your main thing or something you do on the side? Zach Galifianakis is not thought of as a musical comedian, but he used to play piano during sets to juxtapose against his off-kilter one-liners. Garfunkel & Oates (Riki Lindhome and Kate Micucci) are a folk comedy duo who are also both working actors. They were picking up bit parts on TV when they met at the Upright Citizens Brigade in LA and starting writing songs together. When Micucci got a small role on the NBC sitcom *Scrubs,* they got an opportunity to do a couple of their songs on the show. Since then they've recorded albums, appeared on *The Tonight Show* and Comedy Central, and toured the United States and probably other countries, too!

There is a danger of being pigeonholed as a novelty songwriter if that's not what you want to be known primarily for. Many have been able to avoid this, but it helps to know what you want and to diversify what you do.

The Business of Comedy Music

The biggest obstacle for comedic musicians is getting people to see and/or hear you. Maybe you don't want to haul your glockenspiel to every coffee house open mic, but there's really no substitute for a live show. And the steps for making a living are the same if your music is funny or not: play on your own until you feel confident enough to play in front of friends; then play in public at open mics and other nonpaying venues; then eventually open for someone else at paying gigs; and then get your own show at the Staples Center. It's *simple* and *straightforward*.

Alternatively, you can post videos to YouTube, MySpace, and Vine, where many musicians are building audiences by reaching people directly. Nicholas Megalis, one of the most popular Viners (for more on Vine, see chapter 20), quickly racked up a couple million followers, thanks to his innate ability to come up with silly, catchy, visually rich, six-second songs. Likewise, Jonathan Coulton saw early on that there was something to this whole Internet thing, so he quit his day job and embarked on a mission to post a song a week for a year. It's a gimmick that today might get buried under the avalanche of every other online "in a year" gimmick, but in 2005, it got him some attention, steadily built an audience, and forced him to be disciplined about his craft. After he had a few Internet hits, he started doing more live shows, which led to the biggest break of his career to that point: "I wrote a song on the greatest video game of all time," he said. What happened was, after a show in Seattle, a member of the audience introduced herself and asked if he'd like to write a song for this game they were making called *Portal*. He said sure, the game turned into a massive hit, and his song, "Still Alive," is one of the most recognizable in the genre.[2] Today, Jonathan tours regularly, appears on NPR, and is generally a funny famous person with crazy nerd cred.

PUT OUT AN ALBUM

Albums will probably never go away because they offer a nice, tight package that has it all: you, your work, and your aesthetic sensibility. Since most artists make their money on touring and merchandising, it's also one of your best forms of marketing. As the radio host John Moe once said, "Most professional musicians I know are travelers and small business owners who sometimes get to play lovely songs." It's true. You always have to be thinking about almost everything else besides the music.

If you want to make an album, three major distribution options are available: self-publishing, music labels, and comedy labels.

SELF-PUBLISHING In the time of the Great DIY, when most people have at least some technical or digital proficiency, this is an increasingly popular option. It allows you complete creative control, less overhead, and the ability to work on your own timeline. The biggest hurdle, as always, is scale. But there are a few things you should keep in mind, should you go this route.

Distribution. There are a variety of digital and physical distribution options, from iTunes to pressing your own CDs and selling them outside comedy clubs or correctional facilities, since prisoners who are just being released have no idea how to function in the real world and are easily fooled! All distribution options have different guidelines, fees, and licensing percentages, all of which are always changing, so look carefully into this. Or, be clever: sell your album

2 Though it will probably be the biggest audience Coulton will ever have, with millions upon millions of listeners, no one foresaw the game's success, and he was paid a flat rate for his work, meaning he will never see another dime for it.

on thumb drives, or perhaps send email blasts with free copies of your album to get the word out.

Registration. If you are hoping for airplay or any other public use of your music, you should and must register with a performance rights organization (PRO). You've probably heard of BMI and ASCAP, the two biggest PROs. They ensure that your copyrighted music is categorized and tracked so that you can earn royalties. You should register as a publisher (which means you get to pick a cool publisher name) and as an artist. Both charge processing fees, so this is sometimes an impediment, especially to nine-year-old prodigies.

Packaging. Great design and cover art are extremely important to remove any sniff of amateurishness from your work. If you are creative, you probably have creative friends, some of whom might be willing to help you out with your album design. *Be careful about getting work for free, however:* Free equals a favor, and favors have no deadlines or timelines, they impede your ability to give notes or be unhappy, and they bind everyone to a sense of obligation rather than inspiration. I'm not saying to avoid it altogether, but just to be aware of the limitations. Think about what message you want to send. When I see album art or head shots of people mugging it up around goofy fonts, I think, "They need to tell us that they are funny, which means they are probably not that funny." Do something that expresses who *you* are and what your *music* is about.

MUSIC LABELS Major music labels have the most money and resources, and most have smaller imprints that specialize in the comedy genre. As always, it's harder to get a deal with a big label, and if you do, they control the flow of the negotiation. Most places still want to see a demonstrable audience, so much of the work of self-publishing still applies. Some labels will accept unsolicited demos (a sampling of your music), but your best bet, if you don't already have a substantial following, is to hook up with a manager to help break in with the labels.

COMEDY LABELS These include Comedy Central Records, Stand Up! Records, and Uproar Records. You are probably more likely to come across one of these folks, since they tend to run in the comedy industry anyway and are always actively looking for new artists. As with most things, comedy labels offer less money and smaller audiences than major music labels, but so much of the market is pitching to niches now, anyway, that this isn't necessarily a bad thing.

REGGIE WATTS

Reggie Watts is undefinable: Is he a comedian or a musician or an avant-garde artist? His performances are completely improvised, energetic, unpredictable, chaotic, and weird, and yet he seems to be in total control. Watts started as a conventional musician, trained in piano and violin. He played with several groups in Seattle, where he experimented with different genres, composition, and electronic effects, before dabbling in sketch comedy and solo performance. Then he started performing solo at smaller venues, improvising entire songs with his effects pedals. He moved to NYC to concentrate on this form, where he made video shorts for a bunch of comedy websites. One of them, "What About Blowjobs," went, as they say, "viral," raising, as they say, his "profile." People took notice, and he started doing TV and film, in addition to bigger and more frequent live performances. Now he tours the world and appears regularly on screens both big, small, and YouTube-sized—and nobody knows for sure exactly what it is that he does.

An Interview with **Weird Al Yankovic**

"I can shamelessly leech onto whatever new musical trend comes along, and that doesn't make me a sellout or a poseur . . . that just makes me Weird Al!"

I cannot imagine a world without Weird Al. He was there through all the major events and cultural touchstones of my childhood, and some of his parodies have become more recognizable than the original songs. He's adapted to every musical genre, show business trend, and technological innovation while remaining relevant and entertaining. His music is enjoyed by all ages because he's wholesome, positive, and somehow a genuinely nice person.

You've created a kind of perpetual relevance for yourself by parodying popular songs of the day and the current culture. Was this always part of the plan?
When I was recording silly music as a teenager, I had no idea that I'd still be doing this stuff several decades later. When I signed a ten-album record contract in 1982, I thought it was a big joke—"Yeah, like I'll ever have ten albums!"—and as it turns out, I'm currently working on album number fourteen. So it's just fortuitous that I happened to come up with an act that stays relevant by design. I can shamelessly leech onto whatever new musical trend comes along, and that doesn't make me a sellout or a poseur . . . that just makes me Weird Al!

What would you do differently if you were starting out today?
I don't think I'd bother trying to get a record deal. I would probably just do what most other amateurs do: upload stuff to YouTube. That seems to be the easiest and most effective way to get your material out there these days, particularly for my specific kind of comedy.

If what you have to offer is really exceptional, there's a very good chance that people will find it and take notice. Of course, the biggest drawback for me, if I were starting out today, is that I'd be competing with a million other people in a field that I virtually had to myself in the eighties.

What's more important to you: cultural commentary or making entertaining songs?
I'm really just going for the grins. I'm trying to be funny and entertain people, but I suppose sometimes a bit of social commentary slips in there accidentally. Occasionally people glean political messages from my songs that I never actually intended. One website tried to make me into some kind of tort reform poster boy after "I'll Sue Ya." Often I will make my lyrics intentionally vague because I'm actively trying *not* to make a point or take a side. Just as many people thought "Don't Download This Song" was pro-RIAA as anti-RIAA.[3]

How do you choose which songs to parody?
I start with a list of songs that I think would be good candidates—relatively current songs that were big chart hits and got a lot of airplay—and then I just generate as many parody ideas as I can based on each one of those songs. If by some accident or miracle I actually come up with a *good* idea, I start the process of getting permission from the artist so I can turn that idea into a song for the album.

How do you maintain a relationship with your fans?
Well, social media is one way—Facebook and Twitter, mostly.

---

3 The Recording Industry Association of America is a trade group that represents record labels and distributors. Their harsh and draconian crackdowns on file-sharing and piracy are seen by some critics as harsh and draconian.

ACTUALIZATION THROUGH VOCALIZATION™

If this were an actual self-improvement system, it would probably be based around the idea that the first step in making
thoughts a reality is to say them out loud. The act of doing
this involves physical processes (vocal-chord vibration, sound
waves, reception in the inner ear), which thereby bring embodiment to what was once just a neural discharge. Thought has
become form. So go for it. Try saying right now, "I am a professional [blank] and this is a real thing that actually works!"

I really enjoy saying something stupid to three million people every day on Twitter and hearing their reactions. It's gratifying to be part of people's lives and make some kind of connection, even if it's in a very small and kind of ridiculous way. Connecting in person is also fun, so I try to do post-show meet-and-greets as often as possible. Even though by most accounts I'm a reasonably pleasant guy, I do make an extra effort to be courteous to fans, because I know—from the experience of being a fan myself—that the few seconds you share with a celebrity will often shape the opinion you have of that person for the rest of your life.

Do you get permission beforehand from the artists you parody?
I come up with a broad concept and run it by the artist before actu-
ally writing any lyrics. It's pretty rare these days for an artist to turn down permission for a parody, but still I wouldn't want to take a chance and spend weeks working on a song only to find out that the artist has zero sense of humor. Famously, Lady Gaga's manager made me jump through all sorts of hoops, including writing and recording my parody, and then ultimately turned me down for permission . . . only to have Gaga herself reverse the decision after a public outcry from the fans.

What makes a good parody song?

There are a number of things, but here are my big three rules: (1) Either the original song or the subject matter of the parody needs to be topical, timely, or interesting enough to the listener to be considered relevant. (2) The song can't run out of steam after the first chorus. The reveal of a stupid pun in the title is funny exactly once—if it goes nowhere from there, what's the point? A good parody needs to build—it should be just as funny (if not funnier) in the third verse as it is in the first. And (3) the parody should be funny regardless of whether or not the listener is familiar with the song on which it's based.

Chapter 12

ON CAMERA

The vast majority of the comedy seen by the American people will be on TV or film, and yet only the teeniest percentage of the world's already small proportion of funny people ever get to appear on camera. The main reason is simple: you need to be really good at performing on camera because TV and film reach a lot of people, and if you are not good, not a lot of people will see the TV show or film, and then whoever is paying for you to be on camera will not make enough money. Moreover, the final product will not be entertaining, and isn't that ultimately what this is all about?[4]

Even though everyone who's ever made a roomful of people laugh thinks they could make it as a professional comedic actor, success actually has almost nothing to do with how funny you are. That is to say, it has *everything* to do with how funny you are, but being funny is just the baseline everyone must possess.

4 Lol.

Performing Live Vs. On Camera

With a live performance, you practice a thousand times before performing live once, while on camera, you perform it four hundred times to get that one correct take. Most film or TV productions do not use rehearsals for anything beyond staging and technical purposes, and a lot of comedies, especially, are designed to feel improvisational and off-the-cuff. Paul Schneider, an accomplished actor with significant comedic ability, once remarked how amazing it was to him that he spends many weeks rehearsing for a stage show that will only last five performances and be seen by a total of a thousand people, but he spends about five minutes roughly improvising entire scenes for a major network sitcom that will then be broadcast to a sizable percentage of the American populace.

Onstage you are a body. On camera you are a cheekbone. Not only does bigger read better in live performances, but the audience also gets to observe your whole person: your body language, your physical presence and charisma. On camera, especially if you are anything like me, you are a misshapen weregoblin with a reedy, penetrating voice, fudgelike cheekbones, and almost zero "screenrisma." Only a certain percentage of your face and body is visible at any given time, and you've got to be able to "cheat" that for the camera, depending on the shot.

An Interview with **Nick Kroll**

"If someone could invent a way to get a mic on a shirt without having to stick it to my chest and ripping my chest hair out, that'd be great."

Nick Kroll, who started out doing characters in New York's alt-standup scene, has appeared in the TV shows *Best Week Ever, Parks and Recreation,* and *Childrens Hospital,* in the films *Dinner for Schmucks, Date Night, Get Him to the Greek, I Love You, Man,* and in his Comedy Central sketch show, *Kroll Show.* He found that getting to know what everyone does on set, and learning how to interact with them, has allowed him not only to appreciate all elements of production but to become a better performer.

Camera operators, even more so than actors, are the handsomest dudes on set. They're pretty cool dressers and have been known to drive motorcycles. I want to, and need to, get along with them because they need to get the rhythm of a shoot, to be able to follow you around and anticipate the beats. They're the closest thing you have to an audience. If they're laughing, that's always a good sign. You want your operators to be entertained.

The **boom guys** are always the hardest nut to crack, and when you do get them to laugh, you feel like you've really won. Sound guys have seen more of the most perfect breasts in the world than anybody else, which I guess is a perk. Also, if someone could invent a way to get a mic on a shirt without having to stick it to my chest and ripping my chest hair out, that'd be great.

Assistant directors are supremely important, and it's a specific kind of person who constantly wants to tell people to get back to work. Some have aspirations to be directors, and some just love the organizational side of it.

Lighting people are usually quiet, whispering to someone on their walkie. They're kind of like the cowboys on set: Who are they? What are they talking about? A gaffer who can figure out how to light fast is so helpful to the continuity and speed of a set. It took years, but I finally think I know the difference: gaffers are the ones in charge of the lighting, and the grips are connecting the electric together. I think.

You begin and end your day with **hair and makeup,** and you usually see them during lunch and downtime, too. They're around actors a ton, and the makeup trailer can be sort of a home base. There's a lot of information that gets passed around in that makeup trailer, so they need to be someone you can trust. They also need to be able to work with your weird vanities, so it helps if they're someone you like to spend time with.

A lot of my character stuff comes from what I'm wearing, so it's important to have a wardrobe person I can work with who will have some great ideas. I know I'm supposed to be funny, but I still want to look good. And a good wardrobe person can help you make that character better. That's huge for me.

Production assistants have a really tough job. They're working the longest hours, making the least money, and getting the least credit. There's a thing called Five-Dollar Fridays, when everybody puts a five-dollar bill with their name on it in a bucket. Someone pulls one out and whoever's name is on the five gets all of that money. One thing I learned as an actor or producer is to always write the PA's name on that five.

Your relationship to the **director** depends on the project. TV directors might be giving you the note, but it's coming from writers and they're just the conduit. I don't understand directors who play weird power games with people. I like to be complimented but not fawned over. Or I want to be told outright that what I'm doing is not right. I don't love a line read, but I like hearing what they'd like to hear. I worked with Terrence Malick for one day and that was the most amazing, cool experience. He told me I was a torpedo, and my job was to go in and disrupt things. It was a really interesting, fun, gratifying day.

Performing for Your Editor

After you have performed for the camera—be it for a small-scale web video or a major motion picture—that performance will be cut up, moved around, and perhaps augmented with visual effects. All of that stuff, unless you are Tom Cruise (OMG, *are you?*), is out of your hands. It's up to the editor to make you look good, and there are a few things you can do to make the editor's job a bit easier.

GIVE THREE READS This is standard, especially in voiceover recording, and it ensures that your editor has more to work with. They may find a rhythm or moment that wasn't in the original performance or manufacture a reaction from you that didn't exist. Trying lines in different ways—though not wildly different—allows the editor room to play.

PAD IT OUT The editor needs to make everything feel like a condensed version of real life, and a big part of real life is breathing, so make sure you give your takes the smallest of beats before you start. Doing so allows that moment to gain a natural momentum; to breathe. Likewise, don't break character until the director yells

185

cut, and even then, it's not a bad practice to wait a breath or two before laughing with the crew and sharing a high five and drinking a light beer in slow motion.

REACT AS WELL AS ACT Comedy is action-reaction, but a lot of young performers only focus on half of that formula. This is not to say that you need to react like Jim Carrey; rather, you just need to listen and let the moment happen. Give real reactions, and follow the same principles that guide you when you're doing the action part: provide variation, pad the moments, and be consistent.

KEEP ACTING IN THE BACKGROUND Even if you are out of focus, you're still your character, and what you do needs to read consistently throughout a scene and not break the reality.

MAINTAIN YOUR SIGHTLINES This is largely a technical issue that your director or director of photography should be looking out for, but we're all in this together, man. Basically, if you're the only one in the shot, but your scene calls for you to interact with someone or something that isn't there, you need to look at the same imaginary spot consistently. Every time your gaze drifts from this imaginary spot, that take becomes unusable. So just don't do that.

PRO TIP! RESISTING GRANOLA BARS

Production involves a lot of waiting, which brings with it an insatiable urge to wander to the craft services table and snack on one of its mainstays: the granola bar. While these may sound healthy ("granola" and "bar") most brands are laced with sugar, and too much sugar on a shoot makes you fat and tired! Other things to avoid at crafty include bagels, Danish, Cheetos, old bananas, and everything.

REPEAT WHAT YOU DID LAST TAKE. While you can always tweak and explore aspects of your performance, be aware of where your body is and what it's doing in the space, whether it's putting a mug down in the same spot on the table or cocking a shotgun with one hand in that cool way people do right before they say something cool. If you can be your own continuity director, everyone will love you, and you will save at least 50 percent of your takes.

Chapter 13

CHARACTER WORK

Comedy is full of memorable characters, from Ron Burgundy to the racecar driver in *Talladega Nights* to several characters not played by Will Ferrell, as well. Caricature and absurdity are intrinsic to the comedic arts. As conscious beings, we are primed for exaggeration and imitation, which is timeless, transcending language and culture. That is to say, Will Ferrell's male cheerleader character is as funny in English as he is in Chinese.

Though "serious" performances can unintentionally drift into self-parody from time to time, comedy characters tend to be more exaggerated than those we see in other genres of acting. They are larger-than-life, single-minded, laser-sharp versions of the archetypes and personalities that make people so interesting. Characters can include impressions of well-known celebrities or creations of your own invention; goofy and over-the-top or quiet and subtle.

But good characters can go beyond simple impersonation and mockery: they find the humanity in the stereotype and, because they make it so easy for us to laugh at them, because they are fools, they can say and do things that would otherwise be off-limits.

Being able to do good characters is also a highly marketable comedic skill, as evidenced by their prominence in TV commercials, TV shows, movies, web videos, and theater.

Developing Characters

To develop a character, first identify the essence of a person, people, or stereotype, and figure out how to exaggerate it. You probably already do this whether you are conscious of it or not. Every time you relate an anecdote, talk on the phone to someone you don't know, or make fun of a coworker, you create a character with a certain inflection, tone, and manner of speaking. Good characters are funny because of who they are and how they act, not necessarily because they tell jokes; the comedy is in the fully committed embodiment of an unusual or ridiculous or *specific* person and not just silly faces.

For me, watching my five-year-old son reenact his day or describe someone he saw at the park is a perfect lesson in this. My son isn't trying to be a comedian, nor has he been heavily influenced by the caricatures of the mainstream media. He's just trying to communicate the most essential components of the people he's imitating, so he interprets how they look and sound. This is important: your characters should be filtered through you and your unique perspective. Recognizing and imitating an archetype or stereotype

PRO TIP! ESP TECHNIQUE

The key to good comedic character work can be summed up in the acronym ESP: Essence, Specificity, Practice. Distill a character to his or her essence (bubbly, irate, tired, or chivalrous?); choose specific vocal and physical attributes (nasally voice, bow-legged, or short of breath?) and exaggerate them; and, perhaps most importantly, practice (practice, practice, practice).

is one thing, but adding your take on it is what makes it something worth watching.

The most important thing when developing a new character is to make specific choices.

DRAWING FROM PEOPLE YOU KNOW

Anyone in your life can be used to inspire a character, but some people are already halfway to five-sixths of the way there. Let's start with the very first person who comes to mind. For me, it's Coach Caswell, my middle-school gym teacher. He was a huge barrel of a man who could barely move his arms around—they kind of dangled there like a Tyrannosaurus Rex. With his booming voice, beard, and massive smile, he had the bearing of a younger, heavy-drinking Kris Kringle. He would switch from joviality to rage on a dime, and he would spend the summers sitting in his front yard, slamming Coors Lights, and waving to passing cars.

So, I take one of Coach Caswell's signature physical mannerisms and develop his walk like a muscular Humpty Dumpty. Then I add a voice: a more animalistic version of Brad Garrett, who played Ray Romano's brother in *Every Single Person Loves Raymond!* Next, I'll put him in an unexpected situation as a world-renowned ob-gyn. I puff my chest out, swing my arms around aimlessly, and nearly scream all my questions about my patient's last period. Could be funny. I don't know. Let's see. I'll try it right now in front of the mirror. . . .

Yes, it was funny! Might not be appropriate for all audiences, but how many physically intimidating, alcoholic ob-gyn characters are?

This is one example of how you can draw from people you know. A subtler, more realistic character might need only one of Coach Caswell's attributes. A full-on slapstick routine might make use of all of them and escalate even more. It all depends on the kind of comedy you're going for.

Using real-life characters will also help you avoid falling into the familiar rhythms of the cultural clichés and stock characterizations that other performers already use.

Here is a list of essential questions to ask and answer about any character.

WHAT'S THEIR POINT OF VIEW? Most people approach life from a particular perspective. They have one overriding outlook that informs everything they do. If they're angry that nothing ever works out for them, that defensive tension will trickle down to the way they talk, walk, and breathe.

HOW DO THEY SPEAK? What is the quality of the voice: deep, high-pitched, or nasally? Is there a smoker's scratch or a lisp? Identify the thing that makes the voice notable and never stray from it. Then, develop a certain speech pattern: some people cough a lot between sentences; some take exaggerated breaths before answering a question. Others finish everyone's sentence. Accents are a big part of it, too. Many American accents are well-known, such as Midwest, New York, and southern drawls. But make these as particular as possible: which New York borough; which southern state? Try to discern and put across an Oregon accent. Each accent not only betrays a specific place, but also sets the character within a social or cultural context. In what ways does the character fulfill or subvert the expectations of their accent?

WHAT ARE THE THEIR PHYSICAL MANNERISMS? I used to work with a guy who made a very small shrug on every fifth or sixth syllable. He was a specific kind of nerd, so now, whenever I need to do a nerdy character, I incorporate a very small shrug on every fifth or sixth syllable. You should also look at how people walk and sit. Do they shake hands firmly, or do they have one of those creepy dead-fish jobs? Perhaps they have facial tics. Watching myself on tape, I tape, I realized that I blink my eyes about fifty times per minute. I had no idea that I even did it, but it is apparently so instantly obvious that many people assume I am insane. You can use that!

HOW DO THEY LAUGH? The right laugh can say pretty much everything you need to say about a character. First, think about what it is that makes them laugh. What do they find funny and why? Then, how does the person laugh? Is it a light-hearted chuckle or an uncomfortably robotic monotone?

An Interview with **Jamie Denbo** and **Jessica Chaffin**

> *"We are both horrified to discover how similar we really are to these two characters."*

Comedians Jessica Chaffin and Jamie Denbo have made a name for themselves playing Ronna and Beverly, two divorced, outspoken Jewesses from Massachusetts who've interviewed, and humiliated, some of the top names in show business. The characters have a regular podcast, perform live at Los Angeles' UCB theater, and had their own show on Sky TV in the United Kingdom. Jamie and Jessica also appeared in the 2013 Paul Feig–directed comedy *The Heat* as a couple of Boston hard-asses. Jamie answered my questions on behalf of them both.

We first started playing the characters on a whim when we were asked to host a Kosher Christmas Comedy show at the UCB back in 2006 or 2007. We basically had been doing the voices to each other for years, just screwing around, but the minute we put them up onstage that night, it felt so effortless and natural. We knew we stumbled on something with staying power. We knew these women so well from growing up around so many versions of them. It almost felt too easy.

Ronna is very still and confident. Beverly is very jittery and always moving around like a hummingbird or a very nervous guinea pig. The voices seem to reflect that.

Acting without thinking too much about it really helps find nice natural instincts that can lead to further character development. In other words, I wouldn't discount all of the traditional acting techniques people use to "find" characters, but improv has been great for us personally.

I think we are so used to doing the characters at this point that we could probably have an entire conversation going back and forth between ourselves and our alter egos. In many ways, I think we are both horrified to discover how similar we really are to these two characters. And as we get older, maybe we are actually just turning into them. Terrifying.

In a live show, we can feed off an audience and ride the laughs. In video stuff, we have to be a little bit more specific about where the jokes are so they will land. But we can also be subtler. We can be smaller and more intimate in crazy moments. For the most part, I would say these characters don't actually change too much between stage and film. Though you get to see them in more interesting places when you are shooting something. Who doesn't want to see Ronna *in* Ronna's kitchen, right? Or whether or not Beverly *does* in fact have a mini-fridge next to her bed? She does.

Paul Feig directed our Showtime pilot in 2009, back when he was "slumming it in TV." He has been and remains a committed R&B fan and friend. He also produced our English TV show along with his wife, Laurie Feig. So when the time came to flesh out Melissa McCarthy's crazy Boston family in *The Heat*, he knew who to call. Fortunately, we do Boston scumbags pretty well as part of our repertoire.

DRAWING CHARACTERS FROM PEOPLE WHO ARE YOU

While we like to think we know ourselves better than anyone, this is actually a ridiculous notion. We've all created highly detailed personas that we project to the world for our own sense of self-worth, or whatever highly nuanced psychological framework we use to keep ourselves from spiraling into despair. But here's the truth: *we are all living a lie.* What does that have to do with creating characters? All of the real emotions that drive your characters' actions can only be found within you, and the ability to access and reallocate those emotions will make your performances great.

Thus, creating great characters rests on two well-established principles: method acting, and the idea that the best comedy is played straight.

> **PRO TIP!** METHOD ACTING
> An acting technique that taps into the actor's real memories and emotions during a performance. Some of the world's best actors use method acting. It's rarer among comedians, however, as their art is often considered less refined, and more flatulence-driven, than drama.

My Coach Caswell character could very easily stay within the realm of caricature and be a perfectly serviceable ha-ha thing. *He should not be an ob-gyn, and yet there he is, in that exact role!* But if, in the midst of performing an ultrasound, he accidentally turns the device on himself and sees his absorbed twin, lifeless inside him, and has an existential meltdown, and it is played realistically, it can move from just plain silly to bizarrely sublime. Of course, it's an incredibly stupid premise, but if you tap into your own real emotions, and let your body react as it would if this were a real scenario, then you will play the character with authenticity. That is to say: Dr. Coach Caswell, as a character, is an external shell that only becomes real when the performer's actual emotions are filtered through it. To use a different analogy: you are the hardware; your characters are the software.[5]

The components needed to create lasting, dynamic characters are already within you. You have a wealth of experiences, memories, slights, victories, irritations, bouts of depression, bouts of confusion, shameful episodes, happinesses, and humiliations to draw from. The only difficulty is that some of these are ugly, hidden, and not easy to access, but doing so will make for a much richer, and thereby much funnier, performance.

To bring this sort of authenticity to your characters' lives, start by simply being aware of yourself in your own everyday life. Observe your own feelings over the course of a day, and sit with them. Did you act on every impulse? Of course not. But if you had, what would you have done? Within the freedom of your characters, *do those things*. Here are some hypothetical scenarios. How do they make you feel?

- A passive-aggressive email from your boss undercuts your work.
- A boy or girl you like says hi in the hallway.
- You lose your lease and have to find a new apartment at the end of the month.
- A friend posts a photo on Facebook of them with some dumb famous Internet person at stupid South by Southwest and gives it some lame caption.
- Your mother dies.

How many quick, microscopic emotions erupted as you read each sentence? Be aware of them. That's all you need to do. Rather

---

5 The hardware never changes. The speed and power with which it processes information is always the same. But the software is interchangeable, and while there is an almost limitless variety of programs, some work better with the internal hardware than others. That's it for this analogy!

than bury or brush aside what makes us uncomfortable, stay with your feelings when emotional moments occur. Feel how you feel, and then let the feelings pass. Doing this enough will give you a certain kind of mastery over them: you'll be able to predict which emotions are coming, understand their shape, and, in time, call them into being at will. They're just silly, fleeting, common feelings—but at the moment of their birth, they are the only real thing in the entire universe.

That's the sort of aware conviction you want to bring to your characters.

Performing Your Character

As mentioned above, practice is key. You need to feel so comfortable in the body and voice of your characters that playing them—becoming them—is second nature. Anyone can do a voice or a posture for a few seconds, but developing the endurance and muscle memory to maintain a character over a period of time requires practice. Do it over and over and over again. In front of a mirror or on a webcam. Over and over and over. You will look and sound dumb and you will feel even dumber. Over and over. Because a big part of being a pro is feeling dumb for a lot of the time. But then you'll get it right.

LISTEN This is the first thing they teach you in acting class, and it's probably the hardest thing to learn because all of us—especially performers—can usually not wait to start talking again. But listening to the words of the other characters as they're being said allows you to hear them as if for the first time, which leads to new, unplanned reactions. But the listening must be active. Waiting only to say your line muddles the energy of the scene and feels synthetic.

> **PRO TIP!** CHARACTER SHOWCASES
> Most improv theaters, comedy festivals, and a growing number of clubs host character nights or showcases. On the local level, these are great opportunities to get characters on their feet and to workshop them in front of an audience. At the bigger festivals, like Just for Laughs in Montreal, these showcases are by invite only, and virtually everyone in the crowd will be an industry person in one way or another.

SLOW DOWN AND BREATHE We don't do this enough in our own lives, so it's a lot to ask to do it as a character, but it's essential to quiet the neuroses and anxieties that plague us as performers even when we are play acting. Slowing down, even just a hair, is a little bit uncomfortable—which is good. A lot of real and surprising stuff is allowed to come out during those uncomfortable beats when we take a breath before responding. There's no rush. Such pauses will almost never feel as slow on screen as they do in the moment.

MAKE IT PERSONAL Take everything in the scene personally, and inject your own feelings. Recall similar situations in your life. Let those old feelings well back up. When it comes to negative emotions, what feels counterintuitive is actively holding on to them and summoning them again and again.

DON'T TRY TO BE FUNNY There is nothing less funny than a person who is trying really hard, but failing, to be funny.[6] Likewise, great characters don't mean to be funny, they just are. The kind of comedy I'm describing arises out of who the character is and the surprising choices and unexpected reactions they make. Be spontaneous, real, and true to the character, and the comedy will naturally grow out of them.

GETTING INTO CHARACTER

After developing a few characters, it's useful to find ways to quickly click yourself into (and sometimes out of) them. These are usually based in either the verbal or the physical: a certain word, phrase, or movement that kick-starts the whole thing into being. These are also all good practice techniques.

---

6 In the halls of Adult Swim's creative offices in Atlanta, they call this kind of comedy "sweaty." E.g., "His performance in that take was a little sweaty," or "I didn't like that video. It was way too sweaty." It's a perfect evocation because it sums up the strenuous effort, desperation, and general sense of ickiness that accompanies a piece of comedy that's trying way too hard.

VOCAL Once you've nailed down the quirks and cadences of how your character talks, practice doing it consistently. Start by reciting the alphabet, the Pledge of Allegiance, the Miranda warning, or other phrases that you know by heart. The words and rhythm should be second nature, allowing you to identify what is and isn't working in the voice. Then move on to reading entire emails aloud and talking on the phone in character. Pets make excellent scene partners. And when you are really ready to feel lame enough to start acting like a pro, record yourself reading and listen to it later.

PHYSICAL You always read about actors who follow actual bus drivers or assassins around to emulate how they move. Though it may sound like bullshit, it's one of the best ways to find physical inspiration. An old Chinese woman doesn't walk the same way as a cocky investment banker. Look at how people do specific actions, like jump over puddles, tie their shoes, or try to get a waiter's attention.

There's a more inward way to explore physicality: Pick a body part that you think most represents the character you're portraying. Is it their head, feet, butt, or groinal area? Whatever you decide, lead with that body part when you walk, talk, and interact with people. Exaggerate it. It may feel extremely unnatural, but do it enough and it will seep into the rest of your body, and every time you need to snap into that character, you can use that initial movement to get it going.

An Interview with **Peter Serafinowicz**

"The input is more important than the output."

Peter Serafinowicz can act, he can sing, he can write, and he has a truly awesome voice. In fact, Serafinowicz's first big gig was as the voice of Darth Maul in *The Phantom Menace.* He's also been in *Shaun of the Dead, Couples Retreat,* and *Guardians of the Galaxy,* but it was his work on his own sketch comedy show, *The Peter Serafinowicz Show,* where he created dozens of characters and really got to show off his chops as an impressionist.

My show was a lot of TV parodies, so there were some impressions that I felt like I ought to do, like Simon Cowell, though he's not a fascinating person to me. But normally, I look for people and voices that I find really interesting.

People have a hook. There's one thing that they do in the way they speak that will kind of unlock you to that person. And it's often one word, like Iain Glen from *Game of Thrones*: He always says, "Khaleesi," [*Serafinowicz imitates Iain Glen*] and you do that one word for a bit, and the rest of it just kind of happens.

If you're going to do impressions, you probably have a knack for it, but the most important thing when you're starting out is to just listen. It's more important, I think, than copying the voice—like actually physically reproducing the voice. The input is more important than the output. Watch other impressionists and see what they have picked up on. It's the same thing with cartooning as well: you look at somebody and wonder how you could caricature that person, and then you see some brilliant artist do it. Just watch other impressionists. That's what all impressionists do; they just watch people. You start off kind of copying impressionists' impressions. It's borrowing, but then you start to make them your own.

I also try to approach it from an acting point of view. My aim is never to do an actual copy of this person—to pass myself off as this person. The word is "impression," and it's an impressionistic approach rather than an impersonation. It's your interpretation of that person, rather than aping everything about them.

I did this series of actors talking about acting on my show, and I kind of gave them traits that were mainly things from characters they'd played in movies. I made Robert De Niro very insecure, and I made Kevin Spacey super mean, so it was just applying a character's particular flaw or trait onto them. So that made it easier and that made it funny to me.

My final tip is, if you want to do Darth Vader, get a big vase and talk into that. You'll figure it out. Anything you say sounds like Darth Vader in a big vase.

Chapter 14

AUDITIONING

Most every part, be it for stage or screen, usually starts with an audition, that process of proving yourself to three or four strangers in a small white room. Auditioning, like the dreaded writing packet, can be a harrowing proposition, but with experience, time, and a Zen-like detachment from expectation, it can also be not all that bad. For working actors and comics, it's just work. It's like everyone else's version of going on an interview or presenting a big report, but it only lasts two minutes, you do it a few times a week, and several hundred other people who look just like you are doing it, too.

The Basics

AGENTS There are agents that specialize in every imaginable niche, and it's not uncommon for a Comedy Person to have one for acting jobs, one for books, and one for commercial auditions. They put you out for roles they think you'll be good at, and if they're good at their jobs, they do it a lot. You certainly do not need to have an agent to find auditions (see the Pro Tip! below), but they can help open doors and relieve some of the burden of constantly having to look for work on your own.

CASTING DIRECTORS Hired by the producer and director, casting directors tap their contacts and resources to organize and run the casting process. Sometimes they will work on their own; other times the director will be attached at the hip. In time, you'll get to know certain casting directors and they'll get to know you. Like agents, they all have areas of expertise, be it commercials, comedies, or breaking your heart L.

UNIONS There are two major unions for performers: SAG/AFTRA (Screen Actors Guild/American Federation of Television & Radio Artists), which represents film, TV, radio, digital, and voice acting; and Actors' Equity Association (AEA), which covers stage performers. Both have one-time initiation fees as well as annual dues. If a production is a union signatory, they will only cast union actors. There is plenty of nonunion work, as well, but those jobs have no guaranteed pay minimums or restrictions on hours, and many union

JOINING THE UNIONS

To be eligible to join SAG/AFTRA, you must either work three days on a union job or be in good standing with an affiliated union, such as ACTRA (Alliance of Canadian Cinema, Television, and Radio Artists), AEA (Actors' Equity Association), AGMA (American Guild of Musical Artists), or AGVA (American Guild of Variety Artists). Similarly, you may join Actors' Equity during the time that you are working an Equity job or through prior membership in the so-called "Four A's": SAG/AFTRA, AGMA, AGVA, or GIAA (Guild of Italian American Actors).

actors frown on doing nonunion work. In some cases, it can even lead to expulsion.

OPEN CALLS Also known as "cattle calls," these are large-scale auditions that are open to the public with almost no screening before the audition. If you see the notice, you can show up to the audition and feel like a piece of meat right there with everyone else.

PRO TIP! FINDING AUDITIONS

The traditional ways of finding auditions include checking notices in *Backstage* (which focuses mainly on stage productions) and on CastingFrontier.com; poking around on Craigslist and Mandy.com, where you're likely to find anything from student films to network auditions; and, of course, getting an agent. You can also upload your information and headshot to a site like Casting Networks, which allows you to create a profile, network with other actors and casting directors, and respond to casting calls yourself.

CALLBACKS If you do well in an audition, or were otherwise intriguing, the casting director will ask you to attend a callback so they can see more of you and narrow down the field further. Congrats! Someone in this world likes you! It's not generally advised to try anything vastly different from what you did in the first audition during callbacks. Rather, you can use it as a chance to develop that character, home in on specific details about them, and tighten the performance. Even if you don't get booked, casting directors will remember you for future roles. Some even recommend making the callback your main focus and getting cast is just a bonus.

COLD READ This is when you show up and a script or cue card is put in front of you just moments before your audition. Sometimes these are the best auditions because you don't have a lot of time to sit around overthinking three lines of copy. Sometimes they are not.

COMMERCIAL AUDITIONS

Advertising has always used humor, along with guilt and envy, as one of its Three Evil Forms of Public Deception, and a lot of comedy people support themselves through commercial work. Commercials will always need "funny people" to act as the foils or brothers-in-law to the beautiful "normal" people in the advertising world's version of reality. A lot of these comedic roles are for dummies and clowns, but as kids who loved weird, absurd humor grow up into filmmakers and creative directors, this is changing. Commercials still cast almost completely on type, and the types they cast change based on popular culture. It's not much of a surprise that shortly after the success of *The Hangover,* stout, red-bearded gentlemen started appearing in commercials all over TV.

Principles of Auditioning

Whether you're going out for a spot on *Saturday Night Live* or you just got called back for the wet wipe grandpa in a Wet Wipes ad, there are a handful of things to keep in mind at every audition you attend.

KNOW YOUR TYPE Go out for stuff you are more likely to get and own whatever type that is. If your cool-ass Tom Selleck mustache is your moneymaker, make that sacred and do not shave it. Same goes for the quirky girlfriend: rock that pixie hair, girl. Know what you have to sell and sell it. Prostitute yourself for your art, is what we are saying here.

READ THE AUDITION NOTICE CAREFULLY Make sure you know exactly what, if anything, is needed of you, as well as what part you're auditioning for, who the writers and/or directors are, if possible, the physical appearance of the character, and whether or not you are the proper sex.

BE ON TIME No duh, right? Wrong! Be early, dummy.

IF YOU MESS UP, JUST PAUSE AND START OVER Don't ask for permission to start over if you make a mistake. Just do it confidently and without making a big deal out of it because you should never break character.

NEVER BREAK CHARACTER You look amateurish, weak, and uncertain when you break character, and no matter how good your audition is after that, it's hard for the casting directors to shake that image. It's like walking in on someone taking a shit: embarrassing for everyone, weird, and tough to forget. And it smells like shit.

PRACTICE While you can't practice auditions that have not yet happened, you can prepare by reading aloud as often as you can. Read standing up. If you don't have one already, give birth to a child and read him or her stories every night. You'll get better at those cold reads.

BE NICE Remember: It's good professional conduct and the least you can do for people who want to give you a job, but also it's a basic tenet of human decency to be nice, and everyone could use more nice people around them.

DON'T APOLOGIZE No matter how bad you think you were, never say you're sorry. This makes you look like you are making excuses or seeking sympathy.

CONGRATULATE YOURSELF After every audition, take a moment to appreciate yourself and what you just did. Not many people have the chutzpah to audition, and you might even have been good at it. Now, it's over and out of your hands because the casting directors are going to pick someone based on criteria and judgments you will probably never have access to. So cut yourself some slack and give yourself a pat on the back. Even if you sucked—*especially* if you sucked.

Chapter 15

BEHIND THE SCENES

They say that making comedy is harder than making drama, which I don't really believe is true because a lot of times in drama you have to pretend to be Abraham Lincoln or a serial killer, or sometimes both, and people have to believe it. That seems really hard, given how many bad serial killer movies I've seen. A big difference between good comedy and bad—or worse, mediocre—comedy is the quality of the production, from casting to editing, and some of the best comedy minds have left their mark behind the camera. It's not enough to simply Be Really Funny anymore. It pays to know a little bit about TV and film production, not only because it can create opportunities for work, but also because knowing what goes into producing, directing, and editing will help make everything you work on better.

Producing

We know they make a ton of money and that they get to accept the Academy Award when their movie wins best picture and that they have nice sunglasses, but what exactly does a producer *do?* It's a difficult question, and if you're able to come up with a viable answer that you can explain to someone who can give you money, then you are probably a producer already!

Producers have to do a little of everything. They must be able to speak the language of businesspeople and keep them happy (or, at least, at bay) while also satisfying the creative needs of their cast and crew. They are the ones who know what's going on at any given moment, whether that's the star's favorite kind of bagel or how much their international distribution rights cost. They deal with egos, settle arguments, make decisions, fire directors who aren't doing their job, and have an intimate knowledge and passion for the project. But more important, perhaps, than being good at any of these things is knowing what things they're *not* good at and having the instincts and network to be able to hire the right people to fill in those gaps.

ELEMENTS OF A PRODUCTION

Many things go into a production, no matter the size, and a producer has some say in all of it. This is but a mere taste—an *amuse bouche de film de list de book*—of some of those elements. Of course, there are differences between TV, film, independent film, web series, and so on, but for the sake of space and carpal tunnel syndrome, I'm generalizing.

PREPRODUCTION Everything that happens before the shooting starts is called "preproduction." Where a great producer really shines

210

is with staffing and planning. The better the preproduction, the more those involved in the production itself can focus on their jobs.

DEVELOPMENT Before a project gets okayed—that is, money is spent—there's usually a development process. Networks, studios, and dedicated production facilities have people who specialize in development, but producers often have a role to play as well. It basically means getting a project far enough along to improve its chances of success on a creative and business level (see chapter 22).

FINANCING Every production requires money, and sometimes being a producer means that you've actually put up some of your own. Oftentimes, though, producers are tasked with finding investors, getting them excited about a project, and then putting the people in place to make said investors feel like their money is in good hands.

CASTING This is often where a production is really made—especially in comedy. Time spent here can only pay dividends later, since great performers are not only funny but can bring untold value in knowledge and ideas.

ART How a production looks is essential, and excellent set design, props, wardrobe, and overall aesthetic can immediately sell the comedy. Think about the visual differences between a spoof of a 1980s Soviet dating video versus a sketch about Ku Klux Klan ghost hunters. (You don't have to think about it, but I thought it might be fun.) An art department that understands the comedy makes all the difference.

PRODUCTION The action, camera, and lights. Production is hellish, hard, exacting, and exhilarating. And boring. Many shoots feel more like weird existential torture, and much of it is technical:

211

hitting marks, adjusting lights, getting pickups for shots that will be inserted later. Even in the smallest productions, it's a taxing enterprise in which everyone must be focused at all times for long periods of time.

Photography. Framing the action (and making sure you cover it all) sets the basic parameters for what you want the viewer to see. For comedy, crowding the actor in the frame instills a sense of awkwardness, tension, and unease. An extremely wide shot can communicate futility and powerlessness. Both are good comedy themes.

Lighting. No one actually understands lighting except for the lighting guys. That's why they're lighting guys.[7] Lighting setups usually account for the bulk of "delays," that is, reasons actors must wait. But there's good reason to get it right: lighting sets mood, establishes place, and makes everything look beautiful.

Sound. If you're running a production, either get a good sound person or be a good sound person. You can never go back and fix sound the way you can play tricks with video in postproduction, especially if you don't have the ability and money to bring actors back in to do additional dialogue recording (ADR). Audiences are much more likely to forgive mediocre picture quality than they are bad sound.

POSTPRODUCTION Where the phrase "We'll fix it in post" comes from. It's a mantra and a joke, but it's also true. Post has become so important and cost-effective in recent years, with the advanced digital techniques now available, that a lot of people start their careers as editors and motion graphics artists. Post processes include:

Editing. See page 224! I'm not going to write about the same subject twice! That would be a betrayal to you and your hard-earned money!

---

7 Even if those working the lights are women, and many are, I believe the technical term is still "lighting guy."

Sound and music. It's impossible to put a precise number on it, but exactly 78 percent of a film or video's success is due to good sound design. Foley (sound effects work) can be used to great effect in comedy: chewing noises that are just a little too loud, footsteps that sound like tap shoes, vomit. Likewise, the score can bring emotion, while just adding room tone or ambience can propel a piece from flat and off-tone to real and rich and full of life.

Color correction. If you've ever seen before-and-after footage of almost any major motion picture, you know that everything looks like *absolute dog shit* before it's color corrected—which is the process of enhancing film or video through a chemical or digital process in order to balance colors and/or give the piece some desired quality not obtainable through practical means. That is, it looks like *dog shit.* Basic color correction can be done with consumer-level software, but there are also multimillion-dollar facilities that specialize in it.

PRODUCTION COMPANIES

The majority of TV, film, and commercial comedy is made by production companies, independent units that can be as large as a fifty-person crew and as small as a single producer. The production company will handle all aspects of the project, from budgeting to editing and everything in between. A number of Comedy People wind up starting their own production companies because it allows them to take on more work than they would on their own, to develop material from outside creators, to keep in constant contact with agents and networks, and to provide the means for a financial safety net. Making comedy can be an uncertain business, so having the ability to take on smaller, better-paying projects, like directing commercials, while you work on your passions is pretty clutch, as people used to say in the 1990s. Plus, production companies get to come up with those cool logos and slate animations.

PRODUCER HIERARCHY

As a producer, there's nothing more embarrassing than pros-trating yourself before another producer in shame and guilt, only to realize that you actually have the higher-ranking credit! Let this simple chart be your guide through the complicated web of producing titles.

Film	TV
Producer	Executive Producer/ Show Runner
Executive Producer	Co-Executive Producer
Coproducer	Supervising Producer
Associate Producer	Producer
	Coproducer

An Interview with **Judd Apatow**

"I never trust that anything's funny."

Before he became one of the biggest names in comedy, Judd Apatow sought out the biggest names in comedy to learn every-thing he could. As a teenager, Apatow interviewed people like Jerry Seinfeld, Henny Youngman, and Jay Leno. He started as a standup, then as a writer on *The Larry Sanders Show* and *The Ben Stiller Show,* before creating the TV cult classic *Freaks and Geeks.* His company, Apatow Productions, makes TV and mov-ies, with a staff of in-house writers and producers.

On What a Producer Does

Some projects I'm deeply involved in the development of the script, and other times I'm just a champion of someone's vision, trying to help them get it through the system without being watered down.

For certain projects, I'm working with new people who require a lot of guidance because they haven't been through it before, and other times I'm just there looking for problems and trying to anticipate things that could go wrong at any part of the production.

Sometimes you're the producer and you don't agree with what the writers or directors are doing, and then it's incredibly painful because you have to decide how much you want to fight. Are you supporting another artist, or do you have to get involved and say, "I need to try and stop you from doing what you're doing because I don't think it's gonna work"? Because we don't know what's really going to work, so if I stand up for anything, it's gotta be from my gut. But I always know that there's a decent chance that I'm wrong.

On Production

I never trust that anything's funny, which is why I tend to shoot a lot of material. We're not so cocky as to believe that everything we do will work. That makes it a little less scary. The only thing that would be scary would be to go into an edit bay knowing you only have one way to cut a scene. That would be terrifying. The key is knowing the intention of the scene. If you know you have to get from A to B, and you have to hit certain emotions and story points to be clear, you can have fun along the way, but the intention of the scene must be the same.

On Collaboration

I love underdogs, I like people who are self-deprecating, and I'm always a fan of people who are great actors and aren't afraid to go to a deeply honest place. The part that's the most fun to me is to try to figure out what's funny about somebody. If they've been in a lot of movies, it can be great because they're experienced and you know what they can do. But it's a really exciting challenge to figure out how someone would work as the lead of a movie when they've never done it before. It's like popping your cherry on every movie.

Although popping your cherry usually doesn't go well, so maybe that's not a good metaphor. It's like having sex for the eighth time, when you finally get it right, on every movie.

I think it's very hard to give notes to creative people. Sometimes you have chemistry and the process goes well. Other times, the people giving you notes don't know what they're talking about, and it's a very combative situation. Or you could just listen to their notes and ruin your work. I think my career started going better as I figured out which executives and which networks and studios understood what I was trying to do. You find partners who get the joke, and then suddenly those people that you used to hate are your closest allies, and they challenge you and have good ideas. But it took me years to figure out which people had those good ideas. Because when they have bad ideas, you want to kill yourself.

On Finding Work and Mentors

From early on I made working on things that I liked my priority, and I was lucky enough that I had no expenses on Earth as a human being, and that allowed me to not take work on anything that didn't amuse me. I didn't take any crappy shows to pay my bills. I think that's good advice for anybody: don't chase the money. It's better to develop your creative vision and attempt to work with people that you really admire and respect and attempt to learn from them.

I was actively seeking out bosses whom I thought were the greats of comedy. I wanted to be around them. And those people gave me big breaks, and I guess it's always felt organic that I would try to do the same for other people. That feels like what you're supposed to do. You know, you desperately fight to break into the business, and at some point somebody helps you achieve that, and then when you're in a position to do that for other people, that's a priority.

Directing

So much of what makes comedy comedy is a specific tone, and that tone is set and maintained by the director. Take, for example, the difference in two extraordinarily good comedies: *Dumb and Dumber* and *Annie Hall*. The former lives in a world of slapstick, idiocy, and constant physical harm. It is a celebration of the inane, and everything that happens within the movie supports that insanity. The latter is steeped in the intellect, and even as the movie progresses, it is analyzing itself. Imagine the difference in these two movies if *Dumb and Dumber* had been directed by Woody Allen and *Annie Hall* by the Farrelly brothers.

Comedy can come from anywhere, but to make it work over ninety minutes, or even over two, there must be an internal consistency to the world, and all the actors, wardrobes, props, and camera angles must support that world. That is to say, everything must support the main joke. In the case of *Dumb and Dumber*, the main theme is Two Complete Idiots, When Working Against Each Other, Can Successfully Complete a Complicated Adventure. In *Annie Hall*, the main theme is Some Relationships Fail and There Is Nothing that Can Be Done to Make Them Unfail. Both jokes need the proper tone to support them, and it's the director's job to make that happens.

GETTING STARTED

The easiest and most direct way to get directing experience is by doing it yourself and posting it on YouTube. A staggering number of great directors were already making short films when they were children and just never stopped. They simply have it in their blood.

Many directors go to film school where, depending on the curriculum, you'll obtain technical proficiency and learn the language of cinema. In some programs, you'll learn about the more opaque subtleties of marketing, business, and distribution. The most important thing you get at film school is experience and connections, though they come at a price, like forty to fifty thousand dollars a year, which is kind of a lot for normal people.

Most of the best-ranked film schools are located in Los Angeles or New York, including the University of Southern California, the University of California at Los Angeles, the American Film Institute, New York University, Columbia, and Loyola Marymount University. A huge advantage of attending one of these schools is that they are in cities with thriving comedy communities, but you can also find good programs at Syracuse, University of North Carolina School of the Arts, and the University of Texas at Austin.

An Interview with **Peter Atencio**

"You have to love it. You have to want to be on set."

After one year of film school, at the age of nineteen, Peter Atencio took the advice of one of his professors and moved to Los Angeles to get more practical experience. He quickly fell in with comedians and improvisers who were doing work at the Upright Citizens Brigade, and he started shooting short films for them. He eventually wound up becoming the director of the fantastic sketch comedy show *Key & Peele* on Comedy Central.

Every decision I make as a director is influenced by what serves the comedy of the scene the best. I always like to approach everything like, what will make this funnier once the joke is revealed? How much exposition can I put into the style or the look of all of the nondialogue stuff? So much of comedy is hurt by all this exposition

218

to set up the world, or the characters, or the relationships. My philosophy is always the more I can pull out of exposition in what I do, the better it will be.

I'm a big believer in comedic energy—the flow of a scene, the pace of a scene. That's the first thing that dictates what I'm going to do. If the scene feels like it needs to have an energy where there's more life to it, then I'll try to drive my directorial decisions toward giving it that feel, like using a handheld camera. Sometimes the joke has a much more deliberate pace to it, and that will influence the decisions.

Each sketch is such a little world. It's always a process of what is on the page that has to be on the screen versus what's extraneous that can be cut. How do I make it clearer where we are and what we're seeing visually? Where can I put the camera that tells a story? There's a philosophy that comedy needs to be shot wide, that you need to see it all, and I don't believe that at all.

I'm a very top-to-bottom director. I like to be there for the writing process so I can have input on stuff there, and obviously I'm on set, and I like to see it through all the way to the end. I feel like the sound mix is just as important as the color timing, is just as important as the editing. It's all important. I love that whole process. Production's definitely exhausting, but for me, I guess I'm lucky, because this is all I want to do. So I just throw away a personal life when we start making the show, and it's like, for however many months this is going to take, this is going to be my life. You have to love it. You have to want to be on set.

There's sometimes this culture of, "You're better off if you're unhealthy." You're more devoted if everything else suffers but the comedy. Mental health is a huge part of it for me. I've worked to become more mentally healthy because I know it'll make the end product better. The more distracted I am with unhealthy relationships, or bad habits, or if I'm just not taking good care of myself, it shows in the work. You get worn down, or you say, "That's good enough. Let's move on." I want to be as healthy as I can be.

FUNDAMENTAL DIRECTING TECHNIQUES

SET IT ALL UP Know what you want out of each scene beforehand. Think through everything in advance so no one else has to. Make sure everyone knows what's expected of them and that your cast and crew understand each other. This creates an environment in which everyone can do their best work and, ideally, have fun. Comedies that are a bummer to work on are usually a bummer to watch, too.

BE CLEAR With the myriad options and decisions open to a director at nearly every turn, it's easy to fall into muddied waters. Intentions can get lost or compromised by the reality of production, and scenes can become overly complicated. The fastest way to lose an audience is by confusing them, so make sure the material is simple and the concepts are clearly executed.

MAKE YOURSELF LAUGH It's hard to keep laughing over five hours or five months or however long your production lasts, but if you aren't laughing at all, something is wrong. Sometimes you can get so bogged down in logistics and schedules and blocking that you forget about the actual comedy, which becomes just another part of production. But if the ideas and the jokes and the actors are not amusing you, either stop and reassess the material or get yourself a martini.

PLAY OPPOSITES The legendary Texas Hold 'Em player Doyle Brunson had one primary rule: when your hand is weak, play strong, and when you're strong, play weak.[8] Comedy is a little like that: the goofier the scenario, the straighter you should play it. This is by no means a hard and fast rule, but it's a great place to start. The comedy comes more honestly this way, and the audience will respond to that.

KEEP IT ROLLING Never call cut until three beats past when you think you should. If you're working with good performers and the scene is crackling, they'll stay in character after the last line, and sometimes these unscripted reactions, the pregnant pauses or double-takes, are the best thing you'll get all day. There's a lot of comedy in those little moments, and it would stink to miss it.

CHANGE ON THE FLY Watch your actors very closely and be willing to follow their lead. Sometimes you'll see something emerge in what they're doing with the material that can take the scene in a new direction. Likewise, if they're struggling with something in an interesting way, make it about that for a take or two. Finding the awkward, the difficult, the not-quite-right is always ripe for comedy.

HAVE BACKUPS Have two or three extra ideas of where things can go and what actors can do, just in case. It's good to be able to throw a curveball or a Hail Mary or a soccer metaphor of some kind if things aren't working. Worst-case scenario, it gets the actors out of their heads and opens things up.

---

8 At least, I think it was Doyle Brunson who said that. I hope it was him because people have been attributing that to him for a long time. But, you know, he's getting really old and he doesn't look very healthy, so why not let him have this?

An Interview with **David Wain**

"If a joke still makes me laugh two years in, I know it's got legs."

David Wain is one of those Perfect Comedy Guys who comedy people look at and think, "Oh, he's a perfect comedy guy." He's nice, he's funny, and he can write, act, and direct. David was in the 1990s-era troupe The State, and he has written and directed the features *Wet Hot American Summer, The Ten, Role Models, Wanderlust,* and *They Came Together.*

How much directing did you do on The State*?*
I did what we called "second unit." Michael Jann directed the full-production pieces that had a real crew and were shot on Beta or film. My pieces were just me with a Hi-8 or Betacam on my shoulder, and the other *State* guys serving as barebones crew. We did two or three of these in each *State* episode.

What do you like about directing? Is it that you are a total control freak who has to have absolute power over everything in your life, or is it fun?

> **PRO TERM!** SECOND UNIT
>
> The "second unit" refers to the crew, usually smaller, that's sent to film all the stuff that's not part of the main "action"—though a big part of second unit work is stunts and fight scenes. Also includes pickups (shots that were unusable, skipped, or forgotten during principle shooting), b-roll (general background footage that helps give visual detail and fill out a scene), locations (locations), and anything else that would have slowed down or otherwise complicated the tight daily production schedule.

Both of those things are true. It's definitely fun to be able to gather together so many talented people and guide them toward a vision of something that's in your head. And I do like interacting with and meeting different kinds of people. And I love that there are never two days that are even remotely the same. I *don't* love how exhausting and time-consuming it is.

How do you keep knowing that something is funny after two or three or six months?
That's a great litmus test. If a joke still makes me laugh two years in, I know it's got legs! It really should still feel funny through the whole process. But of course by the time I'm finishing a movie I can get really sick of it. Watching with any kind of audience is always a good way to see things through fresh eyes.

How involved are you in the editing process of your films?
I'm a bit of a techie and also just love editing, so I'm usually very hands-on. Also I feel editing is by far the most important part of the process. Depending on the project, I'll pass scenes back and forth with my editor. I really don't feel like I can feel complete in the editing if I haven't done at least one pass of something with my fingers on the keyboard. I like editors who are fast, creative, flexible, and keep their eyes on the big picture.

Are you a heavy outliner?
Yes. I also like to re-outline at various points during the process, including editing.

What's the first thing you do, as a director, when you sit down with a script?
If I didn't write the script, I will read it and simultaneously write a bullet point outline of each plot point, so I can start to understand the underlying mechanics. I'll write ideas and questions that come

to mind at this phase, too. With each scene, I focus first on the core story—what is the character trying to achieve, what's in the way, etcetera—then the visual and comedy ideas flow from that.

What do you do when a scene isn't working?
Try to identify the culprit! Maybe it's a performance choice, maybe it's the writing, maybe it's just a scene that shouldn't exist. Whatever it is, I try to make the right decision, which might be to try something different, or skip it and move on.

Editing

Comedy has always come together in the editing room: you can create moments out of what actually occurred on separate days, or manufacture beats with reactions from unrelated shots. Almost any filmmaker will tell you that editing saves their ass on a regular basis. The performances have to be there, of course, and the material must be great, but a good editor can turn something stilted into something awkwardly hilarious, speed up performances, or cut through the fat and find a new joke to be exploited altogether. In fact, some editors are so good at this that the production team might speed through a shoot and cut corners on coverage, assuming that their editor will be able to do something with it. Somehow.

Editors can take on the glow of high holy shaman, the quiet guru who sits apart from the rest, panics not, and retreats into his or her magic dark room to perform some digital ritual and emerge with an actual, funny thing. And they kind of are like that.

GETTING STARTED IN EDITING

Most computers come bundled with some form of nonlinear editing software that you can use right away, and every phone now has a decent camera attached. With those two things, and a basic tutorial from YouTube, you can get to work learning about editing. Start with small pieces to send to friends or post on Facebook. Practice recutting and recontextualizing commercials, TV shows, and news clips. Record yourself talking about some traumatic event from your childhood and edit it down to a sixty-second piece with supporting footage, photos, and sound effects. All you really need is time.

INTERNSHIPS Interns should be treated and paid fairly, and though they often aren't, I think there's an undeniable value in the intern system. If you don't have any experience or work history, and want some fast, consider one. Despite occasional abuse, internships provide an infrastructure for mentorship; they force neophytes to learn how to work with others and understand processes that they would not otherwise be exposed to; and they foster competition. It's good for interns to see how all the roles fit into the whole and to realize that no one got where they are overnight. An internship is a temporary situation that allows you to soak up as much experience and information as you can, with people who would otherwise never be in the same room as you, before you have to work under pressures and time constraints of your own.

ASSISTANT EDITING Depending on the kind of internship you get, you may or may not be doing the job of an assistant editor. It's grunt work, really: importing and cleaning footage, syncing audio, making selects of the best takes, and flagging problems. It's not glorious, but it will make these basic skills second nature, and you'll start to build your editorial instincts just by the sheer volume of footage you watch and catalog. Moreover, you'll get a chance to learn about workflow—a huge part of the editing process—from the way your editor likes you to organize things. In time, you'll get to start editing stuff on your own.

FREELANCING Most editors work on a freelance or contract basis. Both contractors and freelancers work for a day rate, but contractors will do it for a guaranteed period of time. These rates vary by project, city, and experience level. There are very few staff editors except at production companies and in-house corporate units. Most editors jump around from job to job and will find themselves working with the same people time and again in a tightening circle of collaborators. Once you're established, you can pick and choose your projects.

PRINCIPLES OF EDITING

Comedy editors have to be good at everything, since comedy itself encompasses all genres: action, drama, musical, corporate training, snuff film, sitcom, parody sitcom, medical procedural, foreign film, home movie, and art-house bullshit. The basics of editing remain the same no matter what you're working on.

EDITS SHOULD BE INVISIBLE If the audience is thinking, "There's an edit. There's an edit. Was that a—yup. Another goddamn edit," then it's difficult to enjoy any moving image. There are exceptions to the rule, especially since editing has become its own comedic form, but most edits should not stand out to the viewer.

INTERNAL CADENCE Does every cut feel like it flows naturally from the last? Each scene should establish its own rhythm to help define the mood and emotion of what's happening on camera. A good rule of thumb for finding the right edit is to only make the final cut once you've hit the same point three times in a row. A good rule of thumb for comedy is, don't do that and see if it makes things funnier.

CUT IN MOVEMENT It's generally easier to mask a cut, and give the sense of constant flow, if you cut in and out during an action. Comedy sometimes calls for irregular rhythm and/or parody of existing forms. We made a series of fake human resources videos once, and we purposely chose edit points that halted the action, in order to give the feeling of a stilted and amateurish production.

WHEN IN DOUBT, CUT LONG Leaving scenes a little long will leave you the possibility of cutting more later, which is something you should always want to do.

An Interview with **Doug Lussenhop**

"All you need to know is where you start, not where you finish."

Doug Lussenhop's work on shows like *Tim and Eric Awesome Show, Great Job!, The Eric André Show,* and *Portlandia* rejiggered the parameters for what editing can achieve and offered the world a new, thoroughly modern, digital-age form of comedy. His is a multidisciplinary approach to editing that combines music, rhythms, visual effects, and general awkwardness to achieve something explicitly Lussenhop. He doesn't look at it like changing comedy or inventing new forms. It's just punching up jokes, as far as he's concerned, and finding new ways to entertain himself and the people he works with.

On Starting Out

In high school, I was way into funny movies. *UHF,* Monty Python, *Airplane,* stuff like that. My friend and I had a video camera, and we wanted to make little funny movies. So we did it all in camera and just learned how to edit by shooting stuff. Real time. In college,

227

I gravitated to editing and just felt like I immediately knew how to do it.

I moved out to LA from Chicago to get into the comedy business in 2003 and a year later I met Tim and Eric. I answered a Craigslist ad when they were making *Tom Goes to the Mayor,* and we just hit it off.

On Punching Up

Comedy is a series of little surprises, so a great way to add easy surprises, especially if the jokes aren't there, is to make jokes with the edit. I call 'em bonus laughs! I need to have sound effects. Watching cartoons like *Ren & Stimpy* and all the Warner Bros. cartoons with their sound effects really influenced that. If someone bites into an apple, you could put a different sound effect in there. Or on my web series *Pound House*, we removed a lot of sounds, which is also funny for some reason. Something about removing the sound reminded me of college, when we had to shoot silent films. Have a huge arsenal of a sound effects library, and you can get a comedy bit going from a thousand different angles.

There's a sketch called "Ooh Mamma" where the scene didn't go great when they were shooting it, so they decided to just smash up the room and the set, and they were like, "Here." So I took a look at it, started looping one of the camera angles and took it into Garage Band to try and make something cool out of it, and it turned out really funny.

On Process

In a sketch show like *Tim and Eric* I sit down and watch all the footage and make little marks whenever I think something funny happens. Then I'll make a copy of that sequence and go through and consolidate all the markers. I'll make a really long rough cut with all the jokes, sleep on it, and then watch. If only a few things are hitting, you decide: this bit is gonna be really short, and it's gonna be about this one joke. That's versus working with something that has a narrative, which needs more continuity. Really funny stuff can happen, but they still ultimately need to get from point A to point B.

It's hard to finish things without a deadline. If you want to make something for fun, make sure to give yourself a deadline and force yourself to finish it, whether it sucks or not. The feeling of finishing something and have it suck is way better than not finishing it at all. You can edit something forever and tweak and fix. Things that are done fast are usually better. You got to just crank stuff out.

On Good Habits

I try to always ride my bike to work or I wouldn't get any exercise. I also never work from home. It's too distracting and it's better to be in an office. I edit really fast, in bursts of inspiration, and then I go get a coffee or go watch other people's cuts. It helps a lot to look at other people's work and learn little tricks from each other. It's like skateboarding: doing it all alone you won't really progress, but if you hang out with other people, you'll come up with new ideas.

Don't overthink stuff. You've got to find a balance between refining something until it's good or it's so polished that it has no character anymore. With editing, happy accidents are a big part of it. Sometimes, I'll close the picture window and just move the edit squares around on the timeline. You can lay out a pattern that you think might look cool and then play it and see what you get.

I used to have anxiety looking at all this footage, and I'd get overwhelmed. It can shut you down when you think about it like that. Don't think about the end! I just think about the part I'm working on right now. It's too daunting. All you need to know is where you start, not where you finish.

Part 3

THE VISUAL ARTS

from drawing butts to drawing boobs and everything in between

One has to imagine that the earliest forms of representational comedy were visual. After funny hand gestures were invented, and before puppets were made from the heads of slain enemies, the 2D world must have provided endless opportunities for comedic expression. What's to say that those fertility drawings of robustly endowed women in the caves of Lascaux and Chauvet weren't goofy caricatures of some long-forgotten MILF? Or that the beautifully rendered paintings of men hunting buffalo weren't inside jokes about the one guy, F'gnar, who was always too drunk on wormwine to throw his spear straight?

As children, before our words are sophisticated enough, or our experiences broad enough, we can always draw pictures. Pictures communicate on a gut level, bypassing rational thought or logic. Once drawn images start moving, an entirely new dimension of comedy opens up: animation. Moving images offer a z-axis, a third dimension across which the most absurd ideas, characters, and situations can run and jump and explode in limitless shapes and colors. It is like cracking open a child's psyche and spilling it on a trampoline.

The visual comedian has the ability to tap into an ancient part of the brain to express complicated ideas with sophisticated techniques. Animators and illustrators possess a distinct and often bizarre worldview that words are inadequate to describe. They have style and they have patience: the patience to sit alone and draw, click, or scan to bring their vision to life.

Chapter 16

ILLUSTRATION & COMICS

For a time, the most powerful form of political commentary was the editorial cartoon. It could shift public opinion or make politicians into household names. They were wildly popular and the art was often incredible: vibrant, emotional, and sharp. They could communicate complicated ideas in a single panel drawing (though many are also famously obtuse and convoluted). Nowadays, political cartoons are less influential, as they have to compete with programs like *The Daily Show* and the seven million GIFs and memes that explode out of the Internet each day.

Gone, too, are the days of glorious, full-color illustrations that once graced the covers of glossy magazines. The *New Yorker* is one of the only major periodicals that still commissions such work, and across the board, publications are doing it less and not paying as much for the work they do hire.

Yet there is hope! Those who specialize in static drawn images will always find avenues and venues through which to be seen. Each web page is a visual canvas longing for expression, and niche publishing of books and comics allows artists to reach audiences and put out work that would have been impossible in the past.

Illustration

Most illustrators make their living doing commercial or editorial work—that is, the little doodles, magazine covers, album art, and advertisements that you see nearly everywhere you turn. Few are able to support themselves solely by their personal art, so most turn to commercial assignments. It's not all bad to work for someone else to pay the bills while putting out your own work on your own terms and with less pressure.

GETTING STARTED IN ILLUSTRATION

Some who are active on the opinion-sharing sectors of the Internet believe that the freelance illustration industry is dead. Clients are no longer willing to pay a living wage, and less-experienced illustrators can do less-sophisticated work more quickly, which is sometimes all that matters. Others say there's more work than ever before—you just have to be more clever and responsive. Either way, the landscape is constantly changing, and if you want to work in this field, and you have the talent, you can. Here are a few things that can help.

DEVELOP A UNIQUE STYLE Even if you are capable in multiple styles, try to hone one that you can use for commercial work. It not only makes you easier to identify and reference, but it can help get you work if you are in the same basic genre of a better known, and more expensive, illustrator or artist. Cynical but practical!

DO COVERS AND POSTERS Illustrate book covers, album covers, and posters as much as possible. This helps you gain experience and *possibly* some exposure. You can also offer your services to local newspapers or organizations that otherwise don't have the budgets to commission work as good as yours.

BUILD A PORTFOLIO Accumulate all of your best work in the style that you've chosen to focus on, and put it in one place for prospective clients to see. If you don't have any actual commercial work yet, do your own. Scour your favorite magazines and redo the illustrations in your own style. It's usually recommended that a portfolio include about twenty-four images, with the strongest material at the beginning and the end.

MAINTAIN A WEBSITE Even people with no talent, skills, or products/services to offer have their own websites, so you should certainly have one, too. Make your website simple, easy to navigate, and reflective of who you are.

WORK ON STUFF YOU HATE Since you will often be paid to illustrate subjects you have no interest in, get some practice by doing it of your own volition. Do illustrations for Asian commodities markets and country music awards. If you can make a study on the efficacy of new pituitary gland medications look whimsical, you can make almost anything look whimsical.

BE MULTIDISCIPLINARY Back in my day, kids could play stickball in the streets and never have to worry about getting hit by a car. These days it's all Adobe Illustrator and Cintiq 24HD monitors. Cartooning and illustrating will always boil down to the basic pen-to-paper dynamic, but being able to work in various formats with multiple applications is a must.

BE GOOD TO WORK WITH Be nice. Be courteous. Be prompt, thorough, and professional. No matter how good your stuff is, if you're difficult to work with, people will eventually stop working with you.

SELL YOUR WORK

One advantage illustrators have is that they can sell actual physical things. They can adapt their art into greeting cards, mugs, vibrators, pillow cases, or those weird plastic sheets that you put on cars and buses to advertise energy drinks or whatever.

ONLINE STORE Your website should have a merch section where you can offer LIMITED EDITION prints or made-to-order objects.

THIRD-PARTY SELLERS Having someone else sell for you has advantages: they reach a wider audience and they'll handle fulfillment, shipping, and processing—but they will also take a percentage of your sales. The major options include Etsy, Fab, eBay, Amazon, and Art.com, though others are always coming and going online.

TRADE SHOWS As an artist, fairs, trade shows, conventions, and festivals are a great way to connect with fans and expose your work to consumers. Flea markets and craft fairs are always interesting because you never know who will walk up, and it's fun to reach customers who weren't necessarily seeking comic or illustrator art.

An Interview with **Lisa Hanawalt**

"There's a lot of dumb advice floating around
out there so: be cautious!"

Lisa Hanawalt is one of the funniest, most interesting illustrators in the world, she created the visuals and character designs for the Netflix animated series *Bojack Horseman*, and her book *My Dirty Dumb Eyes* is a visual revelation. She mixes the personal and the surreal and is fearless in her willingness to expose her own fears to the reader in a sometimes funny, sometimes heart-breaking way.

How did you get started?
I just kinda did it! I've always drawn. I never thought, "I am starting to be an artist . . . NOW!"

Who were your favorite cartoonists growing up?
I was raised loving the Sunday funny pages: Gary Larson, Bill Watterson, and, not going to lie, I was really into *Garfield*, too. Steve Martin and Weird Al Yankovic were the funniest people in the world to me. *Ren & Stimpy.*

How does one make money in your field?
Here's what I did last year: I wrote and illustrated articles, designed book covers, sold comic books and zines/prints/T-shirts, made a web comic, sold original art, designed the characters and backgrounds for a TV show pilot, then that sold and I got hired as an art director.

What's the hardest part about breaking in as an illustrator today?
There's so much fresh talent coming out constantly, it's easy to feel lost! I think a lot of illustrators also struggle to find a unique style. Finding creatively fulfilling jobs that also pay well and aren't soul crushing is tricky.

What advice would you have for someone starting out?
Try to actually finish things. Feel comforted that there isn't one path to "success." Try to create something new-ish, instead of just doing the same things the same old way that everyone else is doing them.

What's your favorite publication to work for, and why?
Lucky Peach magazine, because they send me fun places and feed me great foods.

How did the deal for My Dirty Dumb Eyes come about?
Drawn and Quarterly asked me if I wanted to make a book and I said yes. It was just like a high school prom should be.

How important is merch to the overall Hanawalt brand?
It's fun having a few Hanawallets and Hanawal-T-shirts out there in the world, but I'm not incredibly invested in merch. It feels like a nice bonus to the job, not an end goal.

That said, I'd love to work more with textiles. Underwear with my patterns on them?

What's the worst advice you've ever gotten?
I can't think of anything specific, but there's a lot of dumb advice floating around out there so: be cautious!

Comics

Today, the term *comics* covers a broad spectrum of styles and types, from the mainstream syndicated daily and weekly cartoons in newspapers to one-off book ideas to indie and web comics, where just about anything goes. All in all, though, the number of jobs available in comics is, as you might imagine, extremely finite.

SYNDICATED CARTOONS

For traditional, one- or four-panel cartoonists, the good news is that a very specific set of steps exists for getting comics syndicated. The vast majority of such comics are distributed by King Features, which describes its role this way on its website: "A syndicate decides which comic strips it thinks it can sell best. Then it signs a contract with the cartoonist to create the strips on a regular basis. But most of all, the syndicate edits, packages, promotes, prints, sells and distributes the comic strip to newspapers and other publications around the world." To be considered for syndication, here's what your submission package to a place like King Features should typically include:

- A one-page cover letter describing your strip with your contact info.
- Twenty-four daily comic strips on eight-by-eleven paper.
- A character sheet with a one-paragraph description of your major characters.

Expect eight to twelve weeks for a response and check the website for the most recent submissions requirements.

BOOKS

The best-selling original books tend to be compilations of work by widely syndicated cartoonists, but there are still a lot of original titles that do well. Chronicle Books, who published this book, has published the cartoon volumes *All My Friends Are Dead, Zombies Hate Stuff,* and *Darth Vader and Son.* While not strictly "comics," per se, they are humorous, drawn, and follow a story or character. Other publishers also produce comic-based books. For advice on finding a publisher, see chapter 7.

INDIE COMICS

Indie comics have always formed the backbone of alternative comedy in any genre. They've given us Art Spiegelman, Françoise Mouly, R. Crumb, Harvey Pekar, Daniel Clowes, Lynda Barry, Kate Beaton, and Chris Ware. Many of the best original indie comics were self-published, on the cheap and uncompromising in every way. Indie comics are as close as dorks can get to punk rock, and it's getting me all worked up just thinking about it. Because indie publishers don't have to worry about reaching a wide, or tasteful, audience, they can afford to be much more daring—though smaller runs and audiences mean smaller paychecks for artists. The two top indie publishers for comics artists are Fantagraphics Books and Drawn and Quarterly.

WEB COMICS

As soon as people started putting things online, web comics started appearing. Artists immediately found the lack of oversight, the freedom from conventional forms, and the general sense of being able to do whatever the hell they wanted to be exhilarating. Today there are thousands of web comics spanning every imaginable genre, form, and level of quality, though only a small percentage of them are commercially viable. The reason has to do with supply and demand: that same lack of restriction also ensures proliferation. But the creative rewards have been high, with wholly new styles and genres making use of clip art, animated GIFs, and pixel art. This has helped usher in the age of Nerd Culture. A lot of the most popular web comics have historically catered to that very Internet-y series of interests and obsessions—from tech specs to *Star Trek*—that the mainstream used to consider uncool.

WHAT YOU NEED TO MAKE A SUCCESSFUL WEB COMIC

Drawings. You can make these by hand, on the computer, with Photoshop—whatever the heck you want! Just make them! They're really important.

A scanner. Most paper sizes won't fit into your computer. Use a scanner.

Quality. The purest way to stand out is to have a really good web comic. There are other ways to generate website traffic (e.g., "search engine optimization," or SEO), but the main way is to offer a product that people want to read and look at, that they find entertaining and funny and *different.* But don't worry if your web comic is not amazing at first. Quality will come in time.

Regularity. Your comic needs to be published consistently and on time. You've got to build good habits in yourself before you can expect them in your audience, and once you start gaining an audience, they will want more. That's why it's called an "audience," from the Greek words *audi,* meaning "to really, really want," and *ence*, meaning "more web comics." This will give you an advantage over artists whose quality might be higher but who lack discipline.

Community. Web comic artists are a specific breed, to be sure, and the community is passionate. As in any group, there is pettiness and judgment, but there's support and inspiration, too. Connect with your fellow artists. Talk with them and read their stuff. In the end you can choose to support the community as little or as much as you want, but eschew it at your own peril.

Expression. Please, at the very least, do something you want to do. Be daring. Fuck something up. Be weird. Create something you've never seen.

An Interview with **Michael Kupperman**

"A career is the belief that you have a career."

Michael Kupperman is the probably least-known best-known comic artist in the world. His work, including *Tales Designed to Thrizzle* and *Mark Twain's Autobiography 1910-2010,* is widely beloved in the comedy community, and he counts Conan O'Brien and Robert Smigel among his biggest fans. But he doesn't enjoy wide popularity, partly because his work is so specifically, brilliantly insane, but also because he has consciously decided to work outside the corporate system. This creates a natural tension for the modern merchant-artist—especially one who's already prone to tension, like Kupperman—but in so doing, he's been

241

able to create a vast, intricate nebula of work, totally unencumbered by any outside oversight.

I learned to draw in a very academic, fine art-y way at the School of Visual Arts in New York City, and then I felt like I had to sort of go back and deconstruct that. Part of it was going back into drawing as an adventure: you're going into the page and you could be surprised by what happens. Which is part of the reason why, unlike a lot of other cartoonists, I don't have a style, really. It's more like a shifting dialogue with drawing.

My early inspiration was from underground comics and *Raw*—a book-slash-magazine that Art Spiegelman and his wife, Françoise Mouly, created. That was where he showcased *Maus*. It was the greatest marriage of comics, art, and design, probably, ever. Then underground comics such as *Zap* also inspired me. Robert Crumb, Robert Williams. All of these had profane subject matter, so they were freeing on the artistic front, and the humor front, and my mind was blown, so to speak. Art and humor are at their best for me when they're about freedom: freedom of surprise. Freedom of release from expectations.

I was very poorly prepared for life and had no idea how to ask questions such as, "What is my motivation in life?" I didn't even know. I'd been drawing since I was a small child, so it was a language that I was familiar with. It was not hard to learn how to draw; the hard part is putting yourself inside the drawing, to where it's an actual expression of yourself, rather than a mechanical action.

The great cartoonists of the 1950s had careers at a time when they were supported, when people would give them the opportunities and give them the proper environment for them to really develop as artists, and have a satisfying career. We don't have that now. It's a wasteland. It's postapocalyptic, as far as what I do! It's really about what you believe you can make happen, as much as anything.

Getting commercial approval is sort of an all-at-once deal: you get that one thing that gets you that notice, and then you don't have to worry about it that much anymore.

If there's any worth to my work, it's that it's not the same shit. And part of the thing about my humor is that the ball bounces in a different direction than you expect it to. And you either enjoy that or you don't.

Chapter 17

ANIMATION

For most people, comedians and civilians alike, the most formative comedic moments of childhood are animated. Depending on your age, perhaps it was something by Warner Bros. or Pixar or Nickelodeon. Looney Toons set a standard for quality, breadth, and scope that has not been surpassed in any meaningful way—even given the amazing achievements of *South Park, The Simpsons, Beavis and Butt-head, Family Guy, Ren & Stimpy,* et al. You can do things with animation that you cannot do with live action, not only from a production standpoint, but in subject matter. Animation is unconstrained by reality or physics, and this somehow makes it easier for audiences to accept things like extreme acts of violence, weird sexual innuendo, grotesque displays of digestion. No matter how subversive, rude, taboo, surreal, or offensive animation is, it's invariably less threatening because it's *just a cartoon.*

The Basics of Animation

There are two essential forms of animation, 2D and 3D; from these, everything else stems. 2D was the only form before the advent of the various computer technologies and artificial intelligences that now rule every facet of our lives, even down to the childlike pleasure of a simple cartoon. J In the ancient days of yore, all animation was hand-drawn, frame by frame. Today, most animators use some kind of 3D computer software to reduce the number of drawings they need to create and to give them more flexibility of movement. Whatever your tools, they'll all be deployed to the following ends.

CHARACTER DESIGN

No matter what or who your characters are, they need to be rendered with personality, style, and humor, and their physicality should express in some way an inherent anthropomorphic humanness necessary to hold any audience's interest. How this quality is obtained is up to the animator: the noseless, eyeless Pixar lamp has a different kind of human charm than Woody Woodpecker or Jack Skellington or Daria or Totoro or the Iron Giant or whatever the hell the Monchichis were.

BACKGROUNDS

Though you only really notice them when they're bad or not working in conjunction with the story, backgrounds do an incalculable amount of work in animation. From the minimalist approach to the rich, textured worlds of CG film, backgrounds set mood, ground the world in the laws of physics, and generate humor all on their own.

STOP-MOTION ANIMATION

Before computers and CGI, if you wanted 3D animation, you filmed actual objects, like clay figures or articulated models, and created the illusion of movement. This painstaking process is almost like reverse filming: whereas a camera takes many photos per second to capture living things in motion, to make inanimate objects appear to move, you must take one or two exposures at a time and adjust each object, clay arm, or marble eyeball an infinitesimal amount in between each shutter click. Do this over and over and over for a very long time and you will create, for a few brief moments, a living, breathing inanimate world. For some reason, people still do this; apparently, they prefer the lively imperfections of this craft to the sterile precision of CGI. Today, Nick Park of *Wallace and Gromit* fame is probably the most well-regarded stop-motion animator, while the Adult Swim show *Robot Chicken*, known for its *Star Wars* parodies, is probably the best known. It's also a growing medium on Vine and Instagram.

POSES AND MOVEMENT

How your characters move says almost as much about them, and can create as much humor, as how they look. Think of the laborious way Goofy slouches across his world versus the bouncing immediacy of *South Park*'s inhabitants. Poses are the basis of the animation itself: the movement from pose to pose is what determines how they walk, talk, stand, jump, sit, and fly.

FACIAL EXPRESSIONS

One of my favorite animated characters, Meatwad from *Aqua Teen Hunger Force*, has four basic facial expressions: a smile, a frown, eyes closed, eyes open. Yet he's more dynamic than almost any other character I can think of.[1] While the tendency is to exaggerate facial expressions for comedic effect, Meatwad proves that expressions don't have to be complicated so long as they communicate who your characters are in consistent, but surprising, ways.

VOICE AND SOUND

Not all animation includes dialogue, but what and how your characters communicate is massively important. It brings them to life in ways the animation never could alone. Bad or inappropriate voices can leave your animation feeling flat, and bad dialogue—though it can be hidden by great voice talent and dazzling visuals—will ensure that your animation never rises above a certain level. Sound effects, music, and ambience also help construct the highly textured world of animation, so much so that choosing when, or if, to use dialogue is a big part of the animator's job. In fact, animation is perhaps unique in its ability to forgo speech entirely and still be easily understood.

PRO TERM! RIG

In 3D animation, a rig is a digital skeleton of a character that animators can manipulate into various poses by moving its joints and bones around. Some rigs are truly creepy-looking half-formed humanoid things, and others are more fleshed out. They're like clay models without the great clay smell!

---

1 Admittedly, Meatwad's expressions were limited due to financial concerns. The only reason Frylock, another character from *Aqua Teen*, floats is because the animators couldn't afford a walk cycle.

Pitching an Animated TV Show

Due in large part to the proliferation of 3D and motion graphics, animation is one of the fastest-growing creative industries. Most animators receive training in their particular field, especially now that there's such a strong technical aspect to it. But there are exceptions: John Kricfalusi, creator of *Ren & Stimpy*, attended school for a year, but says he barely showed up for class and was largely self-taught, and Dave Willis didn't even know how to draw when he started making *Aqua Teen*.

If you want to develop an animated show for TV, or already have something developed you think could work, here's what you do. In essence, the pitch process is the same as for a sitcom: you're selling an idea or script, but with concept art and perhaps some test animations. Michael Vogel, an animation executive with Sony TV, breaks down the most important aspects of pitching, which are here paraphrased:

FEATURE A STRONG MAIN CHARACTER This has to be the in, the hook, the relatable/lovable/hateable star or stars that audiences will want to watch week after week. They should have a very strong POV and goals for themselves and their world.

ONLY PRESENT ARTWORK THAT'S TV-READY Designs that aren't up to snuff will hurt your pitch. Explaining the kind of artwork you'd like it to be is better than showing up with some shabby-looking talking cats.

KNOW WHAT PRODUCTION ROLE YOU WANT Animator, writer, producer, something else? Be specific and show that you've done your homework. Even if it doesn't work out this time, you'll be remembered for being thorough and professional.

PRACTICE YOUR PITCH AND KEEP IT SHORT Start with the main character and work your way out from there. Cover only what is necessary. Trim all the fat and come in with only the funniest, most essential, and well-thought-out stuff.

KNOW YOUR COMPETITION Be an expert on all the current animated series. Be able to discuss what you like and don't like in the marketplace. Not only will it impress in the pitch, but it will also help you understand where your idea stands and what others are up to. It would stink to have a pitch that's very similar to a show already on the air.

END WITH EPISODE IDEAS Vogel recommends having two completely fleshed out stories and six to eight more that can be summed up in a few lines. Make sure they are consistent with the main character you just spent a bunch of time explaining.

BE CONFIDENT Don't give off the vibe that you don't think you belong there or that you aren't really sure if your idea's very good. Confidence starts with actually liking your idea and believing in your own ability to pull it off.

An Interview with **Dave Willis**

"There are people who laugh because they're expecting it, and there are people who laugh because they're not expecting it. We're going after that audience."

Dave Willis made *Aqua Teen Hunger Force* and *Squidbillies*—two of the best, most enduring cartoons of the 2000s. Before that, Willis was a writer on *Space Ghost Coast to Coast*, a pioneering program on Adult Swim's animation block. Before that he was just some guy who wanted to make comedy who got his first job by having an eight-year-old write him a letter of recommendation and send it to someone at Adult Swim.

On Voices

Any successful cartoon is going to have one great voice that is funny regardless of what the lines are or what's being said. If you look at every successful cartoon, they all have at least one voice that could be funny reading a takeout menu. I love to get people who are great at improv and encourage them to make up stuff and improve upon our script. You work with certain people, like Patton Oswalt or Paul F. Tompkins, and you can see that their thought process is so sharp and they can give you the lines exactly as you want them, but also make them better. But it's more than improv. There's an actual quality to the voice that has got to be funny, in and of itself.

When I read really tight scripts for cartoons, it just seems kind of silly to me. I'd rather come in a little half-cocked, but inspired, and work with really talented people and carve it down from there. To me, it's all process. By the time it's actually being animated, I think a big chunk of the hard work has already been done to make comedy out of it.

On Characters

The best cartoons are character-driven. There's some stuff that's satirical, and that's good, but the best stuff, the most lovable stuff, is when you're with a character that you can really embrace. Some of the pitches that we get at Adult Swim are cartoons that are trying to parody something or capitalize on some trend, but the good stuff is always the same: if it's a great character who's funny to look at and funny to hear talk, then you've got two of the things you need already. Everybody pitches stuff that looks like *Family Guy*. It's like, *Family Guy*'s already done it. Come up with something else.

There are people who laugh because they're expecting it, and there are people who laugh because they're not expecting it. And we're going after that audience.

On Process

For me, cartoons were a means to an end. It was a way to do comedy. *Space Ghost* and *Aqua Teen* were ways that we could make our entire vision happen with the fewest number of steps. We could write it, go in the booth, do a couple voices, and if the joke wasn't working, I could just stand there and make up stuff until something made us laugh. When they handed me the chance to work on *Space Ghost,* I couldn't believe my fortune. And I think I gained confidence just by doing it.

I think of myself as a writer, but only as one step in the process. Compare it to a furniture maker. I don't think of it like, I draw the plan for the chair and then hand it to someone else to cut the wood. I think of it as, I go in with an idea, and then I come out of the building with a chair.

Part 4

THE DIGITAL REALM

LOLS, ROTFLS, URLS, IRLS, and several Ls you've never even heard of*

* Can I tell you something about this section? I am worried that 40 percent of it will be outdated, outmoded, or just plain wrong by the time you read it. I believe, however, that the core principles for success and integrity are the same, no matter the platform, and hopefully those will come across here. In short: If you see details that seem like they might not be right, please Google them.

It's impossible to overstate how profoundly the Internet has changed our daily lives and our way of seeing the world. The more we depend on the Internet to distribute culture to us at increasing speed, the more the Internet winds up *becoming* our culture.

It's like a digital hermaphrodite that impregnates and then cannibalizes itself. Kind of.

At its core, the web's only physically measurable commodity is the click of a mouse. That's it. One can count downloads and ad impressions, but ultimately, the entire Internet economy boils down to billions of index fingers going up and down billions of times per day. So how do you get those fingers to move in a landscape in which you are competing with everything else—be it comedy or not? Most of the competition is all about volume and noise: shotgun blasts of cheap content, optimized for the most popular search terms.[1] How does a humble, well-intended Comedy Person, like yourself, stand out?

Well, the Comedy Person has got to do a little bit of everything. You've got to use Twitter to develop a voice for quick, topical jokes and make friends with other comedians. You've got to use YouTube, not only make your own videos, but to share with your fans and friends the videos that you like. You've got to enter people's commutes through podcasts, as a host or a guest or something in between. Each platform has its own flavor and practical use, and you can put your stamp on all of them.

Look at Chris Hardwick, founder of Nerdist; or Vine's Marlo Meekins; or the podcast resurrection of Marc Maron. They all have their specialties, but they're fluent in more than one medium. The modern Comedy Person has the ability to build a Very Small Digital Media Empire (VSDME) in a relatively short period of time. But you've got to be active. You've got to be inventive. You've got to grab that hermaphroditic digital cannibal by the horns and you've got to create.

---

1 Funny Or Die is so good at SEO (the strategic use of key words and descriptions designed to stand out to search engines) that it is the first result that comes up in a Google search for "Sex."

Chapter 18

YOUTUBE

For a long time, YouTube was the definition of chaos, but it is shifting from a hellish miasma of all that God hath wrought into a linear, organized network that people can easily find, access, and search within. It also represents the most immediate and democratizing form of distribution ever available to the average Comedy Person. Big brands with a lot of money have noticed how large and loyal the audiences are, and YouTube has had corporate partnerships with Disney, NBC, the major sports leagues, and Oprah Winfrey. Whether these media giants will suffocate the little guys or propel them to new heights remains to be seen.

How YouTube Works

YouTube was started in 2005 by two ex-PayPal employees, and in 2006 Google bought it for $1.65 billion. It's not hard to see why it's been so successful: it's simple, intuitive, and allows anyone to be "on TV." Moreover, with its fairly egalitarian ad-sharing structure, it also allows anyone to "make money."

A HANDY YOUTUBE GLOSSARY

Upload. YouTube makes it incredibly simple to upload videos of almost any format. I will not even explain how to upload videos because it would take more time to explain it than it would to go on YouTube and do it. It already has. We're both now that much closer to death because of this!

AdSense. This Google-owned company serves specific, targeted ads to audiences. In other words, it puts ads around your videos, and once you reach a certain threshold of ad impressions, you start to collect revenue.

Search. Tagging your videos appropriately, so that people searching for particular content will find them, can really affect their performance. Search represents a huuuuge part of how YouTube works.

Subscribing. When you subscribe to a channel, you will receive updates whenever that channel adds new videos. The more subscribers you have for your channel, the bigger your audience, the more you can make in ads, the cooler you are.

Favorite. When users tag a video as a "favorite," this favored status is broadcast on social media. Videos also have a Thumbs Up and Thumbs Down feature, which is a great way to immediately regret posting that video of Hodor from *Game of Thrones* saying "I'm gay" instead of "Hodor" after the actor who plays him came out of the closet.

Sharing. The ultimate viewer approval, sharing is when some-one spreads a video through links, embeds, or the various social networks.

Comments. YouTube commenters are a special kind of mon-ster—depraved, ignorant, and outspoken. But there are an equal number of smart and funny people who love to be in on the joke. Watching fans of *On Cinema*[2] pick sides and inhabit the world that the hosts created was an absolute joy to behold. Personality-driven channels thrive on conversations with viewers, response videos, and solicitations of ideas and feedback.

Thumbnails. Small still images, usually of cleavage or someone in yoga pants, that represent each video are called "thumbnails." These can be tweaked and manipulated to entice viewers, especially if they like cleavage or yoga pants.

Annotations. These are those little messages that pop up over videos directing you to like them, or subscribe to their channel, or go here to see more, or leave comments below. Sometimes annota-tions are the funniest part of a video, and they can definitely serve as both an enhancement and an annoyance.

YOUTUBE RULES AND RESTRICTIONS

As freewheeling as YouTube can seem, it does enforce a list of restric-tions: no pornography, hate speech, frontal nudity, extreme vio-lence, or violation of other users' privacy. Users can self-police the site by "flagging" videos and reporting content that violates any of YouTube's rules. In addition, YouTube can automatically detect and remove copyrighted material using other advanced algorithms and God knows what else.

---

2 A hilariously inane movie-review show starring Tim Heidecker and Gregg Turkington.

An Interview with **Kathleen Grace**

"Stop being a douchebag at the Internet party and start conversing."

For four years, Kathleen Grace ran creative development for YouTube Space Los Angeles. Her job was to seek out creators, help them develop their material, and determine who gets which resources to make what. She was also the creator of one of the first well-produced, legitimate web series, *The Burg,* and is also a sometime TV producer.

On Developing Talent

My goals in selecting people to work with were twofold: (1) who will be successful on YouTube, and (2) who is someone that will fit into our community and be a positive member in it. But really I looked at how motivated they were: Are they posting regularly? Do they attend events? Do they keep working at their channel? Can I envision how they will evolve creatively? Are they open to learning?

We looked at this in lots of ways: watch time, subscriber growth rates, views, interviews, and of course just watching the videos and seeing if they elicited a response from us. YouTube is owned by Google at the end of the day, so we used metrics and data to narrow down the pool and then had our team look at them. And we did phone interviews for some of our programs.

On Good Habits

The two key themes I hear myself repeating to creators of all backgrounds are: produce consistently and join the conversation. If I come to your YouTube channel and you don't post regularly on a schedule, that is like flipping on HBO and seeing color bars. If as a viewer I can't count on you, why would I waste my limited time going to your channel?

260

Joining the conversation is the one I see more traditional comedians struggling with online. Now the web is truly two-way and interactive; just broadcasting your thoughts is not enough. You've got to develop a relationship with your audience. The Internet is a party, and no one wants to hang with the guy who just talks about himself all the time. You wouldn't do that in a social situation: just shout your own jokes and not ask any questions or respond to anyone else's material. Stop being a douchebag at the Internet party and start conversing.

On Making Money

Everyone who has a YouTube channel can make money from the ads that run on their channel. That's definitely the easiest and quickest way, but creators are also selling merchandise, raising money on Kickstarter, going on tours, and even getting sponsors. Freddie W. raised $800,000 in two days on Kickstarter, but he did this after two and a half years of building his audience on his channel. The biggest opportunity that YouTube and the web in general brings to creative people is the chance to own your audience. Looking at comedians like Chris Hardwick, I see the future. He owns his audience no matter where he goes. It's an incredibly exciting time to be a writer or director or comedian or actor.

THE CREATOR PLAYBOOK

YouTube's massive success goes beyond its proliferation and ease of use: it's also mastered the metrics of users' searching, watching, sharing, and buying habits, and it communicates the strength of that approach to its creative users. Most of YouTube's findings are outlined in something called the Creator Playbook, which they recommend—almost threaten, in fact—that you follow to the letter. It's comprehensive and invaluable. Here are some highlights:

GET THEIR ATTENTION Make your first shot fascinating; immediately address the audience and tell them what they're watching. Ask them a question and tease the rest of the video. Keep your branding under five seconds.

GET THEM TO PARTICIPATE Speak directly into the camera whenever possible; use end cards to direct viewers to another video or ask them to subscribe, like, and share. Encourage comments with specific prompts.

BUILD AUDIENCE Publish at least once a week, plus whenever something newsworthy happens. Figure out the best time to put up a new video and stick with that schedule. Like, comment, and share other people's videos so your feed remains active.

ORGANIZE YOUR CONTENT Use playlists to group videos that are episodic or centered around a theme. Combine your most popular videos with newer stuff to bring them more attention. Make a "best of" playlist for new viewers, and make sure your playlists all have a fantastic thumbnail.

USE ANALYTICS One of the benefits of using a free service that's owned by Google is access to their vast wealth of data and information. You can keep track of where your viewers are on your channel, how they are finding your videos, and how effective your annotations are.

BUILD COMMUNITY Blog and use Google+ (duh). Respond to commenters within the first few hours of posting new videos. Recognize active contributors by name. Work with creators and channels that share similar audiences.

BE GOOD Make compelling stuff that people will want to watch and use these techniques to enhance their overall enjoyment and expose them to what you do, not to feed some cynical pursuit of fame at any cost.[3]

3 This one is not *technically* in the Playbook.

Chapter 19

PODCASTS

There's an old saying in the Bible: *Vestibulum a erat, et Abraham.*[4] Today there are more than 115,000 podcasts on iTunes on every conceivable topic, in every genre, and representing all levels of quality. Certainly among comedians, they have become somewhat de rigueur and can sometimes feel a little (a lot) incestuous. But there's a reason why so many have taken up the mantel: podcasting is a great way to consistently put out content, it gives you something to show people, and it can provide a forum for topics or ideas you're truly passionate about. It can build audience and it's fun.

However, there's a common misconception that all you need to do to have a podcast is grab a funny friend, turn on a microphone, and just talk about whatever. Podcasts like *Comedy Bang! Bang!, Never Not Funny, WTF with Marc Maron,* and *Who Charted?* are only great because the hosts are talented, the formats are tight and repeatable, and they all work very, very hard to structure and produce their shows on a regular schedule.

When done well, podcasting has a power that goes beyond mere entertainment. Like good radio, podcasts tell a story and build an intimate relationship with the listener, as if each episode were made specifically for them.

4 Even Abraham had a podcast.

Podcasting Technology

Podcasting requires two things: an audio file and a delivery mechanism. What is in those files and how successfully you deliver them varies widely from podcaster to podcaster, but without them, you're really just talking to yourself.

AUDIO FILES MP3 is the most common file type because it can be played on almost any device. Podcasts are usually recorded in a much larger, higher quality format, like AIFF or WAV, and then compressed into MP3.

HOSTING A host is a service that stores your audio files, and it is also the website where you publish your podcast (whether that website is your own or someone else's). Audio files need a permanent address on a host like Libsyn or Blubrry, where RSS feeds and podcatchers can find them to stream or download. It's usually recommended that you do not host your website and your podcasting media files in the same place, mainly because of bandwidth limitations.

RSS FEED This is how you syndicate your podcast to allow listeners to subscribe and receive regular updates. It carries all the information about your podcast: title, date of publication, and metadata. An RSS feed is really just a piece of code, and it is fully automated. Setting up your RSS is relatively easy. You can install it yourself with an XML script or, if you use WordPress, with a simple widget. A web feed management provider, like FeedBurner or the PowerPress plug-in, will host and carry your RSS feed and provide iTunes-optimized metadata, traffic analysis, and ad hosting.

PODCATCHING This is software that captures audio files and brings them to the listener. iTunes is nothing more than the world's largest podcatcher. All it does is watch subscribers' RSS feeds for updates, then obtain the audio file directly from the media host, and then deliver it to their iTunes accounts.

Producing a Podcast

The process of actually making your podcast is the fun part, but it requires equipment, skill, and money. Startup costs can range from a couple hundred dollars to a thousand or more, depending on what equipment you invest in, and hosting can cost between five dollars to over a hundred dollars a month. This is how it works: Talk, sing, or joke into a microphone à the audio is recorded and à goes through a mixer and à gets captured in your recording software and à is edited and produced and à then the raw audio is compressed into an MP3 à which is exported and published.

HARDWARE
In addition to the stuff below, you'll also want to eventually get microphone clamps, cables, stands, and a wind guard.

MICROPHONES Here is a little known but totally true fact: microphones do not actually record anything! All a microphone does is convert sound waves into an electromagnetic signal that can then be captured by a recording device. For general podcast recording, a *dynamic microphone* is usually best. *Condenser microphones* capture a much wider field of sound and are great for acoustic and live music, but are not ideal for most podcasting purposes. I've used my iPhone to record interviews and occasionally audio for videos, too, and I have been pleasantly surprised with the quality. Smart phones are by no means a reliable source of audio capture, but they can be used in a pinch.

DIGITAL AUDIO RECORDERS These are microphones and recording devices in one, and they are a terrific alternative to stand-alone microphones for a few reasons: They store audio internally or on a memory card. You won't lose your recording if you have a power outage or a computer crash. They're portable.

AN AUDIO MIXER A mixer takes multiple audio sources and combines them into a single source to record. These are great when you are recording multiple people or tracks, or you are interviewing someone on Skype. You can get away with buying a very basic one.

AUDIO INTERFACE If you have a non-USB microphone (that is, you have a standard mic with an XLR connector), you will also need an audio interface to connect the mic to your computer to capture sound.

HEADPHONES While technically optional, headphones are vital when you are editing audio, and it's worth investing in a medium-quality pair that will last for a while.

AUDIO SOFTWARE

You will probably spend more time with your editing software than you will recording the podcast itself, and there's a program for just about everything.

GARAGEBAND This editing program comes with most Apple computers. It is fine for podcasting, but it is aimed primarily at musicians and features virtual instruments and customizable loops. It is user-friendly, but in that overdesigned, counterintuitive, clunky, Apple user-friendly way. Lots of plug-ins. Not available on Windows.

AUDACITY This is a free, open-source program that can be used on Mac, Windows, or Linux. It lacks some of the features of other software, but it is more than capable of basic import and editing and is simple to use.

PROTOOLS A professional, and pretty expensive, program, this is made to be used with other Avid hardware. If you're into it, you're probably not reading this chapter.

PROPAGANDA This all-in-one podcasting program can capture audio, edit, and publish the final MP3 files for PC only.

SOUNDBOARD This program allows you to import, store, organize, and play stingers, sound effects, and music while you record your podcast. It can greatly reduce the amount of time you spend on postproduction, since it's essentially like operating the board on a live radio show. Free!

WIRECAST This is live-streaming software so you can broadcast in real-time.

Distribution

The basic distribution process goes like this: you upload your podcast audio file to your media host, then create a new blog post on your website with a link to the file from the media host, and send the link out via RSS. Boom. You are now a podcast. Submitting to podcast directories is how you get your RSS feed to show up in the various podcast marketplaces, and in almost all cases, it is incredibly easy.

NETWORKS

You might also want to try and join a podcasting network. These are the biggest revolution in podcasting and also the most obvious thing in the world. They allow podcasts to reach a much larger audience, share production resources, and go through a development process with experienced producers. These are a few of the most prominent.

EARWOLF Based in Los Angeles, Earwolf produces and/or distributes *Comedy Bang! Bang!*; *The Fogelnest Files*; *Sklarbro Country*; *Yo, Is This Racist?*; *Ronna & Beverly*; and *The Apple Sisters*. Founded by Scott Aukerman and Jeff Ullrich, Earwolf's shows skew a bit indie comedy-heavy, with a lot of improvised conversations, characters, and general we're-all-having-fun goofiness. They draw heavily from the Los Angeles/UCB comedy community and have started expanding into TV production.

NERDIST This wide-reaching comedy network is anchored by über-host Chris Hardwick. The network, whose podcasts account for almost five million downloads a month, places itself firmly at the center of the nerdo-comedic universe: that ambiguous cultural location in which things that used to be not cool are now extremely cool, and everybody wants to know everything about everything they like (and they like almost everything).

MAXIMUM FUN Jesse Thorn's funny, thinky network centers around his pop-culture talk show, *Bullseye*, which also airs on NPR. Their podcasts run the gamut from culture to comedy to music mash up to sketch. They include *Judge John Hodgman*, *The Kasper Hauser Comedy Podcast*, the quiz show *International Waters*, and the history podcast *The Memory Palace*. It is based in San Francisco and also hosts an annual retreat for fans and creators called MaxFunCon.

Marketing

An undeniably disgusting word, marketing is just part of the creative continuum. Consumers are used to advertising, and in most cases, we treat marketing and advertising just as we do "content": we like the good stuff and tell people about it, and we resent and despise the bad stuff. So how you market your work can be just as much an expression of who you are as your podcast is.

Unlike marketing a book or a movie, where you only have to trick people into buying your thing once, with podcasting you are trying to convince them to put you inside their ears for thirty minutes at a time on a regular basis, and that requires trust. But first they need to find you. In that sense, marketing is simply putting your podcast in front of the people who are most likely to be your audience and making them think they've found something special. Here are some useful marketing tips for podcasts:

PROMOTE WORD OF MOUTH This is still number one, folks! Every podcast I've ever subscribed to has been on the basis of a personal recommendation. Most people need someone to tell them something is worth adding to their routine. Malcolm Gladwell would call them culture scouts or recommend-o-trons. You start by reaching the people who *other* people trust and encouraging them to tell their friends. Once you have enough episodes to be proud of, send personal emails, texts, and Facebook messages to friends and acquaintances and be genuine about your need for help. If your podcast is good, they'll tell others.

DON'T BEG FOR ITUNES RATINGS Make people *want* to rate your podcast on iTunes. Or trick them into doing it by speaking very fast. However you do it, don't come across as desperate. People want to feel like their opinions matter, and it's your job to let them know that they do. Science has shown that you need to remind people to do something an average of seven thousand times before they actually do it, so be persistent. Just don't be a nuisance.

GET PIMPED BY BIGGER PODCASTS Anyone who has a big podcast now was helped by somebody when they were starting out, and most people like being in a position to help other people and return the favor. Start with podcasts you genuinely admire or enjoy, and let them know you exist and like what they do.[5] The worst that will happen is that they ignore you and you temporarily feel like shit. The best that happens is that they like what you're doing, they let people know about it, and you become best friends forever!

BE "NEW AND NOTEWORTHY" After you launch in their store, iTunes will list you as New & Noteworthy for a maximum of eight weeks. Take advantage of that window by having multiple episodes ready to go, and if possible, release more episodes at an accelerated schedule. This will increase your download count and keep you near the top of that list.

HAVE A GOOD TITLE Jesse Thorn says of the very popular *Stuff You Should Know* that its name is like daring the listener *not* to listen

---

5 Just don't be an ass-kisser. Most people can sniff that out, and only a specific kind of psycho responds positively to it, and who needs more psychos in their life? They'll probably just wind up murdering you.

to it. A good name is not vital, of course—*WTF* is actually fairly obnoxious, if you think about it—but it's the first thing your audience hears. You want your title to be catchy, short, descriptive, and evocative of the tone of your podcast. Don't try too hard, though: the best title is usually the second name you think of. (While you're at it, have a good description and good artwork, too.)

Making a Good Podcast

BE ENTERTAINING First and foremost, your podcast has to be enjoyable. What's enjoyable? Be totally surprising, or provide comfort, or offer a weird take on a common topic, or create an entirely original world, like they do on *Welcome to Night Vale, The Thrilling Adventure Hour,* or *Super Ego.* You're funny—you can figure it out! One thing that I would recommend you avoid is presuming that your audience will find conversations with your friends to be as captivating as you do. In time, your audience will *become* your friends, and those inside jokes and references will be *their* inside jokes and references. But they've got to be in on it first or else, to be frank, you're just wasting their time.

BE DIFFERENT Modern consumers are like Roman emperors passively perusing the thousands of podcasts in the iTunes store for one that tickles their fancy, so it takes something special to stand out. If you have a great idea for a podcast, make sure there aren't several dozen just like it. When you invariably discover that there are, do not lose heart: figure out what can make yours different.

273

Avoid hyper-specificity and gimmicks, or use these as jumping-off points for something with substance.

BE USEFUL Listeners are more willing to give you their time if they believe the podcast can be useful. Whether or not your podcast actually *is* useful is up to interpretation, but if it offers insight, practical advice, or even exposure to a topic or way of thinking that's unfamiliar to the audience, it certainly stands a better chance of being thought so.

BE CONSISTENT No matter what's going on in the broader world, make you and your podcast something that's reliable and good. Be your audience's rock! You achieve this by consistency, releasing regularly, on time, with the same structure and format, time and time again, for all eternity. *You* need this consistency, too, because parameters will spark growth and creativity in ways that are simply not possible without discipline.

INVOLVE YOUR AUDIENCE This is more than just reading listener mail. It's about active engagement through contests, cruises, live auctions, handwritten postcards, movie screenings, remixes, or soliciting original art. Involvement can involve anything, so long as you do it with enthusiasm and authenticity. Successful efforts will take practice and might feel forced at first, but it's worth it.

An Interview with **Jesse Thorn**

"What few skills I have I've had to teach myself out of desperation."

When he was in college, Jesse Thorn started a radio show with his friends Jordan Morris and Gene O'Neill after they realized that the only real production involved was lowering the volume when a guest talked too loud. That show, *The Sound of Young America,* became popular by appealing to what Jesse calls "the Children of Mr. Show": that is, the protogeneration of comedy nerds who wanted to hear more about their favorite comedians. The show was later distributed by Public Radio International, and in 2012 it was renamed *Bullseye.* Today, Jesse's focus is on Maximum Fun, one of the most successful comedy podcasting networks on the entire planet that we live on.

On Starting Out
When Jordan and I figured out that, if we emailed somebody, they might email us back and come on our show, it was like, holy crap! Matt Besser, Todd Barry, Louis CK were all early guests whom we just emailed. We were presenting ourselves as competent professionals, and that was enough to trick people into thinking it was worth their time.

   In late 2004 and early 2005 I had a friend who was a kind of web 1.0 guru, and he said, "There's this thing coming out called podcasting, and you should check it out for your radio show." I looked it up and I thought, if I can just get, like, dozens of people to listen it seems like it would be worth the extra couple hours. I thought podcasting might be the whole next ten years of talk media, but I didn't know that it would be or believe that it would be. I just thought, baseline, it's worth it to me if I can get together this small audience, and then I'll be ready if by some chance this really becomes a thing.

What few skills I have I had to teach myself out of desperation. I loved public radio, and I wanted to make my show a national public radio show, but nobody was there to teach me audio. So I just had to—by brute force and increments, as my stepmother would say—wrap my mind around editing audio and using FTP software and making RSS feeds and all this crap that I was not naturally suited to but just had to do to make it happen.

On Marketing

I went blog to blog and message board to message board flogging my show relentlessly. And it sucked. I didn't enjoy it. I'm not a natural self-promoter. But I forced myself to self-promote because I knew that, if I didn't promote it, nobody else was going to. And I think that is hard for a lot of people who are of an artistic temperament—and I know that it was hard for me—but you gotta do what you gotta do.

On Standing Out

Unless you are a really famous person or, once in a billion years, you're like a Pete Holmes who has such a crazy distinctive personal perspective, you might be able to break through. But generally, no way. So what I'm looking for when I'm choosing shows to develop is people with really distinctive perspectives and shows that are unusual and compelling enough in their ideas that somebody might give them a try.

A lot of podcast audiences are burned by crappy productions, so they're either looking for a brand they can trust—whether it's a famous person or a broadcasting brand—or they're looking for an idea that's so neat to them that they'll give it a shot.

On Building Audience

My biggest strength is helping people remember that the paramount thing is their connection to their audience and serving their audience's needs. Comedians are used to getting that organically because if they're standing onstage and they're doing something that the audience doesn't like, they're getting a thousand percent feedback right back at them. In podcasting that doesn't exist, and so that's why I think there are so many comedy podcasts that are aimless and format-less.

My preference was always to try to connect my fans with each other so it was a community—like the people who go to the Sturgis Motorcycle Rally—and that was why it occurred to me that maybe we could do something in real life. We were looking at hotels and college campuses for MaxFunCon, and they were so expensive and so stupid. And then we went to the place where we have MaxFunCon, which is a cabin in the woods essentially—it's a hundred cabins in the woods—and I thought "Oh! I understand exactly what this is. This is summer camp for the people that love our shows."

On Independence

I grew up kind of taking care of myself in an inner-city neighbor-hood, and so I'm not naturally inclined to let anyone else do what I can do myself—even if it might make my life better or someone else might be better at it—because it might require me to trust some-one. A lot of times asking someone more successful than you for help, which I always imagine in my head to be a rude imposition, is actually an opportunity for that person to help you, and they would enjoy it and be grateful for the chance to help.

On Mean People

I think I have reached the level of famousness at which I would be very glad to stop becoming more well-known because I am very bothered by people saying horrible things about me. And I don't really want anymore of that in my life, and I'm not that into being famous—it's just not that appealing to me. I usually get precious, smug, arrogant, ugly—a lot of ugly. I'm a perfectly normal-looking person. A nice, solid medium. Any random AV Club thing about me, look at the number of people that hate me. There will always be a thread about how horrible I am.[6]

---

6 Though I haven't been able to peer directly into his soul, my assessment is that Jesse Thorn is not horrible at all. He is gracious, thoughtful, and quite good-looking.

Chapter 20

THE SOCIAL NETWORKS

During the time I spent writing this book, I looked at social media an estimated 5,335 times. That number seems low, actually, but in the interest of self-respect, I have to assume my calculations are accurate. I would check in periodically, letting the social networks be my subconscious' lifeline to the outside world, sometimes for distraction, sometimes for inspiration, but mostly because it's a compulsion—and a very powerful tool for comedy.

Social networking has the ability to expose our best and worst attributes in a giant display of human pathologies. It's got the intimacy of a small town but the scale of the United Nations. It also allows for direct communication, at least on a surface level, with the most powerful people and organizations in the world. It's amazing and terrifying, and it's all free. Each social network has its own distinct flavor, reveals its own layer of human habit—like a Voltron[7] for our souls, the modern Comedy Person needs to be connected to all of them before they can come together as a whole.

What follows is an overview of Tumblr, Twitter, and Vine. I've

---

7 *Voltron* was a Japanese action cartoon from the 1980s in which five separate cat-shaped personal spacecraft, piloted by five *very different teens*, came together to form a giant walking/flying Japanese Viking robot named Voltron that fought evil monsters. No real reason for this footnote beyond my own desire to explain *Voltron* in one sentence.

chosen these three because they seem to be the most accessible and versatile content-creation platforms for comedians. There are other social networks of course: Facebook is great for informing fans of shows and material on other platforms; Instagram is a beautiful way to use oversaturated filters; and Pinterest is . . . whatever Pinterest is. But we will limit this section to the three listed above. Thanks in advance for your understanding!

Tumblr

Tumblr is a little hard to get at first because it takes place on such a vast scale with a speed and a language all its own. It's technically a microblogging site, though that doesn't really do it justice, since blogging usually conjures the written word, and Tumblr is dominated by imagery: photos, cartoons, GIFs, and videos. It's made up of millions (billions?) of extremely short posts that can be instantly gotten, chuckled at, and then shared. It's an incubator for memes.

HOW IT WORKS

SHARING The main way your material gets passed around the Tumblrverse is through reblogging. Someone reposts your post on their own account, thus exposing it to all of their followers. Another way a follower can express their approval, without sharing it with all of their followers, is by liking your post. Lastly, *notes* are basically comments that users make on your posts, and they often accompany a reblog.

ASKING You can allow users to ask you questions, either

anonymously or not. This can be a fun and interesting way to inter-act with other people on Tumblr, or it can be a nightmare scenario that will shake your faith in humanity. This feature can sometimes come off as a bit—how you say?—*narcissistic* if not handled prop-erly, so try to make your answers at least somewhat entertaining.

PRO TERM! *GIF*
Standing for "graphics interchange format," GIFs are compressed graphic files, some of which are animated. GIFs use frames to keep the images small, like movies without sound. The GIF file format was introduced by the ancient online service CompuServe in 1987. After years of battling the inevitable, I have finally conceded that GIF is pronounced "jif." You should, too.

WHAT WORKS

The kinds of accounts that become popular on Tumblr usually share a few traits.

VISUAL HUMOR The Tumblr environment has its own kind of humor, most notably the GIF with caption. These can come indi-vidually or in a series and be used to make commentary or use mov-ing images to recontextualize a familiar situation. Jesus Christ, this is a dry description.

FREQUENT ACTIVITY You've got to update all the time and make conversations with the Tumblrs you like. Reblog, like, leave notes, answer questions.

NOVELTY Tumblr is the home of the million-dollar idea (that will not ever make anyone a million dollars). For instance, photos of celebrities with shrunken heads, adults reenacting photos from

281

MAKING A GIF

A really good GIF makes others think "Of course!" or "Hahahahahahaha," or "I like that GIF." You can make one in Photoshop by creating a frame animation, but it's easier with a tool like GIF Brewery. First thing you need to do is capture your video. If it's from YouTube or a movie, you need to pull it onto your desktop with QuickTime's Screen Recording feature or a program like KeepVid. If you're uploading the video, then you just need to export it to an application (like GIF Brewery) and trim the video to include only the clip you want. The longer the clip, the bigger the file, and the bigger the file, the slower it loads on other people's Tumblrs, which means they will never look at it. You can also add a caption, reduce colors, crop it, and resize the video to make sure it's the smallest file size possible. Post it and wait for the $$$ to start rolling in (JK)!

their childhood, or *Garfield* comic strips with Garfield removed— all may result in a book deal, but they are just as likely to quickly lose cultural steam as well.

POP CULTURE What else?

VISUAL SPLENDIFEROUSNESS M. C. Escher would have killed on Tumblr.

SURREAL DOCUMENTATION Untold millions of random images exist in the world just waiting to be presented for our entertainment, be they awkward family photos to stock photos of white women eating salad.

NAMES THAT DESCRIBE EXACTLY WHAT THEY ARE One of the best ways to get people to follow your Tumblr is to come up with a good idea and then name your Tumblr in a way that describes the idea exactly. Like these:

- Hungover Owls
- Hipsters who Dress like Jackie from Roseanne
- Magical Rappers
- Garfield Minus Garfield
- Fake Science
- Hot Dog Legs

- White Men Wearing Google Glass
- Selfies at a Funeral
- Things Fitting Perfectly into Other Things
- Actresses Without Teeth

An Interview with **Paul Laudiero**

"I really think most writers have a thousand shitty ideas before hitting something good."

Paul was still in college when he got a deal to turn his popular Tumblr, "Shit Rough Drafts," into an actual book. It's an elegant premise: photos of purported first drafts of famous books or screenplays, twisted in some ironic or unexpected way, and usually including an editor's handwritten notes. They're funny, simple, and perfect for Tumblr.

I came up with the idea in an English class in college when I was meditating on just how shitty a writer I am. Then I thought that every writer goes through that. Then it hit.

It took off really quick. I didn't do anything to build the Tumblr audience other than just producing funny and new material every day. I actually knew nothing about Tumblr other than it was easy to use. I was put in touch with my agent by a mutual friend through improv, and she's the one who told me it could be a book. I was twenty-two years old and a senior in college. I was very, very, very happy.

283

I go for the dumbest possible joke, not just because I like dumb humor, but because I really think most writers have a thousand shitty ideas before hitting something good. The drafts that share best online usually just have a few lines of dialogue and one strong joke.

I just handwrite them or print them out and take a pic on my iPhone. I upload directly to Tumblr from there.

As long as they make me laugh, they usually work pretty well. I try to stick to books and movies most people have seen or at least heard of. That keeps it relevant. I also do new books and movies as they are released, and do oldies and classics on their anniversaries or the birthdays of their authors. Stuff like that.

I just want write for a living. Whether it be books, TV, movies, . . . honestly, anything. I really want to write for television some day.

Twitter

Of all the social platforms, Twitter has probably done the most to launch comedy careers. Megan Amram, Kelly Oxford, Rob Delaney, and the guy from "Shit My Dad Says" were all either discovered there or capitalized on the massive audiences they built. Not only is it a fantastic way to interact with people who work in comedy without having to sneak up to their house and hide beneath their bathroom window as they make No. 2, its 140-character limit is tailor-made for jokes: pith, brevity, and a limitless audience all in one simple format.

It also sucks. Twitter has become so huge and overcrowded that it's hard to find quality. Everyone seems to be talking about the same thing all the time and complaining about how so many people are always talking about the same thing all the time. It can be cynical, shallow, and ugly, propelled by a need to post jokes as fast as possible, which often leads to brilliance, but more often leads to tastelessness. Yet we can't get enough, and that makes us hate it even more.

Despite all this, I'm definitely partial to Twitter. I genuinely enjoy it, and I've made so many great professional and personal connections through it that I'll always feel a certain loyalty. It's also introduced me to great comedians and convinced me that a much higher percentage of the population is capable of genius than conventional wisdom would have guessed. This is why it's so compelling. It's like life. But it's not life. It's Twitter.

HOW IT WORKS

Twitter is a microblogging site that allows you to post up to 140 characters of anything you want. People follow you, and your tweets show up in their feeds. In turn, you follow other people (unless you're extremely famous), and their tweets show up in your feed. I have no idea how Twitter makes money, or how it could possibly lose money either. The company went public in 2013.

HANDLE Your username is your Twitter identity. You can use your real name (@randazzoj), a funny name (@fart), something personal yet mysterious (@BAKKOOON), or something descriptive (@HistoryInPics).

AVATAR This image represents you to all the Twitter world. Some people consider it their mark and have not changed it in years, some mix it up with regularity. Your avatar can say a lot about your Twitter persona, for instance, that you are really weird or that you have cleavage.

NAME This is the name that shows up in other people's feeds, and it can be different than your handle or username. You can change it as frequently as you want, as people sometimes do to reflect holidays, current events, or their own insanity.

BIO Your bio is where you can say something flip and funny or give real information about who you are and what you do. If you don't actually do anything definable for a living, just put a link to your website and write "London/NYC/LA."

REPLYING You can talk directly to anyone on Twitter (unless they've blocked you) by using their @handle and typing something. Anyone who follows both of you will be able to read your conversation. It's fun!

FAVORITES This is how you let people know that you liked their tweet enough to notice it, but not necessarily enough to reply to or retweet it.

RETWEETING This is your way of sharing a tweet that you think your followers will love or of kissing up to a celebrity whom you want to notice you.

DIRECT MESSAGES Private tweets that only you and someone who follows you can see are used mainly to exchange contact information and photos of genitals.

HASHTAGS These are used to easily search for themes or topics like #SuperBowl or #endoftheworld. Most comedy people use hashtags ironically: #noshit.

PARODY ACCOUNTS

Parody accounts are the bane of everyone's existence, but they *can* be effective satirical tools and a great way for comedians to make up characters and work in a distinct voice. The speed with which the Twitter succubi register accounts in the name of "@JamesGandolfinisDeadBody"—or whatever the fleeting pop culture sideshow of the moment happens to be—can be horrifying. That's not to say you should not do it! People respond well to clever reactions to big events. Just know that the life-expectancy of the average parody account is getting shorter and shorter.

Still, some of the best ones are sublime. For instance, @dadboner captures an essence of frustrated American masculinity with every unintentionally earnest tweet, and @EveryTweetEver is a brilliant meta-account that reveals just how predictable we all are. Meanwhile, @theTweetofGod started as a promotional account for David Javerbaum's book *The Last Testament: A Memoir by God*, but quickly established a voice of its own, chiming in with divine authority on the most mundane topics and news items. Then, @KimKierkegaard smashes together the daily musings of Kim Kardashian with Søren Kierkegaard's philosophy.

TWITTER TIPS FROM ME, @RANDAZZOJ

GET INTO CONVERSATIONS Though it can be hard to break through all the noise, one of the best parts about Twitter is riffing with other people. People love to respond to tweets with jokes of their own, and while not everyone is a professional like you, these exchanges can be a lot of fun. It also makes you look like not-an-asshole.

DON'T GET INTO CONVERSATIONS Many comedians like their feeds to be nice and clean and to contain nothing but jokes. Content only! It's usually one or the other.

LIVE TWEETING IS ACTUALLY GREAT Even though it can be overwhelming to follow five hundred comedians, all of whom are making jokes simultaneously, commenting real-time on some shared experience is a pretty amazing and wonderful side effect of Twitter. It's exciting to work at that pace, and the reactions you get are more intense and emotional. It's also a way to pick up a bunch of new followers in a short period of time.

BE POSITIVE Sometimes Twitter often feels like a contest to see who can be the most critical, cynical, self-deprecating, and unimpressed by life. You can say nice things, too.

AVOID DEBATES ABOUT RELIGION AND THE APPROPRIATENESS OF RAPE JOKES Seems like you might not be able to figure it out on Twitter?

CHIME IN ON THE NEWS OF THE DAY Everyone has their own nightly monologue at this point, but the right joke struck at the right moment can resonate with the masses. I happened to be attending Super Bowl XLVIII in New Orleans when the power went out, and I tweeted, "Guys I'm AT the #SuperBowl and this power outage is no joke. Most of us have broken into small but loyal factions. I am now a doctor." At last count it had 5,192 retweets and 2,357 favorites. Does any of that matter? I don't know! But it entertained a lot of people and that was a nice feeling.

DON'T TWEET EVERY TIME YOU MEET SOMEONE FAMOUS There's nothing wrong with wanting to share, especially if you get to meet or work with someone you admire. But making a show of it turns people off and can seem insecure and disingenuous and lame and dumb. There's enough of that already.

GET OFF TWITTER Do things with your hands. Write letters. Walk away from Twitter and do not check it during sex. Take a shower and do not think of a tweet while you are in the shower. Paddle a canoe and tell your loved ones that you love them and don't observe how they react and make it into a tweet. Sometimes you can enjoy a witty text exchange with a friend without showing it to 8,431 people. Or even twenty-nine people. Twitter is an extension of yourself and your personality, but it is not real. It's too fast and intense, and emotions are too pared down and immediate to be real. Remind yourself of that every once in a while with a sunset that you do not post any photos of.

YOU DON'T HAVE TO HAVE AN OPINION ABOUT EVERYTHING Just saying!

HOW TO STALK A CELEBRITY ON TWITTER

Stalking can be a very effective way to let someone know that you appreciate their work and were never taught to appreciate boundaries. It's tempting to come right out and tweet, "Oh, my god, I love you so much I want to literally devour your essence!" Still, it's better to take it slow. Only reply to a famous person's tweets when you have something to say, and try to make it witty or useful—like what a real human being might say to another human being that they aren't stalking. Be persistent, but if the person doesn't respond after a few weeks or months or ever, try creating several additional Twitter accounts that you can use for a while. Make one of them a beautiful French teenager! Casually inject knowledge of the star's filmography or personal life in a subtly threatening way. But don't fawn over the person! While celebrities are better than us, and would solve all of our problems if only they would be our friends, they don't always like being told how beautiful and perfect they are. If stalking doesn't work, you might need to come to terms with the fact that it wasn't meant to be. Your best bet at this point is to wait for the next paradigm-shifting social network to come out and track them down there.

An Interview with **Megan Amram**

"My dad is funny in the sense that he left a woman to raise two
babies by herself, which is in a lot of ways the perfect joke!"

Megan Amram's squished-up, triple-chinned face is beloved by
several hundred thousand Twitter followers because below that
face is a constant stream of brilliant one-liners and assorted weird
darkness. Megan's successful Twitter presence has helped lead
to real-life jobs writing for *Kroll Show* and *Parks and Recreation,*
as well as a book called *Science . . . for Her!*

On Developing a Sense of Humor

My twin brother and I were raised by my mom in Portland, Oregon,
in a small, artesian, vegan-espresso machine. My twin is one of the
funniest people I know and has a cool neck-beard. My mom is also
so funny and silly and amazing at puns. My dad is funny in the
sense that he left a woman to raise two babies by herself, which is
in a lot of ways the perfect joke!

I got many laughs *at* me, but I think the first time I realized I
could make people laugh *on purpose* was junior year of high school. I
was running for school president and decided to write a speech with
jokes in it. I so distinctly remember that feeling that I could elicit a
response by just writing *words.* It was very powerful and intoxicat-
ing. And yes I won the presidency, CHYAH.

On Twitter Practice

For the first couple of years that I was on Twitter I didn't do *anything*
but post jokes. No interactions, no retweets, just pushing myself to
write the best jokes I could. Also I honestly think the profile picture
helped a lot. If you think of the jokes coming out of her mouth,
they instantly have a lot more weird subtext.

I mostly keep to myself on Twitter and avoid replying, since there's a nice anonymity in just putting out creative work without conversation. However, I've started interacting more with supporters on Twitter because it really is incredible that I'd ever have any "fans," let alone extremely smart funny ones who have clever replies to every joke I make. I never reply to people being negative since nothing good ever comes from engaging in trolls.

On Writing

I had been writing professionally for about a year before I got the job on *Parks and Recreation*. The creator and show runner, Mike Schur, followed me on Twitter and was a fan before we ever met. Mike is absolutely incredible. He's great at teaching younger writers and keeping the writers' room nice and relaxed.

I am pretty obsessed with my smart phone, so I usually just have to kick it to the curb to focus. Our whole writers' room is very tech inclined, so we sometimes have to just all make sure we're not on Twitter all day. That being said, I always use the Internet to write—I find it to be a good way to get inspiration about subjects you don't know much about. Like small-town Indiana.

Vine

Comedians quickly took to Vine when it debuted in 2013 because, despite its obvious limitations, the possibilities seem endless: six-second looping videos present a unique challenge to distill gags down to their core, and to do it with visual flair. Today, Viners incorporate visual effects, music, stop-motion animation, traditional animation, props, stunts, choreography, and creative editing into their comedy, and audiences, and commercial interests, are noticing.

Vine is extremely popular with tweens and teens. Perhaps because of this, and because it is a visual, short-attention-span medium, a lot of the most popular Viners don't fit the usual comedian mold—that is to say, they're good looking. They're cute. They have big personalities and a broad approach to comedy, and it gets eaten up with a digital spoon.

Andrés du Bouchet, a comedian and writer for *Conan*, has lamented the recent rise of what he calls "Prom King Comedy," and while the biggest Viners are undoubtedly talented and funny, there's a whiff of truth in that phrase. Comedy is no longer relegated to the pastiest weirdos anymore. Anyone can make popular comedy now, right from their phone, and they don't even need to have been the victims of bullying to do it.[8]

No matter what, there is a lot of amazing stuff happening on Vine, and it's only going to get more interesting.

HOW IT WORKS

Vine is a mobile app that allows users to record six-second videos that can then be shared on the Vine social network, as well as on Twitter and Facebook. Using the in-app camera, videos are only

8 Which is good, right?

recorded while the user is touching the screen, making it possible to do real-time editing and to easily create stop-motion effects. Users can add captions, tags, and locations to their videos as well.

VINE STYLES

STOP MOTION Probably the biggest phenomenon to come out of the new platform is stop-motion videos, since touch-screen recording is so accommodating to the technique. The form is inherently funny—which has something to do with the uncanny quality of synthetic movement—and there are a million ways to bring inanimate objects to life, from clay to paper cutouts to clothing and probably filthy sex toys, too.

THE WALK & TALK Viners often shoot themselves as they move through their daily environment, making observations or setting up sometimes elaborate jokes. Ted Travelstead's "Twins Talkin'" series uses this style in a simple, straightforward, and very funny way.

PHYSICAL COMEDY Slapstick is also enjoying a resurgence thanks to Vine. The younger crowd is probably more open to good physical comedy than audiences might be on other platforms—not to mention the fact that people falling through cakes and setting things on fire is hilarious.

MUSIC People use music in so many ways, it's hard to lump every kind of musical Vine into one category. Nicholas Megalis is one of the biggest stars in this genre; he's known for his silly songs and props that crackle with creative energy.

AUDIO DUBS & REMIXES Early on, Nick Mastodon mastered this style by creating funny loops juxtaposing children's animation with hip hop and R&B music. Now it's a whole genre that's constantly being tweaked, altered, and expanded.

MAGIC Vine is rife with optical illusions because, again, touchscreen editing allows for such interesting cuts to be made and covered up in camera.

REMAKES This is when users make their own versions of other Viners' videos for comedic effect, and maybe to kiss a little ass, too!

COLLABS Not just a really cool, really short way of saying "collaboration," it's one of Vine's most popular social uses. Teaming up with other Viners allows you to reach their audience, possibly learn new techniques, and cross-pollinate in such a way as to appear to be in the "cool club." The kids love it.

An Interview with **Nick Gallo**

"Create, post, and repeat!"

Nick Gallo rapidly gained a following on Vine, first due to his series of videos with a local breakfast cart proprietor named Harry. Then, as Gallo's persona evolved, people really enjoyed seeing him smash things and himself. (Who wouldn't?) He developed a style and voice all his own, and he earned the respect and admiration of Viners everywhere. He and I talked about what he thinks makes a good Viner and what doesn't.

What makes a good Vine?
There is a large spectrum of what makes a good Vine, all the way from

a father having a moment with his daughter (user: Bottlerocket) to a person dressed up in a gorilla outfit wearing a suit jacket building a birdhouse (user: Simply Sylvio). My favorite Vines are the ones that are aesthetically pleasing and also make me smile.

What makes a bad Vine?
The number one thing that makes a Vine a bad Vine is when it starts off with "go." This is when the cameraman counts down for their subject and starts filming before cueing the actor to begin. Other things that can contribute is when the camera is shaky or the subjects are inaudible.

Why do you think your Vines are popular?
I try to create surreal moments that pull people out of their day and immerse them into wondering what it feels like to be in the world that I have created. I'm still trying to figure out new ways to create Vines, but I'd say it took me three months to simplify my ideas enough for them to be well-received on the platform.

How long does it take you to shoot one of your destruction Vines?
The most intricate Vines that I have created were a series called "This Makes No Sense" with KC James. It is a series of scenes cut together that make no sense, while we are screaming, "THIS MAKES NO SENSE!" For example, KC is in a bathtub and I am plunging his face, or we smash a toilet with sledgehammers and bright blue paint explodes out of it. They take eight to twelve hours to make. My other destruction Vines take longer to clean up than they do to actually set up and shoot.

Are you a Vine purist?
I guess that you can call me a purist because I prefer to create all of my Vines in-app. I am not against using outside technology, but

I think it should aesthetically fit within the platform and refrain from using special effects. This is just an opinion. I say do whatever makes you happy, and I will continue to do the same for myself.

Have you ever made any money from Vine?
Yes, I have. Companies pay Viners to advertise their brand on the app. I created a series of five ads for a rum company based around Monday Night Football.

What's one indispensable trick or technique you've picked up along the way?
Adding music to help set up an emotion in the environment and then allowing the action within the Vine to juxtapose the emotion.

How has Vine helped your overall approach to filmmaking or comedy?
I have been working in the comedy industry for eight years executing other people's ideas. Given the restriction of a 6.2-second time limit for each Vine, it allows me to bring my own ideas to life without being influenced by anyone else or spending too much time on it. Create, post, and repeat!

Have you ever gotten injured while making a Vine?
Yes! I was shooting one called "Nicky?" I am sitting at a cubicle, wearing a dress, and having a tea party with gasoline and a couple of random items, such as an *Aqua Teen Hunger Force* Mooninite hat and a Fleshlight molded from the anus of the pornstar Stoya. A coworker off-camera says, "Nicky?" and then I scream, "No!" smash my arms down on the table, flip it over, and then do a crazy flip over the cubicle wall. I accidentally didn't let go of the teacup while smashing down on the table. I sliced my palm open real bad. It needed stitches, but I just used gaff tape instead.

Part 5

THE BUSINESS OF COMEDY

No jokes here, all business.

Not long ago, I had the opportunity to observe a focus group watching videos we'd made for a comedy website called Thing X. The entire situation called to mind a sci-fi medical procedure: we sat in a small observation area, looking through a one-way mirror, surrounded by screens and computer modules. One by one, the group of carefully selected demographic representatives walked in, all of the same approximate age, income level, and sex, and timidly took their places at a round table. They placed the headphones over their ears, as instructed, and began consuming the media.

Then they were asked what they thought.

And they thought it was terrible. They all thought it was really, really terrible.

They tore apart every detail, from the site design to the quality of the comedy. Our stuff was too long, they said. The jokes were unclear. Our subject matter wasn't relatable. Once they got the punch line, they didn't need anything else.

Hearing that, and reflecting on it ad nauseam over the next couple of days, had a profound impact on me. I realized something more concretely than I had at any point in my career, and that something is this:

Comedy is a product.

Yes, comedy can be art, and yes, it can be thought-provoking and profound—*and it should be*—but it's important for anyone wishing to make a career in comedy to realize that comedy is also a product. It's like a refrigerator: it needs to function well. It needs to look good. There are customers who know what they like, and they expect it to be packaged and delivered to them in a form they find satisfactory in relation to the time or money they've given in exchange for it. Comedy has value, and it is your job to provide that value.

When considering the business of comedy, these are the core questions:

- What are you selling?
- Who will buy it?
- What do they want from it?
- How does it compare to everything else in the marketplace?

These questions are worth asking yourself about everything you do if you wish to function in the professional realm. But you don't have to ask them alone. There are people whose job it is to think about this stuff, to help the left brain meet the right brain, to make deals, develop ideas, and manage finances. They're the businesspeople.

Chapter 21

REPRESENTATION

The hierarchy of fame and power is like a fortress, with the most famous and powerful occupying the innermost bunkers. Emanating from that central location is a series of battlements, manned by increasingly less famous people. These lesser circles terminate at the outside courtyard and moat, on the other side of which stands "regular people," including me and you, the reader of this book.[1] To gain access to that inner bunker, and, thereby, to the people inside who can help launch a Comedy Career, regular people like us need someone who can navigate the fortress' hidden passageways. Someone who knows the gatekeepers and jailers or can give us the secret password to gain entry. Those people are wizards. I mean, agents and managers!

Whether you want to get one or be one, agents and managers are some of the most important people in the entertainment infrastructure. They always know what's going on and who needs what. They are facilitators. They like bridging gaps and making deals. There are greedy agents, of course, and there are bad managers, but most of them care about their clients and love what they do, which is

---

1 Unless you are a famous person, in which case, Hi! Would you like to work together sometime?

helping the talent get what they need to do the best work they can. In short: Managers help you decide what to work on, and agents help you sell it.

What Managers Do

A good manager will work with you to shape your career over the long term. They usually have fewer clients than agents and are more involved with every aspect of their work, offering guidance, setting up meetings, and giving notes on creative projects. Their job is not necessarily to get their clients jobs but to help them make good decisions. Managers generally get a 10 to 15 percent commission on work they negotiate for you.

PRO TIP! DON'T SIGN THAT CONTRACT

Do not work with a manager who asks you to sign an agreement before you book any work. There is no reason for this other than to lock you into a relationship that you may not be happy with and to tie you to them financially. Your relationship with your manager should be one of trust and compatibility, and you should be able to choose to leave it at any time.

Managers will often act as producers on their clients' projects, which is something that agents cannot do. What's more, managers do not have to be licensed in their trade, whereas agents do. In all states but New York and California, a manager must work with an agent to secure employment for their client.

What Agents Do

Agents are concerned with getting their clients work. An active agent is constantly looking for opportunities, bringing up their clients' name, sending them on auditions, and getting them meetings. Because agents work on commission and must please more clients than managers, they may be more focused on booking whatever jobs come up than looking at the long term. Agents also negotiate contracts for their clients, for which they usually receive a 10 percent commission. Agents must be licensed by the state and should also be franchised by SAG/AFTRA. By law, agents cannot also be producers.

TYPES OF AGENTS

Literary agent: They live in the publishing world and specialize in the buying and selling of books and screenplays, but can also help obtain other writing work.

Commercial agent: These specialists send their clients on auditions for everything from fabric softener to cell phones to whatever else there are commercials for.

Theatrical agents: Stage stuff.

Voice talent agents: There's an entire world of voice acting, and there are agents who specialize in that.

How to Get an Agent or Manager

There are really only a few ways to get hooked up with an agent or manager, but within each point below are an infinite number of possibilities.

BE REFERRED The most common way that agents and managers find new talent is through referrals, either by other agents, other clients, or someone they work with. The way to get referred, of course, is by working with other people. Even if it's just videos you're making in your bedroom, do stuff.

HAVE SOMETHING TO SHOW The best time to look for representation is when you have work that you're proud of, whether it's a great standup set, a couple of scripts, or a bunch of videos. You may literally be the funniest person in the world—or even the one thousandth funniest, which is still pretty good—but unless you have something tangible to demonstrate it, how good you are doesn't really matter.

PERFORM IN SHOWCASES Agents and managers do attend talent showcases, and from time to time, they'll even decide to work with someone they see. It happens.

BE PUBLICIZED Agents or managers might approach you if you do something noteworthy. My former coworker Megan Ganz, for instance, was featured on an episode of NPR's *This American Life* about *The Onion*, and an agent contacted her after hearing it. Once noticed, be ready with other work to show or have a great packet already prepared (for more on packets, see page 78).

BE GOOD The main thing agents and managers told me is that, if your work is good, you will get noticed.

How to Be One

There are many people out there who love comedy and comedians and have impeccable taste, but prefer to remain just outside the spotlight. More and more of them are working as representatives. Like most professional trades, you've got to work your way up, and the majority of agents and managers start as interns or assistants. There are seven million ways to get your foot in the door, be it by socializing with comedians and agents or producing your own shows. Either way, being successful in the field of representation often means having these personality traits:

>   **Outgoingness:** I've never met an agent or manager who was afraid to talk on the phone or meet up for a cup of coffee. It's

THE CAA APPRENTICESHIP PROGRAM

At the world's largest, most successful agency, there's a more direct way to become a talent agent: an apprenticeship. Creative Artists Agency (CAA) has built a training program that pairs aspiring agents with working agents to learn the ropes. All trainees start out in entry-level positions, and those who do well can choose which area or specialty they want to branch off into, be it sports, comedy, or the lecture circuit. While it's not an official program, it functions internally as such, and successful completion of your training almost inevitably leads to employment.

okay to be a little shy, but timidity and crippling introversion are not usually considered advantages.

Professionalism: If you act like you're a professional who should be taken seriously, all of a sudden you might become a professional who is taken seriously. But don't be pushy.

Listeningness: Pay. Attention. To. What. People. Are. Saying. The more you do this, the more you'll learn and the smarter and more engaged you will appear.

Dynamism: You've got to be interesting. People want to work with people who are interesting. The best way to be interesting, it turns out, is to be yourself. (Unless you're boring, in which case, maybe you should be a writer?)

An Interview with **Kara Welker**

"I think that I'm good at helping people find what is— for lack of a better word—sellable about them."

Kara Welker has worked as a manager and producer for two decades, representing Patton Oswalt, Janeane Garofalo, Brian Posehn, Pete Holmes, and Kyle Kinane, among others. She and her longtime business partner, Dave Rath, have produced comedy on every platform at every level with their company Generate, and she has a terrific eye for finding, and developing, new talent. She is also five-foot-three, speaks with an endearing squeak, and started her career as a bouncer.

On Starting Out

When I was in college, I got a job at the Improv comedy club as a ticket girl. Then I started picking up more shifts as a door girl—basically, a bouncer, for all intents and purposes. That was how I got my first look into the business and how it worked. I learned what the different jobs are. I learned what a booker was and what an agent was and what a manager did. There's very few comedy managers who didn't start out as door guys at a comedy club.

By working at the club I got to know a lot of agents and managers. I remember chatting with Drew Carey's manager, Rick Messina, and just getting to know him. Then I got to know Dave Rath, who was working for Rick. I'd talk to Dave about one of his first clients, about how he did the night before, what ticket sales were like, and then one day I mustered up the courage to ask if I could intern at his agency, Messina Baker. And they were like, "Yeah, we need an assistant. Come up and interview!"

After a couple years I got promoted to manager. The reason I think I got promoted was because Janeane Garofalo was a client there, and she and I started working together immediately. I started traveling with her as an assistant, so when she'd go work on a movie, I'd go with her so I could learn about that, too. I'd just tell my bosses, "Hey, I gotta go with Janeane. She really needs me to come along," and they'd say, "Uh, okay."

On Working with Clients

The manager is the core relationship, and it should be the most important relationship in your career. The really dumb metaphor I use is that the manager is the CEO of your company. The client is the brand, that's the top. The CEO then helps that talent bring on all the other elements in their professional life. The sales division, that's your agent. Then there's the marketing person, so we hire PR. And then there's the financial aspect of it all, so we hire a business manager. So the CEO is overseeing all these elements, just like any other corporation, really.

People tell you what they want, but they tell you in different ways. Sometimes you have to coerce things out of people, and that's an important part of my job. It's also trying to help identify what is unique or special about people. I think people know a direction that they want to go in, but they don't always know their own hook. So I think that I'm good at helping people find what is—for lack of a better word—sellable about them.

When I start working with someone, we start with a brain dump. I want to hear everything that's on their mind and what their goals are and what they want to do, and then I take that information and I tidy it up. I'll set up goals from that point, to unclutter their plate, and become goal-oriented. Once we get on track, it becomes my job to help open doors to make those things possible.

On Getting Fired

It'd probably make me throw up if I had to count how many times I've been fired. It happens. If things aren't going to plan, we get fired. Every manager has been fired quite a lot. It's weird! You are not ever really prepared for it, but one of the things my old boss used to say was, "They all leave." He represents giant stars, and that was his philosophy then and now. That's how you prepare for it. You go into it knowing they all leave. Of course, they *don't* all leave, but if you brace yourself in that way, when 10 percent leave, it's like, "Okay, I'm doing all right."

Chapter 22

DEVELOPMENT

Development is the process of bringing an idea from concept to production. Sometimes that means working with the creators to refine their concept into a script; sometimes it means reworking what's already there to make it something that will please investors and audiences. Development people come in all varieties, and their jobs totally depend on their personality, what their bosses want from them, and the project.

Whether it's TV or film—the two kinds of development we are discussing in this chapter—only a small proportion—perhaps 10 percent—of the projects in development ever make it to market. Projects can get killed for any number of reasons, be they creative, financial, or something completely irrational, like an executive's opinion. Sometimes talent drops out or sometimes a similar project gets greenlit first. But unless you're making something completely independently, if there's any money involved at all, you'll probably work with someone to develop your project.

How Development Works

Development varies greatly depending on the situation, but it always refers to making changes to a project before it's been greenlit for production. Sometimes development amounts to little more than pairing the right producer with the right talent. Other times, development is a horrifying series of inane notes seemingly designed to suck all of the life out of a perfectly good script. Generally speaker, however, development is undertaken by two types of entities: production companies and studios or networks.

DEVELOPMENT BY A PRODUCTION COMPANY

Production companies want to find and develop talent and ideas that they can sell to studios, networks, and distributors. Since profit margins at production companies are so much smaller, their development departments are usually slimmer. More often than not, the

PRO TERM! FOUR QUADRANTS

The ultimate prize in movie parlance is a film that appeals to audiences from all four demographic "quadrants": men, women, and those under twenty-five and over twenty-five. Typically, studios executives and their development counterparts want movies to appeal to at least two, and preferably more, of these quadrants. Movies that involve humor, action, romance, and star power have the best chance to become that elusive four-quadrant comedy. Some examples: *The Princess Bride, Ghostbusters, The 40-Year-Old Virgin,* and *The Hangover.*

people who run the production company are also the development department. However, production companies of any size are always looking for new projects to take on, and they will take the time to develop work if they think you or your idea could fit their particular specialty or concentration.

For instance, you bring a pilot script to Producer X, who has a development deal with Fox. (This might mean Fox gets a first look at any new projects, or that they are obligated to buy a certain number of pilots each year. It depends on the deal.) The producer will give notes on the script itself and help shape your future episode ideas to be more in line with the kind of shows Fox likes to air. You'll go back and forth on this for a while until the producer is ready to take the more fully formed project to the development people at Fox.

DEVELOPMENT BY A
NETWORK OR STUDIO

Studios have more money than production companies, and they spend more money on development. Most TV networks and movie studios have a development staff dedicated to working on new projects. Their job is to keep an eye out for new talent and work with them to make something that their bosses are likely to purchase. They tend to be creative people who love the medium they work in, but they can also speak the language of the business people who buy and sell these things.

For example, the development executives at Fox might look at the pilot you put together with Producer X and decide that it would fill a hole in their fall programming if the lead character were about ten years younger, and if there was some way to work in a boyfriend character for an actor whom they really want to work with. After those concerns are addressed, they run it up the flag pole hoping their higher-ups will like it enough to order a pilot. Once the script is bought, money is involved, and a whole new development process begins, with notes and concerns and ideas from other executives, too.

DEVELOPMENT JOBS

Nearly any entity that produces, buys, and distributes content will have jobs in development. Some people come to development from production, some come to it from sales, and some come to it from a different profession altogether. At the entry level, most people start out as assistants and interns and work their way up from the inside. As in many professions, developing good relationships with the people you work with is the best way to earn responsibility and develop a specialty in a given genre. Likewise, keeping a broad range of contacts within the comedy and production worlds is a valuable asset. Another route into development is through the digital world—it's a much more free-ranging landscape than film or TV, with smaller budgets and less oversight.

Tips for Surviving Notes

After you've sold your script or concept to a massive studio or network and provided their accounting department with your routing number for easy direct deposit, your job may be done. Or, you might be a producer on the show or perhaps your contract specifies that you'll be involved with rewrites. Whatever the case may be, you are sure to get plenty of notes. Here are a few things you ought to keep in mind during that process.

ASSUME GOOD WILL AND LISTEN To writers, the development team can sometimes seem like the "enemy," but most of the time they are talented, experienced people who really care about the final product and want it to be the best it can be: for the creator, for the studio, and for the audience. Most development executives have been down almost any road you can think of. They know what works in their genre and, more importantly, their company. Their ideas can help unlock a character, reshape a narrative, or turn a decent idea into something that people will actually pay to watch. They want your show or movie to succeed.

That said, sometimes (often) their job means representing their boss and trying to predict what their boss will want or like. Those predictions can be wrong or lead to creative conflicts. In the most dangerous scenario, you'll come across a development executive whose only job is to justify their job, leading them to make arbitrary changes and suggestions merely to leave their mark on a project. This may not happen as often as rumor would suggest, but it does happen. If (when) it happens to you, will need an advocate.

IDENTIFY AN ADVOCATE You should always have someone who has your back, be it an agent, a manager, a mentor, or a sympathetic executive—someone you can ask to speak on your behalf and advocate for your point of view. Don't lean on this person all the time—you should be your own best advocate—but an outside opinion can be helpful for both sides. Ideally, of course, you will charm and win over the development department, who will become your advocates, as you work together.

PREPARE FOR THE WORST All of the most horrible things you've heard about development are true. The process can be an absolute nightmare with backstabbings, lies, deceit, careless decisions, idiotic notes, and general creative murder. All of those things can really happen. So be prepared for the fact that your project might not wind up being what you started out with at all. If you can approach the process with that in mind, it will be such a pleasant surprise when things don't go nearly as badly.

PREPARE FOR THE LONG HAUL The development process can go through countless unforeseen twists and turns. It can go on, literally, for years. In fact, a project may be shelved—and still technically be in development—and never get made at all.

DON'T TAKE IT PERSONALLY The decision to move forward with something or not is made for a million reasons in a million different moments. Most often, decisions have more to do with the people making them, internal studio politics, or a simple matter of mathematics than it does with you or your project. That's the business part, and it's just business. A network may decide that they have enough family comedies already, or that they'd rather work with David Alan Grier. It can be anything, or it can be nothing. Try not to let it destroy you.

An Interview with **Kate Adler**

"In the most simple terms, you need sustained conflict."

Kate Adler is the executive vice president of comedy development for CBS Television Studios—the creative arm of the CBS network that produces and develops properties to sell to the corporate side. As a development exec and producer, she's worked on such shows as *The Millers, Ed, Survivor, Late Night with David Letterman,* and *Ellen.*

On What She Looks For

What delights us in a pitch is novelty, something that feels somehow fresh or free of cliché, or uses a cliché in a good way. Something that feels genuine, that comes from a real place of having something to say about the world. There should be an agenda, as opposed to just saying, "Well, my agent wanted me to come up with a few ideas."

You have no idea how often we get pitched "Somebody leaves something to someone and they're stuck with it." If your uncle left you a casino in Vegas, and you didn't want to go run a casino in Vegas, you would hire a lawyer to sell it for you. It's the ultimate shortcut for a writer that you don't even have to explain anything. We get so many of those.

We avoid anything too on-the-nose. Like a show about the host of a children's show who hates children. Or a life coach who's completely lost. Or a dating expert who is perpetually single and lonely. Those kinds of reversals are too black and white for most of us. What's interesting is the gray area.

On Characters and Conflict

Any good show usually starts from character. We'll get a lot of phone calls where people say, "Would you be interested in developing a show at a car dealership or an all-girls' school?" And for us that's just a setting. What makes it interesting is: Who are our characters? What are they trying to say? And what are the obstacles in their way? What is compelling? Developing TV is very different from developing a feature because we need to develop something that's going to be compelling to people for years and years and years. So when we hear a pitch, the most important thing we think about is, is this going to be something that's sustainable as a story engine over a long period of time?

In the most simple terms, you need sustained conflict. If it's a very surmountable problem—oh, she can just move out! Or she can just get a divorce—then it's going to be very hard sustaining it. If what a character wants is very clear, and the obstacle is also very clear, then that seems to be the best way to sustain conflict and create story.

On Disappointment

Unlike a writer who is going through this for the first time, we go through this many times a season, and we've been doing this for a long time, so we're aware going in of what the chances of survival are. That each network, out of sixty comedy scripts, is going to order this many pilots, and of those pilots, this small percentage will make it to air. It's a little bit like buying a lottery ticket.

On Starting Out

I worked at a boutique production company that was represented by CAA, so I got to know some agents at CAA and realized that being an assistant there would be like going to graduate school in television development, which was where I felt like I fit in. I knew I didn't want to write, but I wanted to be as close to writers as possible. So I worked at CAA for a year and a half, and then my boss bought me a nice suit, which at the time meant shoulder pads. It was a navy Donna Karan suit that she bought at Barney's, and they set me up with some interviews, and I wound up in my first job at Disney in comedy development.

On Diversity

I'm happy to say that I work in a very diverse environment, and I'd even venture to say that it's female-dominated. CBS has four comedy development executives, and all four are women. The president of CBS is a woman. Development in general, drama and comedy, is heavy on women. Don't get me wrong: there's tons of sexism out there, but at least compared to other industries, in this industry, I feel like I'm in a very protected place.

Chapter 23

LEGAL & FINANCIAL STUFF

And now, to close things out, let's talk about every comedian's two most favorite topics: law and money! Whether it's the differences between a 1099 and a 1099-R, or the intricacies of intellectual property law, there's a lot that affects the creative comedy person without their really knowing it. Once you start getting paid for your work and entering into contracts with other entities, these annoying details become a bigger and bigger part of your life. The laws and principles that bind the worlds of entertainment and finance are far too vast to cover in detail here. This chapter provides general guidance only. Most of all, do your own research whenever contracts or money are involved, and be shrewd enough to talk to a professional about your specific situation. Also: Don't plagiarize and don't fall for pyramid schemes.

Legal Stuff

I am not a lawyer. I once signed up to take the LSAT, and I even bought the study book, but I never read it and I slept through the test. However, I do have some direct experience with a few of the major terms and ideas you will come across in your life as a creative person. Repeat: I am not a lawyer.[2]

INTELLECTUAL PROPERTY

This is the single biggest legal concept that governs the creative industry. At its core is the idea that ideas and creative works can be owned, in whole or in part, by individual entities. This right to exclusive ownership extends from intangible assets like a piece of music to objects such as paintings to the use of words and symbols. It's a complex and complicated area of law that has been at the center of countless lawsuits. This gets especially tricky when it comes to the exchange of ideas: if you are pitching a TV show to a network, when does ownership of that idea shift from the thinker of it to the investor who wants to buy it? Who can claim rights to a movie that was sold as one thing, changed by a writer in the development process, and is now being distributed under another name internationally? Who owns a standup set? Where does ownership begin and end in partnerships?

Most of these questions can be addressed through your contractual agreements, but the lines are still not always clear. It is vital that you take the proper precautions to protect yourself and your intellectual property (IP), especially when you are getting into the pitch process, selling ideas, and dealing with people you may not know creatively or professionally. You should hire a lawyer whenever

2 I am not a lawyer.

you get to that stage, but it doesn't hurt to educate yourself about the basic concepts and rights. The Writers Guild of America and SAG/AFTRA, in particular, are great resources. Even if you are not a member, they can offer services and guidance to get you on the right track and help ensure that you have an advocate and understand the value of your work.

LICENSING VERSUS OWNERSHIP This is one of the most common areas of shared intellectual property, and it can be one of the most confusing. If a network or distribution entity does not outright commission or purchase a work, they might opt to license it from a creator. There are various types of licensing arrangements, but it usually involves a licensing fee, which grants the payor exclusive rights to display and/or distribute the creative works for a set period of time. In these arrangements, the creator still owns the intellectual property, but he or she forfeits certain rights, including, most importantly, the right to make more money through sales or other licensing fees. Again, there are many ways to structure such a deal, but these are the basic principles that govern them.

In other deals, a company may buy outright an idea or creative work. The payee may negotiate for a piece of additional revenue streams (such as international distribution, book rights, merchandising, and so on), but once you've sold your creation, it is no longer yours. Many are the woeful tales of naïve young artists who sell away their greatest asset—their ideas—to the first bidder who offers them rent money. People are, on the whole, more savvy now than they were in the past, but this still happens—and not necessarily out of nefarious motivations, either. The prime directives of business transactions merely dictate that both sides try to get the most value for the least money and risk, and the party with more money and experience clearly has an upper hand.

COPYRIGHT

Copyright is the most common legal method for protecting intellectual property. It grants the owner of the copyright exclusive rights, usually for a set period of time, to sell, license, distribute, cover with fecal matter, trade, or sue over whatever creative work is copyrighted. You can learn about and obtain a copyright in the United States by applying for one from the federal copyright office (copyright.gov).

FAIR USE

There are some areas of intellectual property law that are designed to allow for the free flow of creative ideas, and one of those is fair use. Fair use means you can use a small portion of a copyrighted work for free, without explicit permission from the copyright holder. There are two components of fair use: the interpretive and the literal. In the former, reproduction of a portion of a copyrighted work is considered okay if it is for the purposes of criticism, commentary, or education. Comedians run into this all the time with parody and satire: to legally be allowed to include someone else's work or idea in your own work, you have to do so while making some kind of commentary on the work itself.

In the literal sense, some very restrictive rules govern how much of someone else's work you can use for free. It's considered fair use if you use less than seven seconds of a piece of music or moving picture. For written material, how much you can reprint depends on what type of writing it is or what percentage of the original is copied: you can excerpt a few paragraphs of a nonfiction book in a review, but perhaps one line, or nothing at all, for song lyrics and poems.

If you use someone else's work in your own, and it doesn't fall under fair use guidelines, you should contact the copyright holder for permission and pay whatever fee they ask. If you don't, you put yourself in danger of a copyright infringement lawsuit. While some companies are more litigious than others, copyright becomes a don't-take-chances issue when your work is reaching large audiences and/or making money. If this happens, please have a lawyer, and not this book, at your hearing

PLAGIARISM

Plagiarism is stealing someone's work and passing it off as your own. Every year seems to include a few high-profile examples (see Shia LaBeouf and his weird paper bag fiasco in 2014, or Twitter's youth minister/joke thief, Sammy Rhodes). Particularly in our ever-changing Internet landscape, plagiarism is a big part of the public creator's life. In comedy, joke theft has always been an issue, but it is usually self-policed by writers and comedians. Still, it's a particular problem on Twitter where jokes can be plucked from thin air, tweaked, and reappropriated. Beyond the damage that plagiarism can do to someone's reputation, the copyright owner can sue, especially if they are able to prove that the plagiarism resulted in financial damages to themselves. Ultimately, it doesn't matter legally if plagiarism is accidental or unintentional. Thus, it is always, *always*, always better to err on the side of caution: if it feels like plagiarism, it probably is.

SATIRE VS. PARODY

Though the two are often lumped together, there is a difference between satire and parody. Satire is an act of commentary, usually through exaggeration and ridicule; it's designed to point out injustice, moral shortcomings, or ethical wrongs. Satire uses a work to make a broader comment about society as a whole, and it uses humor to achieve that end, rather than as a means unto itself. That is, satire is not *just* supposed to be funny. Parody, on the other hand, is by design an imitation of a work, genre, or style. It is a form of mimicry, often through caricature and verisimilitude, whose sole aim is to produce a piece of comedy. The difference between satire and parody is the difference between *Dr. Strangelove* and *Hot Shots! Part Deux*.

EXCLUSIVITY

This is a broad concept with very specific parameters that is included in many creative contracts. With an exclusivity clause, the signer is usually restricted from doing any similar work, or making any money, for any competitor of the signee. So, if you sign a contract with Company X to make videos for their website full-time, you are almost certainly not allowed to do something similar for their competitor Entity Y. In most cases it's just standard practice, but sometimes this can be used to take advantage of creators, and it can even entitle Company X to own all the stuff that you create while under contract with them. As with fair use issues, there is a gray area as to what constitutes "similar work" and what could be considered a "competing" company or market, so specify what other work and which companies are and are not

ENTERTAINMENT LAWYERS

There are some artists and creators in the entertainment industry—especially working comics who do their own booking and business management—who choose to forego a manager or agent and hire an entertainment lawyer instead. I would not necessarily recommend this, but for the independent-minded money-saver, it's not a bad option: entertainment lawyers charge about 5 percent (less than an agent or a manager), they handle contract negotiations, they know the ins and outs of a good deal, and many of them work with so many people in your field that they're at least marginally equipped to give good business advice. Ideally, your career will reach a place where you can have all three (plus a business manager, publicist, and personal trainer), but for people just starting out, entertainment lawyers can offer a good first toe-dangle into the wonderful world of entertainment business.

included. Believe it or not, performers and writers often overlook the exclusivity clause, so, you know, *don't do that.* Always read your contract carefully.

Financial Stuff

Most people who work in comedy—be they writers, producers, directors, magicians, cartoonists, actors, comedians, editors, or whatever—are either self-employed or freelance. There are advantages to this, of course: freelancers can make their own hours, work from home, not have a boss in the traditional sense, and feel a sense of ownership in everything that they do. But there are clear disadvantages as well. In the American system, being a freelancer essentially puts you in the financial equivalent of a gulag. You are left to fend for yourself when it comes to taxes, health insurance, and retirement planning, and you don't have any of the security of a full-time job. Fun! Money used to terrify me: it was an evil thing whose powers I did not understand. It still kind of terrifies me, honestly, but I learned that it's better to face money issues head on, rather than pretend they do not exist. Luckily, there are professional business managers and accountants who specialize in this, and who know much, much, much more about the subject than I do.

BUSINESS MANAGERS AND ACCOUNTANTS
People of a creative persuasion, who tend to work unorthodox hours and thrust themselves between states of profound concentration and utter despair, as many comedy people do, *occasionally* need help managing their finances.

BUSINESS MANAGERS These professionals handle all financial affairs, from paying monthly bills to managing investments, to making sure that you are disbursing funds to yourself in a balanced and responsible way. They may handle other things like booking travel and strategizing additional ways to make money. If your manager is the CEO, your business manager is the CFO. A good business manager will relieve the stress and responsibility of dealing with money so that you can focus on what's important: eating noodles alone in a hotel room at 3 am and telling jokes to strangers.

ACCOUNTANTS They primarily watch and count your money. They are absolutely priceless come tax time because they know the ins and outs of freelance laws and will help you navigate the insanely complicated tax code. Accountants can also offer financial advice and guidance, but generally their expertise is going to center around holding onto the money you have, not necessarily turning it into more money.

BECOMING A CORPORATION

Everyone knows that corporations are people, but did you know that people can be corporations? By incorporating, you create a corporation through which you can run all financial and legal transactions. There are tax benefits to incorporating, it can allow you take out loans and employ people, and a corporate business entity offers your personal finances protection from legal liability. It's fairly common to incorporate to create a production company, for instance, and the process itself is relatively straightforward. It can be done with the assistance of a lawyer or an accountant, or you can do it yourself. There are fees associated with the filing stage, and incorporating does require more record-keeping and documentation for tax purposes than filing as an individual. The laws on incorporating also vary from state to state. Your lawyer or business manager will probably know better than you when and if it's time to incorporate, and if you don't have an accountant or business manager, chances are you aren't ready to incorporate quite yet.

TAXES

One of the nice things about working in entertainment is that movies, books, taxi rides, and sometimes even meals at overpriced restaurants can be tax-deductible expenses! Especially if you earn any freelance pay, you should be saving your receipts and keeping track of what you spend, not only on research, but on things like office supplies, agent's fees, classes, wardrobes, head shots, phone bills, and so on.

In addition, if you don't already, you may want to consider paying quarterly estimated taxes. Taxes are usually not taken out by an employer for contract or freelance pay, and at the end of the year, all these unpaid taxes can make a big expense (and could even trigger fines for underpayment). Many accountants recommend estimating your unpaid taxes as the year progresses and paying on a quarterly basis to avoid this.

It will take a little getting used to, but it is extraordinarily satisfying to be on top of your finances in an organized way. I do two things: keep a series of envelopes marked "Research," "Travel," "Meals," and "Other," and empty my wallet of receipts once a week

PRO TIP! PERSONAL FINANCE CLASSES

These are totally worth it. You can easily find personal finance classes at a local college or online, and they'll help get you into the habit of thinking about how to handle money, if nothing else. The expense is usually minimal and will arm you with some basic knowledge of good accounting practices. Plus, it's probably tax deductible, and you'll meet interesting people who would make good characters for your screenplay or sketch ideas!

into one of these envelopes. I also have folders and labels in my email broken into similar categories for easy organization of digital receipts. When tax time comes around, 90 percent of the work is already done, and the rest is just plugging the numbers into a spreadsheet and hand them off to my accountant.

Some expenses that may be deductible include:

- Accounting and tax preparation
- Business gifts
- Charitable donations
- Dues
- Entertainment
- Insurance
- Interest on loans
- Medical bills
- Rent
- Stationery and postage

Note: *You should get an accountant.* It's worth it. They can save you money, and it is *literally* their job to keep up with the ever-changing tax code. Literally.

SAVING

A primary rule in good personal finance is to pay yourself first. Make it a habit, whenever you get paid, to put something away in savings. This should be money that you do not need on a monthly basis and that you will not touch, no matter what, unless it is a dire emergency. Choose a percentage or amount that you can afford to not have access to and put that money away automatically—whether it's in a traditional savings account, a money market account, a retirement account, or all three. It's important, in such an erratic business, to add some regularity, and to use the high times to supplement the low times.

Afterword

HOW ALL OF THIS RELATES TO YOUR INEVITABLE DEMISE

In short: Before too very long, we'll all be dead. That's okay. Everyone who came before us has done it, and they're all fine, so far as we know. We'll survive death. But until that time, we are here, doing this thing. Sometimes it feels wonderful and full of possibility. But it often seems unbearable, hard, and meaningless, too. At its worst, perhaps, life is just boring and dumb. So what are we supposed to do with that? What are we to do in those times when it feels like none of this is worth it? Like life is stupid?

We should think about death.

Most of us do it without much trouble anyway. There's a proud tradition of death-obsessed comedy, from Groucho Marx to George Carlin, from Oscar Wilde to Tig Notaro. For a people who have a tendency toward anxiety, few things inspire more anxiety than inevitable oblivion. But I think some of us are missing the point. Death is not a thing to be avoided: it's the thing that gives us shape. It gives us meaning. It gives us a deadline.

In a job and way of life that is designed in many ways to destroy us, perspective is the most important skill we can possess. Having the ability to see that everything changes, that everything passes, that one job or one standup set are not the end of the world, is sometimes all that can keep us sane. I do a little thing when I get frustrated about work: I imagine myself on my deathbed, surrounded by loved ones. I try to really be there, to feel the moment, and I ask myself if my current petty annoyance will even register as anything worth remembering as I draw my last breaths.

That usually shuts me up.

By the same token, the knowledge that your body is going to rot someday should provide some impetus for Doing Good Work. You now have a standard for yourself, and that is, what will your name mean when you're not around anymore? Will you be satisfied to have just gotten by? To have never quite given it your all because, what if you fail? What does one failure have to do with eternal darkness, I ask you! Take yourself to your deathbed once in a while, and imagine looking back on the work you created. Does it make you proud? Now, not everybody can be Mark Twain but, then again, fuck that—why can't they? If Mark Twain hadn't tried to be Mark Twain, then we never would have had Mark Twain. As Mr. T used to say, "Be somebody," and be guided by the knowledge that you don't have forever to accomplish that.

Lastly, while we're lying here together looking back on it all, there's one other thing worth considering, and that's all the human beings in our lives. We may have written books and shot TV pilots and drawn wonderful drawings, but without other people, all of those things would literally—not figuratively, *literally*—be useless. In fact, if it weren't for other human beings, we wouldn't even exist at all. The work we do will stand on its own for as long as it does, but tastes and sensibilities change. Digital formats change. The thing that will outlast all of that is how we've acted. How we've been, as human beings, in the world.

There's nothing wrong with ambition and ego. It is a big part of why you're reading this and why I wrote it. But cemeteries are filled with ambitious, prolific, talented, groundbreaking people. What is truly remarkable is to be remembered not just for how prolific or talented or groundbreaking you were, but to have been all those things while still making space in your life for other people's well-being.

This way, too, if it turns out that we're not that funny after all, at least they can still say something nice about us.

Acknowledgments

This book wouldn't have been possible without the help and support of a number of generous and talented people. First and foremost, my wife and son, Kat and Cormac, who endured my many moods and hours away, in the dark, typing. My agent, Daniel Greenberg, who put the idea of this whole thing in my head. My editor, Sarah Malarkey, who is patient and wise. Brian Janosch, whose assistance, both organizational and motivational, was so helpful. My manager, Kara Welker, who is just generally the best. My therapist, Oona O'Connell, and my accountant, Harvey Altman. John Hodgman, who is John Hodgman. Copyeditor Jeff Campbell, who is more machine than man, and who made this book so very, very clear and organized. All of my interview subjects. Everyone who was kind enough to talk to me and share their insights for this book, including Tom Scharpling, Wayne Gladstone, Mike Nelson, Mick Napier, Mindy Tucker, Seth Oleneck, and Ken Plume. All of my friends and family at Adult Swim, including Mike Lazzo, Dave Wills, Jeff Olsen, Matt Harrigan, Steve Beslow, John Harris, Max Simonet, Kelly Hudson, Tom Witte, and all of those I worked with every day. My *Onion* friends, too, who offered their help, including Carol Kolb, Todd Hanson, JJ Shebesta, Maria Schneider, and Rob Siegel. My mother, Kathy, my father, Joe, my brothers, Nick and Matt, and my sister, Carli. My in-laws Rob and Jeanne.

My aunts and uncles who were always so encouraging. My best friends growing up, who are my best friends today: Cory, Jim, Evan, Greg, Zac, and Nick. I also drew inspiration and knowledge from Thomas Lennon and Robert Ben Garant, Mike Bent, Ray Richmond, Ernest Becker, Rollo May, Christopher Vogler, Andy Richter, Christina Bouflis, Steve Shipps, Mike Rosovsky, Anthony Beevor, Dan Carlin, Dan Harmon, Josh Clark and Chuck Bryant, Cliff J. Ravenscraft, Rob Sorcher, Matt Harrigan, Frank Boudreaux, Scott Aukerman, Jake Fogelnest, Amy Poehler, Gregg Turkington, Gene Wolfe, Louis CK, Sarah Thyre, Dave Hill, Ben Baumer, Joan Cornellà, Spike Jonze, Sarah Benincasa, San Fermin, Tom Bouman, *Star Wars*, Gil Fronsdal, Zach Galifianakis, Hunter S. Thompson, coffee, Pee-Wee Herman, and all the funny people in the world, big and small, who are just trying to make something happen the best way they know how.

INDEX

JOE RANDAZZO

THE WORLD'S SECOND-OLDEST MAN
HAS DIED OF NATURAL CAUSES,
LEAVING JACK HANDEY AS STILL
THE WORLD'S OLDEST MAN.

—Obituary By Jack Handey